Other works by Bob Thomas:

Nonfiction:

IF I KNEW THEN
THE ART OF ANIMATION
THE MASSIE CASE (*in collaboration*)
KING COHN: The Life and Times of Harry Cohn

Fiction:

THE FLESH MERCHANTS
DEAD RINGER
WILL PENNY (*in collaboration*)
STAR!

For Children:

WALT DISNEY: MAGICIAN OF THE MOVIES
THE DONNA DE VARONA STORY

THALBERG

THALBERG

DOUBLEDAY & COMPANY, INC.

Life and Legend

by (BOB) THOMAS

Robert Joseph

GARDEN CITY, NEW YORK   1969

791.430232
T327Yt

Grateful acknowledgment is made to the following for copyrighted material:

ACADEMY OF MOTION PICTURE ARTS AND SCIENCES AND UNIVERSITY OF SOUTHERN CALIFORNIA PRESS

Speech by Irving Thalberg given at the University of Southern California in 1929. Reprinted by permission.

THE CURTIS PUBLISHING COMPANY

"Why Motion Pictures Cost So Much," by Irving Thalberg and Hugh Weir. *Saturday Evening Post* November 4, 1933. Copyright © 1933 by The Curtis Publishing Company. Reprinted by permission.

HOLT, RINEHART AND WINSTON, INC.

"To an Athlete Dying Young" from "A Shropshire Lad"—Authorised Edition—from *The Collected Poems of A. E. Housman.* Copyright 1939, 1940, © 1959 by Holt, Rinehart and Winston, Inc. Copyright © 1967, 1968 by Robert E. Symons. Reprinted by permission of Holt, Rinehart and Winston, Inc., The Society of Authors as the literary representative of the Estate of A. E. Housman, and Messrs. Jonathan Cape Ltd.

S. J. PERELMAN

"And Did You Once See Irving Plain" by S. J. Perelman. Reprinted by permission of the author.

PRINCETON UNIVERSITY LIBRARY

Lines of a letter which appeared in *F. Scott Fitzgerald* edited by Dan Piper. Reprinted by permission of Princeton University Library as owner of the physical property, and Harold Ober Associates, Inc.

CHARLES SCRIBNER'S SONS

Excerpts from *Crazy Sunday* and The Letters of *F. Scott Fitzgerald;* Excerpt from *The Last Tycoon,* by F. Scott Fitzgerald. Copyright 1941 by Charles Scribner's Sons. Reprinted by permission.

Dedicated to my daughters:
  Nancy, Janet, and Caroline.

ACKNOWLEDGMENT

A biography of this kind requires the help of many persons, and I am deeply grateful to those who gave freely of their time and memories. Howard Strickling, whose longevity as head of the publicity department at M-G-M studios bespeaks his rare capacities, was especially helpful in sharing his reminiscences and affording access to the Thalberg films and to photographs. In the search for photographs, I received the full cooperation of Eddie Hubbell, Dore Freeman and Ben Presser in Culver City and Norman Kaphan in the New York office of M-G-M. Others were helpful in supplying illustrations, and they are mentioned in the photo credits.

The printed sources can be found in Appendix C. I acknowledge my debt to Bosley Crowther for the painstaking and thorough background in his books on the M-G-M history and Louis B. Mayer, *The Lion's Share* and *Hollywood Rajah*. Without his research, much of the M-G-M saga would have been lost to history. Many of the important figures have died in the ten years since Crowther began his books.

For assistance in my research I am grateful to the Academy of

Motion Picture Arts and Sciences, the Los Angeles Public Library, the New York Public Library's theater collection at Lincoln Center, the Museum of Modern Art, and the UCLA Library.

The bulk of information came from those who knew and worked with Irving Thalberg. For recollections and insight I owe my gratitude to:

Margaret Booth	William Hawks	Edward G. Robinson
Milton Bren	Helen Hayes	Rosalind Russell
Clarence Brown	Lucien Hubbard	Morrie Ryskind
Olive Carey	Talbot Jennings	Dore Schary
Lenore Coffee	Edwin Knopf	Adela Rogers St. John
George Cohen	Junior Laemmle	Budd Schulberg
Joseph J. Cohn	Mervyn Leroy	Irene Mayer Selznick
Joan Crawford	Albert Lewin	Laurence Stallings
George Cukor	David Lewis	Howard Strickling
William Daniels	Edwin Loeb	Robert Taylor
Howard Dietz	Anita Loos	Benjamin Thau
D. A. Doran	Alfred Lunt	Franchot Tone
Jimmy Durante	John Lee Mahin	Lee Tracy
Sidney Franklin	Frances Marion	King Vidor
Arthur Freed	Groucho Marx	Minna Wallis
Willis Goldbeck	Chester Morris	Walter Wanger
Frances Goldwyn	Conrad Nagel	Lawrence Weingarten
Samuel Goldwyn	Ramon Novarro	Eddie Welch
Billy Grady	William Powell	Arthur Wenzel
William Haines	Allen Rivkin	Ralph Wheelwright
Howard Hawks	Hal Roach	Darryl F. Zanuck

. . . Smart lad, to slip betimes away
From fields where glory does not stay
And early though the laurel grows
It withers quicker than the rose.

Eyes the shady night has shut
Cannot see the record cut,
And silence sounds no worse than cheers
After earth has stopped the ears:

Now you will not swell the rout
Of lads that wore their honours out,
Runners whom renown outran
And the name died before the man. . . .

—A. E. Housman,
To an Athlete Dying Young

CONTENTS

INTRODUCTION

During a lifetime in Hollywood and a quarter-century of reporting films, I had become acquainted with the Thalberg legend. His precocity in commanding production at Universal at the age of twenty. His remarkable genius for developing stars and doctoring scripts. His ideal marriage to Norma Shearer. His creation, in partnership with Louis B. Mayer, of the greatest film factory the industry has known. His bitter estrangement from his longtime partner at M-G-M. His untimely death.

The name of Irving Thalberg continues to be revered in Hollywood more than thirty years after his death. The homage is expressed at the Academy awards with the presentation of the Irving G. Thalberg award for "consistent high level of production achievement." With the passing of time, Thalberg has achieved a position akin to sainthood.

"But he was not St. Irving," says his onetime employee and admirer,

Anita Loos, and indeed, sainthood seems scarcely possible in Hollywood, then or now.

The legend is complicated by the fact that F. Scott Fitzgerald chose Thalberg as hero of his final, unfinished novel, *The Last Tycoon*. Many readers have accepted the character of Monroe Stahr as an accurate depiction of Irving Thalberg. Therefore it seemed best for me as biographer to examine first the background of Fitzgerald's research and the similarities and differences between the fictional figure and the real man. Then I could proceed with the Thalberg story.

I

LEGEND

"How old are you?" she asked suddenly.
"I've lost track—almost thirty-five, I think."
"They said at the table you were the boy wonder."
"I'll be that when I'm sixty," he said grimly.

—The Last Tycoon

I

F. SCOTT FITZGERALD had been drinking too much, as had been his custom during his second tour of scriptwriting duty in Hollywood. His friend and fellow writer at M-G-M, Dwight Taylor, had brought him to the Sunday afternoon party at the beach home of Norma Shearer and Irving Thalberg and had tried to watch over Fitzgerald. Fitzgerald had been circumspect at first, greeting the hostess fondly and exchanging words with the guest of honor, Frederick Lonsdale, the London playwright. Having had experience with alcoholics, Taylor remained close to Fitzgerald, and both dutifully declined the appetizing martinis that were offered the guests. But the two writers were separated by the gay swirl of the party—all the famous names of Hollywood were there—and Fitzgerald no longer faced the restraining influence of his chaperon.

Taylor anxiously asked a few friends if they had seen Fitzgerald. Robert Montgomery replied that he hadn't, but would like very much to meet the noted author. At that moment Fitzgerald appeared, and Taylor provided the introduction.

During his brief absence, the Fitzgerald charm had vanished. He stared scornfully at the actor, who had just come from polo and was wearing white riding breeches and black boots.

"Why don't you bring your horse in?" said Fitzgerald without a trace of humor. Montgomery murmured something and left.

Taylor realized that his vigil had failed. He knew how desperately Fitzgerald, with his wife Zelda mentally ill and his literary reputation in disrepair, needed the M-G-M job. Taylor hoped that he could spirit Fitzgerald from the Thalberg house before something untoward occurred.

Fitzgerald had other ideas. He called for silence, and the startled assemblage quieted down. He announced that he wanted to sing. Under the best of circumstances, this could not be a popular proposal in a roomful of the most accomplished exhibitionists in the world. But Fitzgerald was insistent.

Miss Shearer, the gracious hostess, asked him what he wanted to sing. Fitzgerald replied it was a song about a dog, and the maid was dispatched to bring Miss Shearer's dog to him. Ramon Novarro was enlisted to play a piano accompaniment. The guests milled before Fitzgerald with an air of discomfort and apprehension.

The eminently confident Fitzgerald began his recital. The song went along the lines of:

> In Spain, they have the donkey
> In Australia, the kangaroo,
> In Africa, they have the zebra
> In Switzerland, the zoo.
> But in America, we have the dog—
> And he's a man's best friend. . . .

There was a faint murmur of approval as Fitzgerald addressed the final line to the dog he held in his arms. He then launched into the second verse, which proved to be only a slight variation of the first. When no particular point to the song appeared, the crowd began to grow restless.

A third verse ensued, and Fitzgerald began to sense the makings of a fiasco. But he was unable to plot any escape, and he launched into a fourth verse.

Miss Shearer remained attentive, and Thalberg watched indulgently from the back of the room, his hands stuck into his back pockets. But the rest of the audience was becoming rebellious. Midway in the fourth verse, the unmistakable sound of hissing was heard; it came from two of the more irrepressible members of the film colony, Lupe Velez and John Gilbert.

The song came to a miserable conclusion, and the guests, with a natural fear of the contagion of failure, moved away from Fitzgerald. Only Miss Shearer feigned amusement, and on the following day she sent a telegram to Fitzgerald:

I THOUGHT YOU WERE ONE OF THE MOST
AGREEABLE PERSONS AT OUR TEA.

The message helped raise Fitzgerald's fallen spirits. He feared his performance had endangered the $1200-a-week paycheck which was necessary for Zelda's medical bills and for the education of their daughter Frances.

"This job means a lot to me; I hope I didn't make too much of a jackass of myself," he told Taylor. "I don't know why I chose yesterday of all days to go off. I always do that—at just the wrong time."

The two writers lunched under bizarre circumstances in the M-G-M commissary. The studio was making a film called *Freaks*, and sideshow performers were eating in the lunch room. When Fitzgerald observed the Siamese twins consulting each other on a meal selection, he excused himself and hurried from the commissary.

He was fired the following week.

2

In December of 1931, Fitzgerald left Hollywood to return to Montgomery, Alabama, where Zelda had been living at her childhood home between breakdowns. At first he intended to write of his five weeks at M-G-M in an article to be called "Hollywood Revisited." He began work on it, then decided to incorporate the experiences in a short story. The result was "Crazy Sunday." The story was turned down by *The Saturday Evening Post* and *Scribner's*. *Cosmopolitan* also rejected it, and Fitzgerald suspected the Hearst publicity men killed it because of possible offense to Norma Shearer, Irving Thalberg, John Gilbert or Marion Davies. The story finally sold to Henry L. Mencken of *The American Mercury*, and Fitzgerald commented bitterly, "Think Mencken bought it for financial value of name."

One of the best of the Fitzgerald short stories, "Crazy Sunday" offers special interest because it displays beginnings of the author's last, unfinished novel, *The Last Tycoon*. "Crazy Sunday" begins with Joel Coles, a writer new to Hollywood, facing an afternoon party at the home of the distinguished director, Miles Calman. In view of the scene that follows, the reader might expect Coles to be Fitzgerald. But Coles is described as being twenty-eight—Fitzgerald was thirty-five at the time—and the Europe-educated son of a famous actress. The description obviously fitted Dwight Taylor, son of the Broadway star, Laurette Taylor.

Coles arrives at the party and is greeted by the hostess, who is the famous actress, Stella Walker. He comments on the fact that she has a baby, as Norma Shearer did in 1931, and he pauses to chat with the host's mother—the elder Thalbergs were inevitably in evidence at their son's parties.

Although he vowed not to, Coles takes one cocktail, and then another. After hearing a singer perform, he gets an idea. "Possessed by the hunch, his blood throbbing with the scarlet corpuscles of exhibitionism," he proposes a performance of his own. The hostess cheerfully agrees, and the crowd quiets down to hear his recital. It is a monologue based on the ignorance of a prominent independent producer noted for his malapropisms. Coles tries hard to engage his audience, but fails ignominiously.

"He felt the undercurrent of derision that rolled through the gossip; then—all this was in the space of seconds—the Great Lover, his eye hard and empty as the eye of a needle, shouted 'Boo! Boo!' voicing in an undertone what he felt was the mood of the crowd. It was the resentment of the professional toward the amateur, of the community toward the stranger, the thumbs-down of the clan."

Only the hostess greeted his performance with equanimity, and later she sent him a telegram:

> YOU WERE ONE OF THE MOST AGREEABLE
> PEOPLE AT OUR PARTY. . . .

The rest of "Crazy Sunday" concerns screenwriter Coles' involvement in the marital problems of Stella Walker and Miles Calman. They are at odds over his confessed infidelity, and both are undergoing psychoanalysis. Calman flies to South Bend to see the Southern

California-Notre Dame football game, and Coles takes Stella home after a movie premiere. But his notions of an easy seduction are dashed when the telephone rings and she learns that her husband has died in a plane crash near Kansas City. As cars begin to arrive at the house, Coles leaves, contemplating Calman's achievements: "Everything he touched he did something magical to. He even brought that little gamin alive and made her a sort of masterpiece."

Then he added: "What a hell of a hole he leaves in this damned wilderness—already!"

The phrases seem to comprise an epitaph to Irving Thalberg, yet they were written more than four years before his death. Coles' evaluation of Calman might seem to be a tribute to Thalberg, with the substitution of "producer" for "director"—"He was the only American-born director with both an interesting temperament and an artistic conscience. Meshed in an industry, he had paid with his ruined nerves for having resilience, no healthy cynicism, no refuge —only a pitiful and precarious escape."

In reality, though the character of Calman may have been based on Thalberg, the situation of Calman's marriage came from Fitzgerald's acquaintance with King Vidor, who was undergoing a divorce from Eleanor Boardman during the author's 1931 visit to Hollywood.

Fitzgerald had first become fascinated with Thalberg during his visit to Hollywood in 1927. He was enjoying the full glory of his literary fame when United Artists hired him to write an original story for Constance Talmadge. Thalberg was then engaged in a romance with Miss Talmadge, and the two men became acquainted. Their first time alone together was over lunch in the M-G-M commissary. Years later, Fitzgerald recorded his remembrance of Thalberg's comments:

"Scottie, supposing there's got to be a road through the mountain and . . . there seems to be a half-dozen possible roads . . . each one of which, so far as you can determine, is as good as the other. Now suppose you happen to be the top man, there's a point where you don't exercise the faculty of judgment in the ordinary way, but simply the faculty of arbitrary decision. You say, 'Well, I think we will put the road there,' and you trace it with your finger and you know in your secret heart, and no one else knows, that you have no reason for putting the road there rather than in several other different courses, but you're the only person that knows that you don't know why you're doing it and you've got to stick to that and you've got to pretend that you know and that you did it for specific reasons, even though you're utterly assailed by doubts at times as to the wisdom of your decision, because all these other possible decisions keep echoing in your ear. But when you're planning a new enterprise on a grand scale, the people under you mustn't ever know or guess that you're in doubt, because they've all got to have something to look up to and they mustn't ever dream that you're in doubt about any decision. These things keep occurring."

The conversation was interrupted by others arriving at the table, but Fitzgerald remained impressed "by the shrewdness of what he had said—something more than shrewdness—by the largeness of what he had thought and how he had reached it by the age of twenty-six, which he was then."

Fitzgerald's script for Constance Talmadge was rejected by United Artists, but he was unconcerned. He and Zelda had lived in elegance at the Ambassador Hotel in an apartment bungalow they shared with John Barrymore, actress Carmel Myers and author Carl Van Vechten, and the Fitzgeralds had savored the gay life of 1927 Hollywood. Five years later, Fitzgerald returned to Hollywood a different man. Dispirited, uncertain of his talent, he accepted the assignment of fashioning a script from the Katharine Brush novel, *Red-Headed Woman*. The leading role was to be played by Jean Harlow, and Thalberg wanted a sympathetic approach to the portrayal of a girl who improved her lot by sleeping with the men who could help her. But Fitzgerald had no empathy for the character and could not produce what Thalberg wanted. He became obsessed with the mechanics of scriptwriting and pumped other screenwriters for advice on how to plan camera angles, etc. They counseled him to forget such matters and concentrate on what he did best: creating characters, scenes and dialogue. But he insisted on catechizing the mumbo-jumbo of camera instructions.

His general demeanor was depressing to those who had known him in other times. He would knock tentatively at the door of Anita Loos, who also occupied a writer's office at M-G-M, and inquire, "May I come in?" After pouring out his travails in learning the scripting trade, he would mutter, "You don't want me here, do you?"

It was disheartening to Miss Loos, who had seen Scott rip up the Riviera while roaring drunk.

Fitzgerald had been working on the script of *Red-Headed Woman* with Marcel deSano, a Rumanian-born director who was devious and eccentric, but touched with brilliance. Fitzgerald later wrote to his daughter of the experience:

". . . Life had gotten in some hard socks and while all was serene on top, with your mother apparently recovered in Montgomery, I was jittery underneath and beginning to drink more than I ought to. Far from approaching it too confidently I was far too humble. I ran afoul of a bastard named deSano, since a suicide, and let myself be gypped out of command. I wrote the picture and he changed as I wrote. I tried to get at Thalberg but was erroneously warned against it as 'bad taste.' Result—a bad script. I left with the money, for this was a contract for weekly payments, but disillusioned and disgusted, vowing never to go back, tho they said it wasn't my fault and asked me to stay. I wanted to get East when the contract expired to see how your mother was. This was later interpreted as 'running out on them' and held against me. . . ."

Fitzgerald returned to M-G-M for a six-month contract beginning in June of 1937. He recognized the drift of the studio in the year following Thalberg's death, and he could reiterate what Joel Coles had said of the death of Miles Calman in "Crazy Sunday": "What a hell of a hole he leaves in this damn wilderness."

3

While working on such scripts as *Three Comrades*, *Madame Curie* and *Gone with the Wind*, Fitzgerald dreamed of writing a novel about Hollywood. He was impatient with the novels that had been written about the film capital, dismissing them as shallow and sensational. He wanted to conceive a novel that would encompass the entire scope of the movie industry, its business intricacies, its power struggles, its human tragedies. More and more he pictured Thalberg as the hero of his tale.

"Thalberg has always fascinated me," Fitzgerald wrote to Kenneth Littauer, editor of *Collier's*. "His peculiar charm, his extraordinary good looks, his bountiful success, the tragic end of his great adventure. The events I have built around him are fiction, but all of them are things which might very well have happened, and I am pretty sure that I saw deep enough into the character of the man so that his reactions are authentically what they would have been in life. So much so that he may be recognized—but it will be also recognized that *no single fact is actually true*. . . . This is a novel not even faintly of the propaganda type. Indeed Thalberg's opinions were entirely different from mine in many respects that I will not go into. I've long chosen him for a hero (this has been in my mind for three years) because he is one of the half-dozen men I have known who were built on a grand scale. . . . Certainly if Ziegfeld could be made into an epic figure, then what about Thalberg who was literally everything that Ziegfeld wasn't?"*

Thus Fitzgerald idealized Irving Thalberg in the role of Monroe Stahr, just as he had patterned Dick Diver of *Tender Is the Night* after his friend, Gerald Murphy. Throughout his literary career, Fitzgerald borrowed his heroes from friends he admired, and inevitably a bit of Fitzgerald entered the characterizations. "When I like men," he once wrote, "I want to be like them—I want to lose the outer qualities that give me my individuality and be like them."

There were similarities between Fitzgerald and Thalberg. Both possessed a magnetic kind of masculine beauty. Both had been prodigies: Thalberg was in command of a film studio before he was twenty-one; Fitzgerald was acclaimed for *This Side of Paradise* at twenty-three. Both produced a remarkable amount of first-class work during their young lifetimes. Both were subject to heart ailments that presaged their early deaths: Thalberg at thirty-seven, Fitzgerald at forty-four. "Show me a hero and I'll show you a tragedy," said Fitzgerald.

The author began writing *The Last Tycoon* in October of 1939. Desperate for money, he tried to seek advance payments from *Collier's* and *The Saturday Evening Post*, but the editors of both magazines said they would need to see more than the fragments he submitted before making judgments. He continued work on the novel, although his physical resources were diminishing. He worried that the novel of Budd Schulberg, with whom he had collaborated on the disastrous *Winter Carnival*, might take the edge off his own

---

* In 1936 M-G-M had released an expensive production based on the life of the Broadway showman, Florenz Ziegfeld.

Hollywood book. But when *What Makes Sammy Run?* appeared, Fitzgerald dismissed it in a letter to Maxwell Perkins: "It's not bad but it doesn't cut into my material at all."

After a year's work, Fitzgerald wrote to Edmund Wilson: "I think my novel is good. I've written it with difficulty. It is completely upstream in mood and will get a certain amount of abuse but is first hand and I am trying a little harder than I ever have to be exact and honest emotionally. I honestly hoped somebody else would write it but nobody seems to be going to."

A day or so later, he suffered his first heart attack. Still he continued to work. On December 20, 1940, he conquered a particularly difficult passage and decided to take Sheilah Graham to a press preview of *This Thing Called Love* as a celebration. He collapsed after the performance, and the following day he was dead. In contrast to the state funeral of Irving Thalberg four years earlier, Fitzgerald was laid out in the back room of an undertaking parlor near downtown Los Angeles. One of the few persons who came to view the remains was Dorothy Parker. She looked at his waxen face and delivered the epitaph that was spoken at the funeral of Jay Gatsby: "The poor son of a bitch!"

Fitzgerald had originally planned *The Last Tycoon* to be a novel of 60,000 words. But by the time of his death he had written 70,000 words and had told only half of his story. The manuscript, together with the author's notes about characters and Hollywood itself and his outline for the remainder of the book, was assembled by Edmund Wilson and published by Scribner's in 1941. In his foreword Wilson proclaimed that the novel was, "even in its imperfect state, Fitzgerald's most mature piece of work."

Wilson added: "It is marked off also from his other novels by the fact that it is the first to deal seriously with any profession or business. The earlier books of Fitzgerald had been preoccupied with debutantes and college boys, with the fast lives of the wild spenders of the twenties. The main activities of the people in these stories, the occasions for which they live, are the big parties at which they go off like fireworks and which are likely to leave them in pieces. But the parties in *The Last Tycoon* are incidental and unimportant; Monroe Stahr, unlike any other of Scott Fitzgerald's heroes, is inextricably involved with an industry of which he has been one of the creators, and its fate will be implied by his tragedy. The moving-picture business in America has here been observed at close range, studied with a careful attention and dramatized with a sharp wit such as are not to be found in combination in any of the other novels on the subject. *The Last Tycoon* is far and away the best novel we have had about Hollywood, and it is the only one which takes us inside."

The reviews of *The Last Tycoon*, though perhaps tinged by acknowledgment of the neglect of Fitzgerald in his last years, were generally favorable. Stephen Vincent Benét wrote in the *Saturday Review of Literature:* "*The Last Tycoon* shows what a really first-class writer can do with material—how he gets under the skin. . . . It is character that dominates the book, the complex yet consistent character of Monroe Stahr, the producer, hitched to the wheels of his own preposterous chariot, at once dominating and domi-nated, as much a part of his business as the film that runs through the cameras, and yet a living man. Had Fitzgerald been permitted to finish the book, I think there is no doubt that it would have added a major character and a major novel to American fiction."

James Thurber wrote in *The New Republic:* "It is the last work of a first-rate novelist; it shows his development, it rounds out his all too brief career; it gives us what he had done and indicates what he was going to do on the largest canvas of his life; it is filled with a great many excellent things as it stands." But Thurber pointed out the unfinished nature of *The Last Tycoon* and yearned for the polish of rewriting which a craftsman like Fitzgerald would have provided in time.

The character of Monroe Stahr might well have become more rounded and fictional if Fitzgerald had lived long enough to give *The Last Tycoon* the benefit of rewriting. In the published version, Stahr bears close similarities to Thalberg.

4

The remark most frequently heard about Thalberg's career is that "he never put his name on a picture." This is said of Stahr in the early pages of the novel, and the author wrote in his notes about the character: "Never wanted his name on pictures—'I don't want my name on the screen because credit is something that should be given to others. If you are in a position to give credit yourself, then you do not need it.'" Thalberg many times made the remark in almost the same words.

Stahr's work habits coincided with those of Thalberg: "He seldom left the studio before eleven (P.M.)"; ". . . he had been able to figure costs in his head with a speed and accuracy that dazzled. . . ."; he "apparently derived some rare almost physical pleasure from working lightheaded with weariness."

There are also similarities in appearance and background. Fitzgerald's notes for Stahr might have described Thalberg: ". . . he was a fighter even though he was a small man—certainly not more than 5'6½", weighing very little (which is one reason he always liked to see people sitting down)." Fitzgerald describes "a kindly fatherly smile Stahr had developed inversely when he was a young man pushed into high places." Stahr, like Thalberg, had been a "boy wonder" who headed a large studio in his early twenties.

Fitzgerald wrote: "Though Stahr's education was founded on nothing more than a night-school course in stenography, he had a long time ago run ahead through trackless wastes of perception into fields where very few men were able to follow him." The same could have been said of Thalberg, as well as: "He (Stahr) was a marker in the industry like Edison and Lumiere and Griffith and Chaplin. He led pictures way up past the range and power of the theater, reaching a sort of golden age, before the censorship."

In another passage, Fitzgerald wrote: ". . . Stahr like Lincoln was a leader carrying on a long war on many fronts; almost single-handed he had moved pictures sharply forward through a decade, to a point where the content of 'A productions' was wider and richer than that of the stage." Stahr had even raided the stage of its directors when sound came in, to the distaste of the old-line silent directors—"'It put them on their toes and made them learn their jobs all over, but they never did really forgive me.'"

Fitzgerald explained further about Stahr's relations with directors: ". . . up to his arrival the director had been the King Pin in pictures since Griffith made *The Birth of a Nation*. Now, therefore, some of the directors resented the fact that he reduced their position from one of complete king to being simply one element in a combine." During his years at M-G-M Thalberg had subordinated the role of the director, but he enjoyed close personal relationships with several directors.

"Stahr knew he had a working knowledge of technics, but because he had been head man for so long and so many apprentices had grown up during his sway, more knowledge was attributed to him than he possessed. He accepted this as the easiest way and was an adept though cautious bluffer." But Fitzgerald added: ". . . it should be remembered that he came out of the old Hollywood that was rough and tough and where the wildest bluffs hold. He had manufactured gloss and polish and control of the new Hollywood, but occasionally he liked to tear it apart just to see if it was there." Such generalizations might—or might not—apply to Thalberg.

With his subjective view of the motion picture industry, Fitzgerald quite naturally concerned himself with Stahr's relationships with writers. Here the feelings of F. Scott Fitzgerald, the unsuccessful screen writer, color his views. A writer complained of Stahr: "He may have ten writers working ahead of me or behind me, a system which he so thoughtfully invented." Fitzgerald himself had been rankled by Thalberg's practice of having different writers working on a script unbeknownst to each other.

In one scene Stahr explains his philosophy to a Communist writer: "I never thought that I had more brains than a writer has. But I always thought that his brains be*longed* to me—because I knew how to use them. Like the Romans—I've heard that they never invented things but they knew what to do with them. Do you see? I don't say it's right. But it's the way I've always felt—since I was a boy."

One of the major factors that had attracted Fitzgerald to the Thalberg saga was the conflict that the producer had in his final years with Louis B. Mayer. The Mayer figure is represented by the studio boss, Brady, a man of gross habits (the most startling and un-Fitzgerald-like scene in the book comes when Brady's daughter opens the closet door in his office and out falls his nude, nearly suffocated secretary). The final half of *The Last Tycoon* was to have centered on the power fight between Stahr, the old-fashioned paternalistic employer, and Brady, the unscrupulous despot. According to the outline of the remainder of the book as pieced together by Wilson, the struggle sickens Stahr and he thinks of quitting, but "it is difficult for him to surrender to Brady." The author apparently planned to have Stahr defeated by a trumped-up scandal and betrayal by labor unions.

"Stahr is now being pushed into the past by Brady and by the unions alike. The split between the controllers of the movie industry, on the one hand, and the various groups of employees, on the other, is widening and leaving no place for real individualists of business like Stahr, whose successes are personal achievements and whose career has always been invested with a certain personal glamor. He held himself directly responsible to everyone with whom he has worked; he has even wanted to beat up his enemies himself. In Hollywood he is 'the last tycoon.'" Thus "tycoon" seems more related to its origin as a title for the Japanese shogun than to its more recent American acceptance, meaning a leader of industry.

Two doctors had predicted an early death for Stahr, but his end was to come in an accidental plane crash. Thus he would meet the same fate as Miles Calman in "Crazy Sunday."

Despite the obvious parallels, Anita Loos, Albert Lewin and others who worked intimately with Thalberg declare they do not recognize him in Monroe Stahr. There is little resemblance to Thalberg's personal life; Stahr is depicted as a widower, and his romance with Kathleen is related primarily to Fitzgerald's with Sheilah Graham. It is in the playing out of the scenes that the resemblance of Stahr and Thalberg becomes obscure, for one was a melodramatic creation and the other was a human being.

Yet to a generation of students of Fitzgerald and of Film, Irving G. Thalberg has been The Last Tycoon.

II

BEGINNINGS 1899–1923

The astounding thing about him is his gentle, dreamy air; his almost placid personality—except in the midst of an argument. A frail boy, he has terrifying energy—enormous vitality.

—*Jim Tully*

I

W HY should he have become the architect of the American film? There existed no really compelling reason. Most of the men who wrested control of the motion picture business had been immigrants. Eager to succeed in the new land, they recognized films as a field of endeavor that offered unlimited growth, one that was open to those of humble origins because the more respectable members of the community shunned it as being beneath their dignity. The film pioneers were rough, uneducated men; they were utterly unaware that movies might be conceived as an art form. If better films might extend their power and wealth, then they were interested in making better films. If they believed their best interests would be served by repeating the same formulas, such would be their product. They were unconcerned with aesthetics.

Irving Thalberg was different. Although largely self-educated, he gave the impression of having intellectual depth. Oddly, this did not disqualify him from membership in the industry's high council. Not at all. He was accepted, even revered, as a sage and a savant. He was respected not merely for his intellectual leadership; that would not have been enough for survival in Hollywood. He also possessed all the requirements for leadership: the ability to inspire intense loyalty, to make quick, apt decisions, to produce a large body of creditable work.

Nothing in Thalberg's family background or youth seemed to equip him for such eminence. He came from a mercantile family of German-Alsatian Jewish origin; none of his forebears had the remotest connection with the entertainment world. Nor did Thalberg indicate any predilection in that direction during his early years. His youthful ambition was to become a lawyer. When that was rendered impossible, he entered the business world. Only by chance did he later seek employment with a company that was in the business of making and selling motion pictures.

He was born on May 30, 1899, at 19 Woodbine Street in Brooklyn. It was a comfortable brownstone house in a middle-class neighborhood that was populated largely by Germans. Nearby lived John F. Hylan, later the Mayor of New York City, and Frederick A. Cook, polar explorer. Thalberg's mother, Henrietta, was the daughter of the founder of the department store, Heyman and Sons. Her husband was William Thalberg, an immigrant from Germany who operated a lace importing company at 9th Street and Fifth Avenue. Irving was their first-born; later came a daughter, Sylvia.

The daughter of a hard-driving merchant, Henrietta Heyman Thalberg, was a woman of strong ambition. She was petite and slender but filled with nervous energy. The intensity shone in her eyes, so deeply black that she appeared to have no pupils. The man she married was bland, affable, and ineffectual. Henrietta poured her ambition into her son.

19 Woodbine Street

Her hopes for him went beyond the usual ones of a Jewish mother for her son. From the beginning she believed him to have a special quality, stemming from the circumstances of his birth. He had been born a blue baby. The cyanosis, or blueness of the skin, was caused by imperfectly oxygenated blood, and doctors told Henrietta that the condition usually resulted from a congenital defect of the heart or lung. Their judgment indicated Irving would not know a normal, nor a lengthy life.

The prognosis was both a sorrow and a challenge for Henrietta Thalberg. If her son's life was to be short, she meant it to be productive.

Irving was small like his parents. He grew to five feet, six inches, and he seldom in his lifetime weighed more than one hundred and twenty pounds. His shoulders were broad, and his chest was well-formed; he had the body of a flyweight boxer, except that his arms and legs never developed beyond a painful-looking thinness. The most striking feature was his head. The hair was darkly luxuriant with a slight wave, the ears close to the head. The nose was long and ascetically thin, the mouth wide and sensitive, the eyes deep, like his mother's. His eyes were penetrating, almost hypnotic, appealing to men and women alike.

His early years were spent like most Brooklyn boyhoods in the first part of the century. Henrietta enforced a strict schedule of school work. But there was time for baseball in the street, and Irving was an enthusiastic player, if limited in his capabilities. Sometimes he played too hard, and he was forced to spend days in bed to recover his strength. But Henrietta did not allow him to remain there for long. As soon as he seemed able, she forced him out of bed and back to school.

He attended Public School No. 85, then in February of 1913, he transferred to Boys' High School, where he remained six terms. He became interested in the world around him and dabbled briefly in socialism. His grades were good, but not exceptional, perhaps because of his many absences for health reasons. He was unable to return for the fall semester of 1916 because he was stricken with rheumatic fever.

At first Henrietta was terrified, because doctors told her of the heart damage that could result from rheumatic fever. But again she considered Irving's illness a challenge, and the six months that followed proved to be the most important period of his young life. Racked by high fever and painful joints, he lost all ambition and wanted to do nothing but linger in bed. Henrietta would have none of this. She trudged to Boys' High School and interviewed teachers for work her son could do at home. She forced him to study, not only the curriculum he would have been undergoing at school, but extra reading as well. She walked to the public library to withdraw volumes of Kant and Schopenhauer and Hegel. She stood over Irving to make sure he read them.

His incentive returned as the fever lessened. He became insatiable in his quest for knowledge, and he devoured novels, plays, sociological works, philosophy. He was profoundly affected by the writings of William James, especially in his philosophy of pragmatism. James himself had been a youthful invalid and had overcome his condition by exercise of his own strong will. In the triumph of that will he had arrived at what he considered to be the truth, and his findings impressed the ailing seventeen-year-old in Brooklyn:

> The true . . . is only the expedient in our way of thinking, just as "the right" is only the expedient in the way of our behaving. Expedient is almost any fashion; and expedient in the long run and on the whole, of course; for what meets expediently all the experiences in sight won't necessarily meet all further experiences equally satisfactorily. . . .

> Like dead men, dead causes tell no tales, and the ideals that went under in the past, along with all the tribes that represented them, find today no recorder, no explainer, no defender. . . .

> Who gains promotions, boons, appointments but the man in whose life they are seen to play the part of living hypotheses, who discounts them, sacrifices other things for their sake before they have come, and takes risks for them in advance. . . .

Armed with such beliefs and goaded by his mother, Irving began to think about his future. His dreams of a career in law were now destroyed; the rheumatic fever had left its toll in a damaged heart, and doctors doubted that he could withstand the disciplines of attending college. With his newly pragmatic attitude, he decided he should

prepare himself for a life in business. He also devised his own maxims
for his venture into the outside world:

Never take any one man's opinion as final.
Never think your own opinion is unassailable.
Never expect help from anyone but yourself.

He went to work as a clerk in his grandfather's department store
so he could earn enough money for a business education. This was
acquired in night courses at New York University and at a private
business school in Brooklyn where he learned shorthand and Spanish.
He taught himself how to type, and he earned a few dollars by writing
advertisements for the *Brooklyn Eagle*. After six months of training
himself, he figured he was ready to enter the world of business, and
he placed an advertisement in the *New York Journal of Commerce:*

SITUATION WANTED: Secretary, stenographer, Spanish and English.
High school education, inexperienced. $15.00.

He received four inquiries from the ad, and one of them led to a
position at the stipulated salary with a small trading company on
East 41st Street. The job did not last long, and he became stenographer to Hugo Windner, export manager for the firm of Taylor,
Clapp and Beall. He performed ably enough to rise to assistant
manager of the export department within a year. But Thalberg was
restless. He found the work uninspiring and he realized it would be
a long time before he progressed further in the company. Convinced
that there must have been some other line of work more suited to his
talents, he resigned.

Thalberg then made a fateful journey to the cottage of his grand-
mother on Long Island, intending to take a brief vacation before
seeking another situation in the business world. It happened that
Carl Laemmle, the head of Universal Pictures, had a summer house
next door. On warm evenings, Laemmle set up a projector on the
front porch and showed his latest movies on a bed sheet. He invited
all the neighbors to attend, and he listened carefully to their comments and reactions. As many as a hundred neighbors appeared, among
them the slender, dark-eyed boy from next door.

Irving was fascinated by the flickerings on the front-porch screen,
and he had cogent things to say about the films. He also was cordial
to Laemmle's two young children, Rosabelle, and Carl, Junior.

Laemmle saw promise in young Thalberg and offered him a job at the Universal headquarters in the Mecca Building on Broadway.

What happened next is clouded by legend. The official version of Thalberg's studio biography: the idealistic young man spurned the offer because he didn't want to acquire a job through family influence; later he hired himself to Universal without Laemmle's knowledge. A more credible explanation is that Henrietta Thalberg persuaded Laemmle to employ Irving, and her pragmatic son accepted the position. Whatever the circumstances, Irving Thalberg found himself in 1918 at work for Universal Pictures at a salary of $35 a week. He began his education in motion pictures under the able but eccentric Carl Laemmle.

2

Laemmle was a cheerful man who loved a good fight. Born in 1867 at Laupheim in the south German kingdom of Württemberg, he learned the rules of survival early. His father was a Jewish dealer in country estates, and there were thirteen children; eight died in a scarlet fever epidemic. Young Carl attended Latin School until he was thirteen, then was indentured to a trading firm for three years. He was seventeen when he paid $22.50 for a steerage ticket from Bremerhaven to New York. Twelve years later, he was an American citizen and manager of a clothing store in Oshkosh, Wisconsin. He was determined to make his store the biggest in Oshkosh, and he did so by flooding the countryside with catalogues and giving turkeys to purchasers of more than $15 worth of clothing.

Despite his success, Carl was restless to accomplish something big before he was forty. He quit Oshkosh for Chicago, where he invested $2500 in *Hale's Tours*, a motion picture device which offered scenic films to audiences seated in railway coaches. The enterprise was an immediate success, and Laemmle expanded with more theaters and a film exchange. By 1909, his expansion ran into conflict with the Motion Picture Patents Company, the trust that exacted tribute for the use of all movie equipment. Carl Laemmle rolled up his sleeves for a fight.

He launched a series of trade paper advertisements that attacked the Trust with scathing humor. Backers of the Trust became alarmed, and they offered concessions to Laemmle, who was their biggest

Carl Laemmle takes a flier

customer. He spurned their overtures and in June of 1910 wrote his
fellow exhibitors: "Again I renew my pledge to you that I will rot
in Hades before I will join the Trust, or anything that looks like a
Trust. How is *your* backbone?"

That month he formed Independent Moving Pictures (IMP) to
make films outside the Trust. His first release was *Hiawatha*—"Length
988 feet. Taken at the Falls of Minnehaha in the Land of the Dacotahs.
And you can bet that it is classy or I wouldn't make it my first
release."

In his campaign to beat the monopoly, Carl Laemmle managed to
create the star system. Before 1910, the leading players in films were
known only by the characters they played or the company they
worked for—The Biograph Girl, Little Mary, The Vitagraph Girl,
etc.; actors were never billed by their own names. Florence Lawrence
was one of the most popular performers, the public recognizing her
only as The Biograph Girl. Laemmle lured her away from the
Biograph Company with promises of publicity and a bigger salary.
When a New York newspaper reported that Miss Lawrence had been
killed in a trolley accident in St. Louis, the resourceful Laemmle
dispatched the actress and her leading man, King Baggot, to St.
Louis to prove she was still alive. Thus the first personal appearance

by a film figure. The reception was clamorous, and Laemmle capital-
ized on the publicity by featuring Miss Lawrence's name on the
screen and in advertisements.

Laemmle next hired Biograph's bright young star, Mary Pickford,
with an offer of $175 a week, $75 more than her previous salary.
The Patents Company was losing patience with its gadfly, and it
loosed a torrent of litigation that made it virtually impossible for
IMP to continue making films. When the movie companies tried to
continue shooting, thugs threw rocks at the casts and crews. Laemmle
responded by shipping seventy-two of his film makers, including
Mary Pickford, Owen Moore, Jack Pickford, Thomas Ince and King
Baggot, off to Cuba to establish a movie production colony. The
émigrés fed movie subjects to the New York IMP office for nine
months, then the miserable conditions drove them back to the United
States.

Eventually the tenacious Carl Laemmle won his fight. In 1912,
Democrat Woodrow Wilson was elected President, and the new ad-
ministration put an end to the monopolistic practices of the Patents
Company. Laemmle sailed forward with his company, now called
Universal Pictures. In 1914, he purchased two hundred and thirty
acres of land in the San Fernando Valley, just over the Cahuenga
Pass from Hollywood. There, across Lankershim Boulevard from the
spot where California was ceded to the United States by Mexico,
Laemmle built Universal City for the production of motion pictures.

Universal became a major power in the film industry, but Carl
Laemmle continued to run his enterprise in the same helter-skelter
manner as when he was fighting the Trust. The looseness of the
organization in 1918 astonished the male secretary who had been
newly hired by Universal. One of the lessons that had been instilled
in him by his mother was to speak out when he saw something that
was wrong.

Thalberg, who was assistant to Laemmle's assistant, D. B. Lederman,
began composing memos to the company president, suggesting how
administrative operations could be improved. At first Laemmle was
too busy to read the memos, but they came with such frequency that
he couldn't ignore them. He was surprised to discover that they
made good sense. At the age of nineteen, Irving Thalberg became
private secretary to Carl Laemmle.

He was diligent in his service, toiling long hours in the Universal offices at 1600 Broadway, performing the boss's orders with dispatch and continuing his counsel on the efficiency of the company. As secretary, Thalberg was the first to see the letters and telegrams that came from the studio at Universal City. The place seemed like another world to him, far-off and chaotic. Judging from the reports he read, it was a miracle that the studio was able to produce films. As Laemmle screened the new product in his projection room, the boy was beside him, pad and pencil in hand. Thalberg saw the results of the jumbled studio operation. The films were standard replays of the same themes and techniques that had been used for a decade; they lacked originality and excitement. Laemmle himself was becoming more and more disturbed by the quality of the Universal films.

Thalberg gave early evidence of his faculty for dealing successfully with people of all temperaments, especially the volatile performers and creators of films. He listened to their problems and placated them, and they seemed to find in his dark eyes more wisdom than his years would indicate.

One day Lucien Hubbard appeared for an appointment with Laemmle. Hubbard had been writing films for Edison and Pathé, and Laemmle was considering him for the post of scenario editor at Universal City. As was often the case, Laemmle's appointments were running late, and Hubbard was left sitting in the anteroom. Finally he went to the Dutch door that led to the secretary's office and snapped, "If he wants to see me, I'm here. If not, I'll leave."

The slim young secretary looked up and saw Hubbard's angry face. Thalberg rose from his desk and went out to speak to Hubbard in the anteroom.

"Now, look, Lucien," said Thalberg, addressing a man fifteen years older whom he had never met. "They want you out there on the coast. This could be a very important advancement for your career. Why ruin it by acting like a star?" The chastened Hubbard agreed to wait patiently, and he was rewarded with appointment by Laemmle to the studio post.

Laemmle was entirely pleased with his new secretary, although he didn't always heed the young man's advice. After Thalberg had been with him for more than a year, Laemmle remarked one late afternoon: "I'm going out to the studio, leaving on the train tonight. I want

you to go with me. We can get the correspondence done on the way across the country. Can you go?"

"Certainly, Mr. Laemmle," Thalberg replied. His heart was pounding when he returned to his desk. He had scarcely been out of New York City in his lifetime, and now he was going to California! He quickly telephoned his mother to tell her the news.

Henrietta Thalberg was overjoyed, too. She had a twinge of concern that her son would be going three thousand miles away and she would not be able to see that he ate properly and got enough rest to protect his damaged heart. But that worry was overshadowed by the realization that Irving was coming up in the world by accompanying the president of Universal Pictures to the studio in California. She and her husband brought Irving's bag to Pennsylvania Station and kissed him goodbye as he left for his great adventure. All three were crying as the train began its departure from the city of his boyhood, the city to which he would return only as a visitor.

3

Hollywood was a dazzling sight to Irving Thalberg. He was awed by the brilliance of the sunshine, by the expanse of citrus groves and brush-covered hills in contrast to the cityscape in which he had lived. He was impressed by the vitality of the movie people he met. These were not the film sellers and bookkeepers of the Eastern offices, those who talked of movies only in terms of footage and how much return could be achieved. These were the creators of film entertainment, the people who gave life to the screen.

He met them under the best of circumstances. As private secretary to Carl Laemmle, he was close to the throne. His counsel was sought, his friendship was treated as something of value. More than one pretty actress cast her vampish looks in the direction of the handsome young assistant to Mr. Laemmle. That delighted Thalberg, too.

The studio was in incredible disarray. Laemmle's attempt to run the operations on both coasts had resulted in a displacement of authority that seemed almost insoluble. He would return to Universal City after months of absence and issue orders that were forgotten with his departure. During the interim Isadore Bernstein tried to operate the studio as general manager, but his authority was constantly undercut. Laemmle and other Eastern officials wired instructions they ex-

Irving Thalberg and Carl Laemmle under the Universal emblem

pected to be carried out. And many persons at the studio claimed to have directions from Laemmle himself about how things should be run. Numerous relatives and friends from the old country were sent by Laemmle to the studio, and they were given jobs regardless of the capabilities.

Thalberg followed Laemmle about the studio, making mental note of the conditions. After a four-month visit, Laemmle announced: "I have to go back to New York tomorrow."

"All right, I'll start packing," said the secretary.

"No, I want you to stay here," said Laemmle. "I need someone to keep an eye on things for me."

And so Irving Thalberg moved into a bare little office in a frame building on the Universal City lot. He came to work with hair slicked back, wearing a stiff collar and immaculate suit—and underneath, in accordance to instructions by his mother, long wool underwear. With Laemmle safely out of the state, Thalberg's fellow workers granted him less deference than they had before. They could not conceive that a boy who was barely twenty could exert any influence in such a big company.

Thalberg didn't interfere in the studio operation. His employer had left no instructions on what his responsibility would be, and the boy realized he would make no headway with Bernstein, who was twenty years his senior. Thalberg merely observed. He studied scripts and cost reports. He visited the sets and watched the progress of shooting. He made voluminous notes.

When Laemmle returned four months later, Thalberg was ready for him. "The first thing you should do is establish a new job of studio manager and give him the responsibility of watching day-to-day operations," said Thalberg.

"All right," replied Laemmle. "You're it."

Thalberg was surprised but not overwhelmed. He knew what needed to be done, and he set about to do it. He was hampered by a division of authority that remained at Universal City. In typically devious style, Laemmle had appointed a triumvirate to manage the studio operations: Isadore Bernstein, Samuel Van Runkle, and young Thalberg. Within six months, the two older men had left the studio, and Thalberg was in complete command.

The news of his ascendancy astounded the film community. It

Studio manager of Universal Pictures, age twenty

was accustomed to prodigies; the movie industry was a young man's business. But a twenty-year-old boy in charge of a big studio! By contrast, other leaders of the film industry included Samuel Goldwyn, thirty-six; Thomas Ince, thirty-eight; Cecil B. De Mille, thirty-nine; Mack Sennett, forty; D. W. Griffith, forty; Jesse Lasky, forty; Adolph Zukor, forty-seven. Thalberg was the talk of the Alexandria Hotel and other places where the movie people met. Their most delectable piece of gossip was something that happened when Carl Laemmle bustled off to Europe and left Thalberg on his own. When payday arrived, the controller had to tell the studio boss the embarrassing truth: that he, Thalberg, was underage and could not sign the company payroll. But Thalberg was not too young to co-sign for a million-dollar loan which Laemmle badly needed to finance his production schedule. Thalberg gave his signature without hesitation.

Only one person was not surprised to learn of Irving's youthful eminence: Henrietta Thalberg. When he relayed the news to her by long-distance telephone, she reacted the same as she had when he brought home good marks from school. She wanted to know what he could do next that would be better.

4

As general manager of Universal City studios, Irving Thalberg's biggest problem was Erich Von Stroheim, the *homme terrible* Carl Laemmle had hired on a whim in 1919. Von Stroheim, who looked entirely like a Prussian officer and earned a good living in such a portrayal during two World Wars, was Vienna-born, graduate of the Austrian Military Academy. He became an army officer, then turned to journalism, emigrated to the United States and worked for newspapers and magazines until his natural sense of the dramatic pushed him into acting. He toured in a vaudeville sketch based on a novel he had written, later wrote a Broadway play, *Blind Husbands.*

The war proved a boon to his career. He went out to Hollywood where he was in demand as actor, drill instructor, and technical adviser on the anti-German films that were being poured out by the studios. Armistice brought a drought to his career; producers had no need for the bemonocled actor with bullet head and ramrod spine. Von Stroheim roamed the studios with his script for a proposed film version of *Blind Husbands.* No one would listen to him. In desperation he called one evening at Laemmle's home. The butler explained that Mr. Laemmle was dining.

"I only want to see him for ten minutes," Von Stroheim protested.

"Who wants to see me for ten minutes?" asked Laemmle.

Von Stroheim introduced himself and explained his mission. Laemmle granted the ten-minute audience, but warned it could be no longer, as he had a theater appointment. Von Stroheim was still expounding his views at midnight.

Von Stroheim, whose real name was Erich Oswald Hans Karl Marie Stroheim von Nordenwald, starred in and directed *Blind Husbands* for Universal, and the results were extremely pleasing to Laemmle. So much so that he signed an advertisement in *Photoplay* which declared:

> In all my years as a producer of the best photoplays that the art has created I have not known more delightful entertainment than is provided by this amazingly artistic drama, written and directed to the uttermost detail by Erich Von Stroheim, who, furthermore, plays the leading part.

Curiously, the critics agreed. Many of them remarked upon the detail which Von Stroheim lavished on the film: the careful attention to costume and scenery, the glances and gestures that indicated the depth of the characters, the intimations of the psychology that motivated them. Such perception had seldom been seen in American films, which had largely been devoted to one-dimensional figures engaged in enough activity to warrant the term, moving pictures. Von Stroheim introduced a new element of sex relationships; *Blind Husbands* concerned a triangle: an American doctor, his neglected wife, and a courtly Austrian who gave her the attention she needed.

Von Stroheim continued his treatment of sexual motives and the inadequacies of the American male in *The Devil's Passkey*, which caused almost as much comment and business as *Blind Husbands*.

Irving Thalberg recognized the creative talent of Erich Von Stroheim, but he was disturbed by the director's profligate tendencies. The Austrian seemed obsessed with detail, so much so that he neglected all the economics of film making. This failing became extreme during the filming of his third Universal film, *Foolish Wives*. Von Stroheim insisted that the studio build him a life-size replica of Monte Carlo, complete with casino and Hôtel de Paris. Thalberg, who had recently assumed command of the studio operation, had no alternative but to agree.

But the land-locked acres of Universal City could not duplicate all of Monte Carlo, and Von Stroheim insisted that another set be constructed by the sea. The only area that would satisfy him as a duplicate of the Riviera was on the Monterey peninsula three hundred and fifty miles north.

The Monterey location shooting stretched on for weeks. During one sequence, Von Stroheim wanted a shot of pigeons flying in from the sea. But the wind blew constantly from the Pacific, and the pigeons flew against the wind only. The director spent days trying to photograph the birds in the flight pattern he sought.

Thalberg was barely twenty-one years old when Von Stroheim began shooting *Foolish Wives*. Almost a year later, the director was still photographing the film, which had cost a million of Laemmle's dollars, by far the biggest outlay for a Universal picture. Thalberg visited the set one day and drew Von Stroheim aside.

"I have seen all the film, and you have all you need for the picture," said Thalberg. "I want you to stop shooting."

"I am not finished as yet," Von Stroheim announced, eying the young man coldly.

"Yes, you have," Thalberg replied. "You have spent all the money this company can afford. I cannot allow you to spend any more."

The director fumed. "If you were not my superior"—he made the word sound like an insult—"I would smash you in the face."

Thalberg's dark eyes displayed no emotion. "Don't let that stop you," he replied.

Von Stroheim stood glaring at the young studio boss, then turned on his heel and stalked off. In late 1921 *Foolish Wives* concluded production.

When *Foolish Wives* proved to be the biggest success in Universal's history, the troubles with Von Stroheim were almost forgotten. But not quite. As Thalberg studied the returns from theater rentals, he realized the margin of profit was not as high as on the company's other big pictures, because of the million-dollar production cost. Thalberg had no objection to paying more for film entertainment, but he knew the excessive charges to *Foolish Wives* were due to the director's extravagances and the expense did not appear on the screen.

Although the film was hailed in some quarters as an advance for the movie art, it also came under some criticism as being anti-American. *Photoplay* attacked *Foolish Wives* as "an insult to every American" and cited "continual innuendoes as to American ideals; sly little thrusts at our traditions and sentiments."

Thalberg was willing to engage Von Stroheim for a fourth film, *Merry-Go-Round*. Again the director's lack of discipline was evidenced. For days he produced no more than a few hundred feet of film. Then he decided that night shooting better fitted the mood of the picture. Despite the added cost and the inconvenience to the cast and crew, he filmed exclusively at night. After five weeks he had spent $210,000 with little finished film to show for it.

Late one evening, Von Stroheim was summoned from the set of *Merry-Go-Round* to the office of the general manager. Thalberg had asked the Universal attorney, Edwin Loeb, to be present. Loeb had prudently stationed his young secretary, Minna Wallis, behind a door to record what was said.

Von Stroheim swaggered into the room and gazed contemptuously at the small figure in the big chair behind the desk. Thalberg rose and was prepared to shake hands with the director, but Von Stroheim responded with a click of his heels.

"Mr. Von Stroheim, much as I regret it, I have to report that Universal can no longer afford your unreasonable behavior in the shooting of this picture," said Thalberg. "You are being replaced as director."

Von Stroheim was incredulous. "That is impossible," he scoffed. "*Merry-Go-Round* is *my* picture. I conceived it, and I will see it through to the end. No one can take Von Stroheim off a Von Stroheim picture."

"Perhaps that was impossible in the past," Thalberg remarked, "because you appeared in your other films. But you are not acting in *Merry-Go-Round*. And so you can be replaced."

The director realized his error. He continued his arguments, but they were unavailing. He was removed from the picture and replaced by Rupert Julian, most noted for his wartime film, *Beasts of Berlin*. The film colony delighted in telling how the slight, unassuming young boss of Universal had fired the autocratic Von Stroheim.

The gossips had something else to talk about. They sensed that a romance was blossoming between Irving Thalberg and Carl Laemmle's only daughter, Rosabelle. Indeed the young man dined regularly at the Laemmle house, and he often escorted Rosabelle to dances in the ballroom of the Garden Court Apartments and to openings of new pictures. There could be no denying his attention to the young lady, nor any doubt that her father approved of her friendship for his brilliant studio chief.

Rosabelle Laemmle was a bright, attractive girl who had qualities that Irving Thalberg admired, qualities that were also possessed by his mother. Carl's wife had died when Rosabelle was young, and the girl had to assume the role of the woman in the family. She did so with skill. She often traveled to Europe with her father, and she learned the social graces. She was an expert hostess in the Laemmle homes in New York and California, and she supplied the gentility which her father sometimes lacked. Thalberg admired her assurance, her efficiency. There was only one problem in his fondness for Rosabelle: Henrietta didn't like her. Mrs. Thalberg voiced no objection to the Laemmle daughter, but her attitude was apparent. She believed her son could do better.

5

During his two years as head of production at Universal, Thalberg developed some of the office habits that were to remain with him throughout his career. He realized that first impressions were important, and so he adopted a mannerism he believed would present him as a busy, efficient executive. When a newcomer entered the office, Thalberg was usually standing behind his desk shuffling papers or intently reading a letter. He gave no indication of noticing the visitor, and when he looked up, he seemed to be somewhat surprised. He immediately put the visitor at ease, and he listened with complete concentration to the problem or presentation. The visitor felt that he was receiving the most careful and sympathetic consideration, and thoughts of the tenderness of Thalberg's years were minimized by his mature manner. Although his sense of humor was adequately developed, he rarely joked. Levity would have underscored his youth; hence he was generally solemn.

Thalberg thoroughly enjoyed the exercise of power, but he was not entirely satisfied with his position at Universal. His hopes for more efficient operation of the studio were thwarted by the abundance of relatives and immigrant friends of Laemmle's, who could not be discharged. As was true throughout his career, Thalberg believed strongly that he should be paid in accordance to his contribution to the company, and he did not feel that his $450 weekly salary met that standard. But Laemmle would pay him no more. In the wake of the Von Stroheim excesses, Laemmle was becoming more conscious of costs. He was constantly admonishing the studio to hold down expenses. Thalberg was convinced that only by pouring more quality, hence money, into pictures could Universal take its place with Famous Players—Lasky, Fox, and other first-rank producers.

Laemmle agreed to Thalberg's ambitious plan for a film to be based on the Victor Hugo classic, *Notre Dame de Paris*. Thalberg wanted to make it a spectacle, rather than just a horror picture, and he ordered construction of a huge square, including a replica of Notre Dame. For the key role of Quasimodo, the Hunchback of Notre Dame, he chose Lon Chaney, who had been coming into prominence as portrayer of grotesque heavies.

The son of deaf mute parents, Chaney had of necessity learned to express himself through pantomime. He played in road-company musicals, then drifted to Hollywood, where he joined the Universal City stock company in 1915. He left to free lance with other studios, usually being cast as a heavy because of his coarse features. His ability as a contortionist won him the role as a crippled beggar in *The Miracle Man*, and he followed with the part of a legless pirate in *The Penalty*. Thalberg was impressed with his Fagin in Jackie Coogan's *Oliver Twist* in 1922 and assigned him the title role of the new film, *The Hunchback of Notre Dame*.

As with all his roles, Chaney approached the make-up with almost masochistic zeal. He wore shoulder pads that attached to a seventy-pound rubber hump. A leather harness prevented him from standing erect, and the whole rig was covered by a rubber suit affixed with animal hair. Chaney stuffed mortician's wax into his mouth to push his face out of shape and added putty cheeks, fangs, matted hair and a popping false eye. So contorted, he worked for the three months of the film's duration, and his portrayal of suffering was eloquent.

When Thalberg viewed the finished film, he recognized the unique quality of Chaney's performance. The New York office was clamoring for the film, but he refused to ship it. He knew the distributors would release *The Hunchback of Notre Dame* immediately to fulfill the never-ending demand for theater product. Thalberg believed it deserved better treatment.

He ordered the director, Wallace Worsley, to return the company for additional crowd scenes, thus adding $150,000 to the cost. It was a long chance. Laemmle had been grumbling about the film's expense, the biggest since Von Stroheim's debauch with *Foolish Wives*. But Laemmle was in Europe and wouldn't know about the added scenes until his return. And by escalating the cost, Thalberg would force the New York office to sell *The Hunchback of Notre Dame* as a special attraction.

The ruse succeeded. Astonished at the film's cost, Laemmle ordered a special campaign to promote it. The picture was Universal's biggest moneymaker to that date, elevating the company's prestige and establishing Lon Chaney as a top-flight star.

Laemmle still refused to reward his young general manager with

a bigger salary, and Thalberg grew more restive. At night he worked with Lucien Hubbard and a prominent director, Rollin Sturgon, in developing a script they planned to produce independently. Each contributed to the $30,000 cost of a film called *Daughters of Today* starring Patsy Ruth Miller, who had been the Esmeralda of *The Hunchback of Notre Dame*. It was designed to capitalize on the flaming-youth cycle of films, and the trio of film makers planned to launch their own company if it was a success. But when they had an offer to double their investment, they sold out to Lewis J. Selznick, who subsequently earned $750,000 with it. That was the end of Thalberg's outside production.

The restless young man cast about for a position with another production company. He paid a call on Cecil B. De Mille, whom he knew slightly. De Mille and Jesse Lasky were operating a studio on Vine Street just south of Hollywood Boulevard, and De Mille was impressed with Thalberg's achievements. He proposed to his partner that they hire the young man.

Lasky asked how much Thalberg was earning at Universal. De Mille told him Thalberg's salary was $450 a week and he wanted more.

"We can't do it, Cecil," said Lasky.

"But Jesse, this boy is a genius," De Mille protested. "I can see it. I know it."

Lasky remained firm, and De Mille had to tell Thalberg they couldn't hire him. Next, Thalberg began negotiations to join Hal Roach, and a contract was almost completed. But then a talented creator of comedies, Dick Jones, left the Mack Sennett studio, and Roach hired him instead of Thalberg.

The youthful chief of Universal production was determined to improve his position. In the three years since he had taken over direction of the studio, he had proved his worth. The Universal pictures had improved enormously, and the credit was largely his. He had displayed an uncanny sense of story, so that the Universal scripts no longer possessed a slapdash flavor; always he insisted that a script be tightly constructed before filming began. He also showed a remarkable capacity for working with actors, casting them aptly and advising them on their careers.

He enjoyed his work. He was stimulated by dealing with diverse temperaments and combining them to create a piece of entertain-

ment. He was excited by the Hollywood life, the plenitude of
beauty and talent, both of which he admired profoundly. He had
quickly become one of the most attractive figures of Hollywood's
loose-knit society, a young man sought as guest for dinner parties.
Already a figure of power at twenty-three, he bore the promise of
greater importance.

Thalberg knew his future: it was in films. But not the chaotic
kind of movie business as it was constituted in the early 1920s,
when thirty or forty companies of varying size provided an effusion
of film to satisfy the public's fascination with movies. There was no
continuity, no direction, no building for the future. These conditions
needed remedying, Irving Thalberg believed. Soon he was to make
contact with another man who shared his ideas.

Patsy Ruth Miller, center, in Daughters of Today

III

MATURITY 1923–1929

Irving was a motion picture man utterly. He was also extremely young. I used to go into his office with the feeling I was addressing a boy. In a moment, I would be the one who felt young and inexperienced. I would feel he was not one but all the forty disciples.

—Lionel Barrymore

I

THEY SEEMED to have little in common, except that both were Jewish and both had mothers they adored.

Irving Thalberg was an insatiable reader, a man who could talk to writers in their own language, who could explain why Theodore Dreiser was a better writer than Jakob Wasserman—"not so superficial." Louis B. Mayer preferred to have screen stories told to him by his studio's Scheherazade, Kate Corbaley, who narrated the tales in graphic style.

Thalberg was shy in public and shunned the spotlight; although his relations with reporters were cordial, he avoided interviews. He made public appearances only if by so doing he could further his studio and the film industry. Mayer adored playing the mogul before the world. Politics was an avocation, and he liked nothing more than to hobnob with Presidents and visiting dignitaries.

Thalberg was aesthetic in his tastes; Mayer developed a great fondness for horse racing. Thalberg practiced moderation in all things; Mayer was a man of lusty appetites. Thalberg lived by an almost chivalric code; Mayer was less scrupulous in achieving his ends.

Despite such disparities, Louis Mayer and Irving Thalberg for a momentous decade comprised the most successful partnership in Hollywood—until the inevitable forces of greed, jealousy, and power pulled them asunder.

Mayer was thirty-seven and Thalberg was twenty-three when they first met in 1922. Mayer was impressed by the young man's sagacity, his devotion to picture making, and his loyalty to his mother. Thalberg often visited Mayer's house, and the pair talked about the film business far into the night. Thalberg respected the experience of Mayer, who had been exhibiting and producing movies for fifteen years.

He had been born in Minsk, Russia, a fact he did not like to refer to—nor would he reveal what had been his name at birth. He called himself Louis Burt Mayer after his parents had moved to New Brunswick, Nova Scotia, where his father dealt in salvage metal. Like William Thalberg, Jacob Mayer was not an aggressive man, and much of the family drive was supplied by his wife Sarah, who augmented their bare income by selling live chickens from door to door. Young Louis looked to his mother for guidance and love.

The boy collected used metal for his father's trade, to combat the taunts of the Canadians, to whom a Jew was something strange and faintly ridiculous. Young Louie acquitted himself well with the village toughs. He was small of stature, but the years of lifting metal gave him a powerful build; he was a rugged fighter, as he continued to demonstrate even into middle age. After attending public schools, he went into the Mayer business, which now included salvaging of sunken vessels. But Louis was restless, and he left home to try his hand at the salvage metal business in Boston. Then, by one of those unexplained strokes of fate that befell many of the film pioneers, he was attracted to the movie business. In 1907, a friend showed him an ad for the sale of a theater in Haverhill, Massachussetts. Mayer decided to invest in it, and one of his first attractions was a hand-tinted film depicting the Life of Christ. The Catholic workers of the shoe mills flocked to the theater, and Mayer decided he had happened onto a good thing.

Married and the father of two daughters, Mayer worked hard at his new enterprise, and he was able to establish theaters in other nearby towns. Soon he was distributing films from headquarters in Boston.

After making a huge profit with *Birth of a Nation,* he began eying the gold that could be reaped from producing films. He realized that he needed a star, and in 1918 he spirited Anita Stewart away from Vitagraph. Her first film for Mayer's company, *Virtuous Wives,* was a success, and the onetime junk dealer from Nova Scotia was in business as a movie producer.

In late 1918, Mayer followed the migration of film makers to California and set up his operation on Mission Road in east Los Angeles at the site of the Selig zoo. William Selig had established a zoo and film studio there ten years before. The combination seemed wry to some observers of the movie business, but it proved a convenient one for the making of films with animals. Within three years, Mayer had a bustling operation on Mission Road. Films about women appealed to him, and most of his stars were female: Anita Stewart, Mildred Harris Chaplin, Renée Adorée, Kathleen Mac-Donald, Barbara LaMarr. His directors were Fred Niblo, John Stahl, Reginald Barker, and Hobart Henley, and the writers included Bess Meredyth, Frances Marion, and Kathleen Norris.

Mayer recognized his own inadequacies as a producer. He was an indefatigable persuader, a man who made his will prevail by means of cajolery, flattery, tears, threats, physical violence or any other technique. But while such methods often succeeded in making deals, they were not always effective in making pictures. He admitted the need for someone of a more sensitive and creative nature to oversee production.

"I will go down on my knees to talent," Mayer said, and he often did so in his most persuasive moments. He saw in Thalberg a talent of exceptional rarity, a young man with a fine consciousness of the creative process, yet with a sound business mind. Mayer had dreams of expanding his operation into a giant studio, and he knew that he could do so only by a widespread search for talent. He saw in Irving Thalberg the key to his search.

Mayer's timing was good. In late 1922, Thalberg had despaired of making order out of the tangled affairs at Universal City or of achieving an increase in salary from Carl Laemmle. After making inquiries at other studios, Thalberg began negotiating with Mayer. An agreement on a salary of $600 a week was reached.

On February 15, 1923, Thalberg at the age of twenty-three assumed

the position of vice-president and production assistant of the Mayer
Company. Carl Laemmle was furious over the theft of his young
general manager and would not speak to Louis Mayer for long afterward.

Thalberg plunged into his job at the Mayer studio with the same
zeal he had displayed at Universal. This time he was not hampered by
the abundance of relatives and hangers-on, and he made rapid progress in fashioning a program of creditable films. Mayer was delighted with his new production assistant. Thalberg had the ability
to placate such a flammable personality as John Stahl, with whom
Mayer had clashed furiously. Mayer was amazed with the facility
Thalberg displayed in analyzing a script's ills and suggesting remedies
to scenarists. The studio was developing an *esprit* that Mayer had long
striven for, and he was most gratified by the splendid returns that the
improved features were bringing at the box office.

2

From the start of their association, Louis Mayer and Irving Thalberg
agreed that one of their prime objectives would be to develop new
stars. Only by so doing could they hope to attract wide patronage
from a public that was crazy about Mary Pickford, Douglas Fairbanks,
Charlie Chaplin, Rudolph Valentino, William S. Hart, and other
top-notch attractions. In his search for new personalities, Thalberg
recalled an actress he had admired in a 1920 film called *The Stealers*.
Her name was Norma Shearer, and she played a minor role in the
picture, but he was impressed by her vivacity and her cool beauty.
While he had been in charge of Universal studio, he made inquiries
about the girl. But she was in New York and nothing came of it.

In 1923, Thalberg proferred a contract with the Mayer Company
at $150 a week, plus railroad fare for her mother and herself to
come to California. At the same time Hal Roach was in New York
seeking a leading lady for a serial he had contracted to make for
Pathé. He saw Miss Shearer and made her a better offer than she
had received from Thalberg. She felt inclined to take it, and Roach
departed for California after instructing his attorney to draw up the
contract. The attorney devised what he considered a brilliant publicity scheme: the contract would specify that the actress would assume
the name of the character in the serial. Miss Shearer declined to

change her name, and she accepted the offer with the Mayer Company.

During her three years of working in the New York studios, Miss Shearer had heard much about the lavish treatment accorded players who went to Hollywood, and as her train neared Los Angeles, she grew more excited. When the car jolted to a stop, she gazed up and down the platform. There were no photographers, no reporters. She and her mother stepped down from the train. There were no publicists offering baskets of fruit and bouquets of flowers, no liveried chauffeur to usher them to a Rolls-Royce. Not even an office boy to greet them.

Disconsolately, they hired a taxi to take them to the Hollywood Hotel. That afternoon, Miss Shearer decided to face her new employers. She took another long and expensive taxi ride to Mission Road. As she entered the studio, she heard the roar of a lion from the zoo, and she felt a fleeting kinship to early Christians.

She was somewhat gratified when the young man in the reception room said, "Oh, yes, Miss Shearer, we've been expecting you. Follow me, please."

She followed him down a long corridor and into a small office. Then she was surprised when the dark, slight man sat down behind the desk.

"Then—you're not the office boy?" she asked.

He smiled. "No, Miss Shearer, I'm Irving Thalberg, vice-president of the Mayer Company. I'm the man who sent for you."

She recovered her equilibrium and began expounding about the

Miss Lotta Miles

number of offers she had received from other studios. "Universal
wanted to sign me a year ago for two hundred dollars a week, but
I was too tied up with pictures in New York," she said.

"Yes, I know," he replied.

"You know?"

"Yes, and it wasn't for two hundred dollars. I was in charge of the
studio at the time."

She decided not to say anything more, but to place herself in the
hands of this self-assured young man. He advised her to be patient
and trust him to make the right judgment in the planning of her
career.

Patience had not been one of the prime attributes of Edith Norma
Shearer. She was persistent, shrewd, perhaps ambitious. But not patient. Like many film actresses of the period, her drive was supplied by
a determined mother. So indulged was young Norma that she didn't
go to school until she was ten; she stayed home and took piano and
dance lessons.

Her Montreal childhood was a happy one. Her father was president
of a construction company, and little was denied to the Shearer
children, Athole, Norma, and Douglas. Norma went to all the dances
and had all the partners a girl could desire. At fourteen she won a
beauty contest. Encouraged by her mother, she took part in the high
school theatricals and could give a rousing recitation of "The Face on
the Barroom Floor."

Andrew Shearer's business went sour during World War I. He sold
out and put the money into investments that failed. The resilient
Edith Fisher Shearer gathered up her two daughters and set out for
New York to find theatrical careers for them. "Girls, let's make an
adventure of it," she suggested, and they said they'd try.

Norma won an audition with Florenz Ziegfeld, but she couldn't
sing, and she was too short to be a show girl. "Go back to Canada
and forget the stage," Ziegfeld advised her. She drew a tiny role in
D. W. Griffith's *Way Down East*, but the great director said she
would never be a movie actress. "Your eyes are too blue," he told
her.

The two Shearer girls landed a job as extras in a film being made
in Mount Vernon. Each morning they took the train from Grand
Central Station at six-thirty and returned home at midnight with the

salary of five dollars apiece. When that job ran out, the work stopped coming. Mrs. Shearer tried to find work in a department store but failed. Norma sought jobs as pianist in movie houses but was told she couldn't be hired because she didn't belong to the union. Reluctantly, Edith Shearer telegraphed her husband for money to return home. Andrew Shearer replied he had none to send.

Norma began working again. Herbert Brenon gave her a small role at $25 a day, and it lasted several days. She began posing for illustrators like James Montgomery Flagg and Charles Dana Gibson. She drew work with advertising agencies and found herself on a billboard at Columbus Circle, peering through a Springfield tire as Miss Lotta Miles. She worked in such films as *The Restless Sex*, *Channing of the Northwest* and *The Stealers*, which had made such an impression on Irving Thalberg.

His faith in her did not seem entirely justified during her early months with the Mayer Company. Her first assignment was *The Wanters*, directed by John Stahl. He was unimpressed when she appeared in an overly sophisticated gown, and he relegated her to a minor role. The demotion shook Miss Shearer's confidence, but not Thalberg's. He cast her in *Pleasure Mad* as a flaming debutante who was forced to choose between her father and mother in a divorce.

"You don't seem to know what it's all about," declared the director, Reginald Barker, as she continued to deliver a colorless performance. The young actress was too nervous and frightened to do otherwise.

She realized that Mary Alden, who played her mother, was running away with all their scenes. Yet she couldn't muster the fire that was required for the madcap heiress. That fire was supplied by Mayer, who called her into his office and accused her of being yellow. Her Irish aroused, she answered him defiantly and stormed back to the set with fierce determination. She gave a performance that fulfilled Thalberg's confidence.

3

The forces of consolidation were running strong in the motion picture industry during the early 1920s. Independent producers were being gathered into a few giant companies which could maintain big studios and control large chains of theaters.

Louis Mayer perceived the advantages of bigness. It pained him to see actors, directors, and cameramen sitting idle because he did not have the scripts nor stage space to keep them working all the time. He often expounded to his young production manager how much better it would be to have fifty stars instead of ten, twenty stages instead of three, so the company could pour out a steady supply of motion pictures. His concept achieved reality because of a pair of studios which were bigger, but not as healthy as his.

In 1920, Marcus Loew had bought Metro Pictures with the idea of using it to feed much-needed product into his huge chain of Loew's theaters. His plan worked well for a while, especially with the production of *Four Horsemen of the Apocalypse* starring Rudolph Valentino. But production costs began to climb as theater business sagged in a postwar depression, and the Metro operation started to register large losses.

Goldwyn Pictures was also ailing. The company no longer had the services of hustling founder, Samuel Goldwyn, who had been forced out of the organization in a power play by Joseph Godsol. Goldwyn Pictures had a huge studio in Culver City, formerly Thomas Ince's Triangle, and it was caught in the same economic crush as Metro.

Marcus Loew and Joseph Godsol began having conversations about consolidating their losing studios. But neither had a production boss in Hollywood who seemed capable of handling such an immense enterprise, and they began casting about for such a person. Enter Louis B. Mayer.

It was just what Mayer had been looking for: a chance to broaden his film making into a large-scale operation. Now that he had the partner to help him fulfill that vision—Irving Thalberg—nothing could hold Mayer back. Mayer was fortunate in having as his attorney J. Robert Rubin, a handsome, persuasive man who had learned the ins and outs of politics as an assistant district attorney of New York City. Rubin also happened to be attorney for Loew's, and he suggested to Godsol and Loew that Louis Mayer was just the man to head the new studio.

The negotiations were lengthy. Mayer, a vigorous walker, went to New York, and he and Rubin spent hours treading the Manhattan streets as they discussed the proposals and counterproposals. Meanwhile Irving Thalberg was carrying on the studio operation at 3200 Mission Road.

One spring day in 1924 he was in conference with his associate, Paul Bern, director Fred Niblo and writers Bess Meredyth and Lenore Coffee on a script to be based on the successful play, *Captain Applejack*. The story of a reformed pirate, it had become famous for its line, "I am in a mood for dalliance."

Thalberg was called from the meeting, and he was absent for a lengthy period. When he returned, he stood in the doorway with a broad smile on his face. The others in the room were surprised, because they had grown accustomed to a studied solemnness in the young man.

"Ladies and gentlemen," he declared, "I have the pleasure to announce to you that the merger of the Metro, Goldwyn, and Mayer companies is now an accomplished fact."

The news was a stunning surprise to his listeners, and they were further surprised by the next remark of the businesslike Thalberg: "I think we'll do no more work today, for I find myself in a mood for dalliance."

The formation of Metro-Goldwyn*—Mayer was added to the corporative name two years later—was announced on April 17, 1924. The merger meant immense new power for Louis Mayer, who was designated first vice-president and general manager of the studio at a weekly salary of $1500. It also brought huge responsibility for Irving Thalberg as second vice-president and supervisor of production at $650 a week. Not yet twenty-five years old, he found himself in charge of a directorial staff that included Victor Seastrom, Fred Niblo, Erich Von Stroheim, John Stahl, Reginald Barker, Robert Z. Leonard, Frank Borzage, Rex Ingram, Marshall Neilan, Victor Schertzinger, and Hobart Henley. His stars included John Gilbert, Lon Chaney, Mae Murray, Eleanor Boardman, Ramon Novarro, William Haines, Renée Adorée, Norma Shearer, and Conrad Nagel.

Most of the new company's talent was on hand for the inauguration ceremonies at the Culver City studio on April 26, and Mayer beamed

---

* No longer in the management of the Goldwyn company, Samuel Goldwyn remained a stockholder. But he disapproved of the merger, and his interests were bought out. He never was a part of Metro-Goldwyn-Mayer, although his name was retained.

upon them from the bunting-wrapped, flower-filled platform. He and Thalberg and Harry Rapf, who was to take charge of the minor films, posed for photographs before a giant key marked "Success." Mayer made a fervent speech, messages from President Calvin Coolidge and Secretary of Commerce Herbert Hoover were read, and Will Rogers arrived late on horseback. He apologized for being late, explaining that he had to return home for his chewing gum.

The ceremonies over, Irving Thalberg settled down to the immense task of fashioning a production program for the new company. One of the first problems he had to face was *Ben-Hur*.

4

In an attempt to revive its fading fortunes, the old Goldwyn company had committed itself to a huge outlay for the screen rights to *Ben-Hur*, the best-selling novel by General Lew Wallace and for years a big attraction as a stage spectacle. Now the commitment became Metro-Goldwyn's, and at the time of the merger a company was shooting in Rome with Charles Brabin directing and George Walsh in the title role.

Ben-Hur was not Thalberg's kind of picture. He preferred films that dealt in human relationships, rather than the crowd-filled spectacles. But he realized the value of *Ben-Hur* to the newly formed company. It was being made in Italy on a huge scale, with a mammoth replica of Joppa Gate of Jerusalem and sea battles involving fleets of galley ships. If the film could reflect excitement and dramatic power as well as bigness, it could be a perfect vehicle to establish Metro-Goldwyn as a giant of the industry.

But it wasn't coming off. Thalberg hastened to the projection room as soon as the latest supply of film arrived from Rome. He sat in the darkened room and shook his head over the footage. The scope and size of the spectacle was there, but what was happening up front was drab and lifeless.

Thalberg voiced his concern to Mayer, who agreed that *Ben-Hur* was not going well. This was no news to the Loew's executives in New York, who were aware of the troubles in Rome. But they had done little except complain about the spiraling costs.

Mayer was gravely concerned, realizing that his dream of a film empire could be destroyed by a disaster of the magnitude that *Ben-*

Hur was threatening to be. He and Thalberg agreed that the director and star should be replaced, even though the subsequent loss might amount to a half-million dollars. But who could sell the Loew's brass on such a bold scheme? Not the youthful, unproved Thalberg. Mayer himself headed for New York to exercise his considerable powers of persuasion.

One Sunday noon, Ramon Novarro was lunching at his home when he received a telephone call. He instantly recognized the young voice of Irving Thalberg, with whom he had worked on Mission Road. "Can you come to the studio?" Thalberg asked.

"Today? Now?" asked the Mexican actor.

"Yes, now."

Novarro drove to the studio and reported to Thalberg's office. The young executive didn't bother with preliminaries. "How would you like to play Ben-Hur?" he asked.

Novarro was stunned. "Are you crazy? Of course I'd like to play Ben-Hur."

"All right. I want you to leave tomorrow." Then Thalberg added: "I want you to make a test today."

The actor took a long chance. "No," he replied.

"Why not?" Thalberg demanded.

"You know what I can do, Irving. And if you're worried about my legs—you saw them in *Where the Pavement Ends*. There's nothing wrong with them."

Thalberg smiled. "All right, Ramon, no test. Now listen. Tomorrow I want you to leave from the Pasadena station, not Los Angeles, where you'll be noticed. No one is to know."

Thalberg also dispatched two other stalwarts of the Mayer Company, director Fred Niblo and writer Bess Meredyth. They met in New York with Marcus Loew, who was to lead the pilgrimage to Rome. "If they interview you at the boat," he instructed Novarro, "just tell the reporters that you're going on a vacation with me."

The mission succeeded, and Brabin and Walsh were supplanted by Niblo and Novarro. Miss Meredyth and another Thalberg favorite, Carey Wilson, fashioned the unwieldy script into manageable shape, and production resumed.

But Thalberg was dissatisfied with the new footage. The scenes lacked definition because of too little lighting. The costumes seemed grotesque. Novarro himself complained of the long hair and turban he was required to wear: "I look like Pola Negri." Thalberg continued pressing for the company to return to Culver City, where he could keep a close eye on the shooting. Marcus Loew resisted any change in locale, and Mayer himself decided to travel to Rome and see what was going on. He was shocked by the amount of money that was being wasted. When he returned to New York, he used all his persuasive powers to convince Loew to order the company back to Hollywood. Loew finally acquiesced, and the *Ben-Hur* troupe left Rome after spending two million dollars during more than a year of shooting. Less than a third of the film was completed.

Now the New York executives were anxious to finish *Ben-Hur* as quickly as possible. But Thalberg would not be hurried. He realized that the sea battle and the Joppa Gate scenes would establish an epic size for the film; reducing the scope to hurry *Ben-Hur* to a finish would be false economy. He also knew that excitement was needed to raise the film above the level of a religious tableau. The chariot race had supplied thrills in the stage presentation of *Ben-Hur*, which featured real horses racing on a treadmill. Thalberg decided to film the chariot race in a style that even the Romans would have admired.

He ordered the expenditure of $300,000 for construction of the Antioch Coliseum on a field near the studio. When studio designers showed him the plans, he approved the vastness of the set. But he added: "The audience is going to think the set is a fake unless we prove to them it isn't. What we need are some statues, huge statues we can place the extras beside so the audience will get a sense of the scale."

Doug and Mary watch the chariot race

The designers returned with sketches of crouching figures which would be placed in the center of the track. "That's it," Thalberg said approvingly. The statues were fashioned out of plaster, and an alert press agent helped publicize them by posing a visiting troupe of midgets.

The chariot race brought a day of rare excitement to Hollywood. The film colony had been watching the construction of the huge Coliseum, the biggest set in Hollywood history, bigger than Griffith's Babylon for *Intolerance*. Now the time had arrived to photograph the race, and a special platform was built as a vantage point for visiting celebrities. Hollywood's own royalty, Mary Pickford and Douglas Fairbanks, were among the invited guests.

Thalberg wanted to shoot as much as possible in one day, and he ordered forty-two cameras stationed throughout the arena to catch the action. He arrived early and watched with cool detachment as the trainers exercised the four-horse teams. Soon the stadium began to fill up with extras; the casting department had enlisted them

from everywhere possible, including skid row. Thalberg eyed the
crowd and called over J. J. Cohn of the production department.

"How many people have you got, Joe?" Thalberg asked.

"Thirty-nine hundred," Cohn replied.

"Not enough. Get some more."

"But where? How can we find them at this hour?"

"I don't care. Pull them in off the street. The set needs more
people."

Cohn enlisted the curious onlookers to don robes and join the
throng, and his assistants scoured Culver City for others. Four hundred more Antiochians joined the Coliseum throng.

A fog had drifted in from the Pacific and hung over the Coliseum
so that filming was impossible. Ten o'clock passed, and not a
camera had turned. Ten-thirty. Thalberg walked silently about the
set, with only an occasional glance at the sky betraying his anxiety.
Director Fred Niblo was less calm.

"Can't we do something?" he asked. "How about getting some wind
machines to blow the fog away?"

"You'd just blow some more in," an assistant pointed out.

Finally at eleven o'clock the California sun began poking through
the grayish haze. In a half-hour, the scene was bright enough for
photography, and Cohn suggested filming a couple of shots before the
lunch break.

"But these people are hungry," Niblo said, gazing at the crowd.

"Get the horses," Cohn told the assistants.

"Joe, don't rush us," said Niblo.

"I said, get the horses."

"Joe, you'll have a riot on your hands," Niblo warned.

The cost-conscious Cohn replied, "So it'll look like they're cheering
for the race."

Two shots were completed before lunch, then the major part of
the race began afterward. The staging was in the hands of an action
expert, Reeves (Breezy) Eason, and he made sure the racing would
be spirited. Before the race began, he gathered the stunt-men drivers
together and told them: "The man who wins the race gets a hundred
and fifty dollars. The second man gets a hundred, and whoever comes
in third wins fifty dollars. Now let's see you give us a race."

They did. For such prizes the stunt men would have fought lions,

and they raced around the arena in breathtaking style. One mishap provided the race's biggest thrill. On the second lap, a wheel came loose from one of the chariots, and it swerved. Three more chariots crashed into the wreck, and a fourth leaped over it.

Thalberg was pleased with the day's shooting, but he ordered more closeup shots to heighten the audience's participation in the race. Camera cars sped before the onrushing teams—an innovation in filming. For days, Ramon Novarro and Francis X. Bushman stood on the back of chariots as horses charged furiously behind them. One slip could have meant serious danger for the stars, and an assistant crouched on the floor of each chariot to prevent such a catastrophe.

During the latter stages of filming *Ben-Hur*, the concern over the immense production and the output of energy to initiate the great new enterprise took a toll in Thalberg's delicate health. He suffered a collapse and was taken to a hospital in grave condition. Doctors examined him and discovered his weakened heart. They gave him no more than an even chance to recover.

The workers at Metro-Goldwyn-Mayer were plunged into depression. Irving Thalberg symbolized the vast hope that all of them felt for the young company; his loss would be a staggering blow to its prospects. Louis Mayer was terrified. He locked himself in his office and waited there, red-eyed and ashen, fearful of the news that might come from the hospital.

Finally the good tidings came: Irving had passed the crisis and would recover. The experience had shaken Mayer, who had pinned his hopes for the new company on the frail shoulders of his young partner. But Mayer's concern was soon alleviated by the amazing recuperative powers of Thalberg and his insatiable capacity for work. Even before the doctors would allow him to sit up in bed, Thalberg was viewing the rushes of *Ben-Hur* as they were projected on the ceiling of his bedroom.

Thalberg personally supervised the cutting of the chariot race, and the sequence proved the best in the picture. *Ben-Hur* finally reached the theaters at the end of 1925, and it became an immense attraction. Because of its cost—almost four million, double that of any previous film—and the fact that the owners of the theatrical rights took half the profits, the film was not extremely profitable. But it did accomplish what Mayer and Thalberg had hoped: to establish the new company as the creator of films of prestige.

He learned an important lesson from the experience. Because of the chaotic conditions in Rome, *Ben-Hur* had cost more than twice what it would have in Culver City. Only in rare instances would he ever allow films to be shot on far-off locations, beyond his watchful control.

5

The merger brought Irving Thalberg face-to-face once more with the forbidding visage of Erich Von Stroheim. After Thalberg had fired him from *Merry-Go-Round* at Universal, Von Stroheim had moved to the Goldwyn Company and had involved himself in a film based on the Frank Norris novel, *McTeague*. He aimed to capture the breath of reality in the film, to be titled *Greed*, just as "Dickens and De Maupassant and Zola and Frank Norris catch and reflect life in their novels." To accomplish this, he eschewed all studio sets. He rented a house on Laguna Street in San Francisco and insisted that

On location with Greed. *Von Stroheim with megaphone; Zasu Pitts and Jean Hersholt are behind him*

his actors, including Gibson Gowland, Zasu Pitts, and Jean Hersholt, actually live in the rooms so they would feel at ease playing scenes in them. Von Stroheim photographed the house with natural light from the windows, augmenting it with artificial lights only when necessary.

The studio people urged Von Stroheim to shoot his Death Valley scenes on the dunes at Oxnard, only thirty miles from Hollywood, but he refused. Instead, he led an expedition of forty-one men and one woman into Death Valley itself. He later bragged: "We were the only white people who had penetrated into the lowest point on earth since the days of the pioneers. We worked in 142 degrees Fahrenheit in the shade, and *no* shade. I believe the results I achieved through the actual heat and the physical strain were worth the trouble we had all gone to."

When Von Stroheim had finally completed shooting, he had spent $470,000 and amassed forty-two reels of film, enough for four lengthy movies. He cut it down to twenty-four reels, then decided he could eliminate nothing more. At that point the merger was completed, and the new head of production, Thalberg, had to deal with the

*Gibson Gowland and Jean Hersholt
on the Death Valley salt flats*

oversized *Greed* and an intractable creator whose enmity he had already incurred.

Thalberg urged Von Stroheim to make further cuts. The director agreed—and then edited out a dozen feet of film here and there. He secretly sent a print of *Greed* to his friend, Rex Ingram, who returned it with six reels eliminated. Ingram had made the cuts at Von Stroheim's request and said he wouldn't speak to his friend again if another foot was removed. Von Stroheim reported this to Mayer, who was unimpressed. He hated Ingram, and he gave Von Stroheim the ultimatum: cut *Greed* to ten reels.

Von Stroheim had no heart for shortening the work to which he had devoted two years of creative effort. The job was done by a cutter under Thalberg's supervision, and *Greed* was released with little fanfare. It brought only modest returns at the box office and represented a loss for the new company.

Proponents of Von Stroheim have long castigated Thalberg for his treatment of *Greed*, and possibly he should bear at least part of the responsibility for damaging what might have been a masterpiece. Perhaps if he had stood up to Mayer and the bosses of the East, he might have been able to preserve *Greed* more in the form that Von Stroheim had intended.

Thalberg's adherents argue that there is no real evidence that the original version of *Greed* was indeed a masterwork. Nor was it probable that the postwar movie audience, doting on the escapism of Mary Pickford's innocence and Rudolph Valentino's seduction, would have been receptive to three unrelenting hours of man's lust for money. At any rate, Thalberg was an extremely young commander of a new and untried production team, and he could not afford any conspicuous mistakes. It was safer to release *Greed* at normal length and let it chance the film market.

Although Thalberg regretted Von Stroheim's excesses, he recognized the Austrian's unique talent. He assigned Von Stroheim to direct and write one of the most important projects of the new company, *The Merry Widow*.

There were disagreements from the very beginning. Von Stroheim wanted to cast himself in the role of the villain, Crown Prince Mirko. Thalberg demurred. He had learned his lesson at Universal: never allow Von Stroheim to assume a position where he can't be fired. Roy D'Arcy was given the role, and he was coached in all the Von Stroheim mannerisms by the master himself.

Thalberg assigned Mae Murray and John Gilbert in the leading roles. Von Stroheim objected. He detested the star system and prided himself in directing relative unknowns in star performances. Thalberg was convinced that audiences wanted to see stars, and he needed the insurance of well-known performers in a film as expensive as *The Merry Widow* promised to be. Von Stroheim acquiesced.

But the director remained firm to his resolution that *The Merry Widow* would not be the inflated meringue it had been on the operetta stage. He saw in the subject a chance to depict the decadence of the European aristocracy that he had grown to detest in his Austrian youth.

The clash between Von Stroheim and Mae Murray could be foreseen in remarks he made in an interview at the time: "They call me hateful, and say I talk to my people as if they were dogs, that I am in truth a typical pre-war German. But I know what I am doing. It is my method. I must undermine this surface of acquired false technique and bring out the real feeling that is like a kernel beneath a girl's superficial charm. I glower at them. Never in their lives have they been spoken to as roughly as by me. I crush them, beat them down with satire, with harsh words, with scorn. They are ready to quit. Then I get at the real soul and guide its natural unfoldment. With Mary Philbin in *Merry-Go-Round* it was simply a process of development, for she had no previous training to be ripped from her childlike naturalness. Mae Murray's artificiality in most of her films, her self-consciousness and cuteyisms had to be torn away, gossamer garments that concealed her real capacity for feeling and her capability for expressing it."

The technique proved effective, for Miss Murray provided the

A Von Stroheim orgy for The Merry Widow. *Roy D'Arcy, center*

single substantial performance of her career. But the experience proved to be hell for Thalberg, who was repeatedly forced to arbitrate between the two massive temperaments.

"That madman is making a filthy picture!" Miss Murray exclaimed to Thalberg. "All this business of a dirty old man kissing girls' feet and drooling over a closet of women's shoes! It's repulsive."

Von Stroheim complained that the star paid no heed to his instructions and on more than one occasion called him a "dirty Hun."

She railed that he neglected to take closeups of her, and when she played her love scene with Gilbert, the director turned his back and commented, "Let me know when it's over."

After a pitched battle during the filming of "The Merry Widow Waltz," Von Stroheim stalked off the picture and was briefly replaced by Monte Bell. He returned after Miss Murray agreed to an apology.

The warfare continued throughout the twelve weeks of filming. Von Stroheim's extravagant ways did not change, and he insisted on working his actors day and night. The studio was forced to engage

two shifts of crew workers, and even then, the director worked into the morning hours. The production manager, Joe Cohn, solved this by cutting off electricity to the set at midnight.

Thalberg again took over the editing at the conclusion of *The Merry Widow*, and he eliminated some of the fetishism that Von Stroheim had injected. Still, it was Von Stroheim's picture, and he crowed: "They butchered *Greed*, but this time I have outwitted the lousy buttonhole-makers. *The Merry Widow* may not be another *Greed*, but it's not milk-soup, either. It's oxtail. The boobs won't know where the guts of this picture lie."

Von Stroheim and M-G-M were destined to part company. An enterprise as vast as the one Mayer and Thalberg were building demanded a degree of conformity, and the Austrian lacked the capacity to conform; that was the source of his genius and the cause of his downfall. His departure from M-G-M was determined one day during a heated exchange in Mayer's office. In arguing with Mayer about the portrayal of women in *The Merry Widow*, Von Stroheim casually remarked, "Well, all women are whores, anyway."

Mayer stared at him incredulously. "What did you say?" he demanded.

"I said, all women are whores," the director repeated.

"You have a mother?"

"Of course."

"And still you say that?"

"Yes."

"Why, you filthy Hun!" Mayer exclaimed, and he landed a fist in Von Stroheim's face. Before he could recover from the blow, the director found himself being thrown out the office door by Mayer, who then threw out Von Stroheim's hat and cane after him.

Von Stroheim made a few films after leaving M-G-M, but his extravagances proved to be too costly for Hollywood economics. He returned to being an actor, and it was in that capacity that Thalberg hired him once more, to appear with Greta Garbo in *As You Desire Me* in 1931.

6

Another director Thalberg inherited as the new production head of Metro-Goldwyn-Mayer was King Vidor. He was a thoughtful young man from Galveston who had risen from prop boy to director, winning acclaim as a portrayer of the common man. While his contemporaries dealt with the jazzy superficialities of postwar life, Vidor addressed himself to basics. Thus when Thalberg asked him what subjects he would like to pursue for the new company, the director answered: "Steel, wheat or war."

Thalberg and Vidor discussed the first two possibilities and then decided to search for a story about the World War, which was still vivid in the minds of all Americans. The director pored over writings about the war but could find nothing that carried the spark of reality he was seeking. Meanwhile Thalberg went off to New York to hunt for talent and properties and to bring his mother out to California for a visit.

What Price Glory? was then the sensation of the New York theater because of its hard-bitten attitude toward war. Thalberg was impressed with the play and tried to buy it for M-G-M, but Fox beat him to it. Thalberg then spoke with Laurence Stallings, who had written *What Price Glory?* with Maxwell Anderson. Stallings, a Marine captain who had lost a leg at Belleau Wood, could both recall the war and recount it with a dramatist's sense. He and Thalberg discussed an idea for a screen play, and Thalberg was so enthused he telegraphed Vidor that their search was over.

Thalberg insisted that Stallings accompany him to Hollywood, and the two men and Henrietta Thalberg made the journey across the country by train. She had one drawing room, and Thalberg and Stallings occupied the one adjoining. It was a hot summer, and Thalberg spent the days in his underwear, discussing the plot with Stallings. By the time they arrived in Los Angeles, they had developed an outline. The title was supplied by Stallings: *The Big Parade.*

Stallings and Harry Behn worked on the script under Vidor's supervision, and the film was cast with two of M-G-M's brightest stars, John Gilbert and Renée Adorée. The brilliantly erratic Gilbert had found favor with a series of flashy portrayals, and *The Big Parade* was planned to cash in on his popularity. The budget was in keeping with other Gilbert films: $205,000.

But Vidor was determined to make it more than a routine vehicle for a popular star. He devoted time and thought to the character relationships, particularly between Gilbert and Miss Adorée. In one on-the-set improvisation, he happened on the idea of having Gilbert introduce Miss Adorée to the American habit of chewing gum, a means of communication between the pair who didn't speak each other's language.

While watching reel upon reel of Signal Corps film in preparation for *The Big Parade*, Vidor had come across a scene in which the soldiers marched to a different tempo from the ordinary pace. He discovered the company was parading in a funeral procession. Vidor measured the beat with a metronome, then repeated the tempo when he filmed the scene of the doughboys marching into battle in a forest that resembled Belleau Wood. The metronome's beat was conveyed to the actors by a bass drum, and all the actions in the sequence conformed to the same unrelenting pace. The result was a scene of extraordinary power.

Thalberg followed the production of *The Big Parade* with intense interest. After Vidor had assembled the film, Thalberg took it along on a vacation to Coronado with his parents. One night he arranged to show *The Big Parade* at a local theater; he had adopted the custom of testing each movie before an actual audience, rather than relying on the sterile atmosphere of a studio projection room.

Thalberg possessed an uncanny knack of gauging the pleasure or displeasure of a theater audience. He recognized that the Coronado citizens were gripped by the story of the three American men who encountered the agonies of war. Thalberg was especially pleased with the reaction to John Gilbert. The actor had attracted attention with a series of flamboyant portrayals at Fox in *The Count of Monte Cristo, Cameo Kirby* and other films. In *The Big Parade*, Vidor held down Gilbert's mannerisms but allowed him to display his natural vivacity. The result was an intensely human portrayal.

When Thalberg returned to the studio, he reported to Mayer: "It's a fine picture, but it isn't finished."

"Why not?" Mayer asked.

"It doesn't have the war in it."

Thalberg proposed broadening the scope of *The Big Parade* by injecting battle scenes. Mayer agreed, but both realized they would have to sell the Eastern office on returning the film to production. The New York salesmen saw no value in reshooting a picture after it had been completed; they sought only "a John Gilbert picture" to fulfill the season's schedule.

"I'll sell them on it," announced the confident Mayer, and he boarded a train for New York with a print of *The Big Parade*. He showed the film to the dubious executives, then demonstrated in dramatic style how the addition of scenes of battle would enhance the project. Mayer's persuasion worked, and the Loew's officials agreed to the additional scenes.

Vidor had filmed a prologue and epilogue depicting Gilbert in his well-to-do home in America. Thalberg decided the sequences should be built up for two reasons: to heighten the sentimentality for female moviegoers who might find a war story unappealing; to underscore Gilbert's conversion from playboy to fighting man. The sequences were entirely refilmed with the addition of more important players, Hobart Bosworth and Claire McDowell, as the boy's parents.

A second unit director had been sent to Fort Sam Houston in Texas to film the "big parade" of men and equipment to the front. The Army helpfully supplied five thousand troops, two hundred trucks and a squadron of airplanes, and the director shot twelve reels of film. Vidor looked at the footage until two in the morning, then called Thalberg in despair.

"It doesn't have what I want," said the director.

"What's that?"

"A straight line of trucks moving down a long road."

"Then I guess you'd better go down there and shoot it yourself."

Vidor went to Fort Sam Houston and achieved the scene he wanted. Thalberg also wanted him to direct the added scenes of battle, but Vidor was already working on *La Bohème* with Lillian Gish, John Gilbert, and Renée Adorée. George Hill was assigned to direct the night battle scenes, which added another $40,000 to the film's cost. The bombardment shots were done in miniature, with five thousand explosions being fired.

The Big Parade had its premiere in New York on November 19, 1925, and fulfilled Vidor's ambition at the outset "to make a picture that stays in town longer than a week." It played ninety-six weeks at the Astor Theater and earned almost fifteen million dollars. Unlike *Ben-Hur*, the profits were all M-G-M's, and on an investment of $250,000 they were considerable.

The experience strengthened Irving Thalberg's resolve: never release a picture until it's as good as you can make it.

Youthful M-G-M executive steps off the 20th Century Limited

Mayer and Thalberg pulling most of the load. Left to right: unidentified, Mayer, writers George Kann and Richard Schayer, Lawrence Weingarten, actor Edward Brophy, agent Frank Orsatti, Harry Rapf, Thalberg

7

The structure of Metro-Goldwyn-Mayer was forming under the watchful guidance of Louis Mayer and Irving Thalberg. Both wanted the studio to have an *esprit*, a family loyalty that didn't exist in the other film companies. The layout of the Culver City studio lent itself to such a purpose; the buildings opened onto a large courtyard, so there was easy access from one office to another, and the comings and goings of all could be observed. Mayer and Thalberg themselves were peripatetic, often striding to the sets or holding conferences in the California sunshine.

Studio picnics were organized, and Mayer and Thalberg joined in the tug-o'-war and the baseball games. The team spirit was demonstrated every time a studio executive left for New York or arrived home from the East. Such occasions became ceremonial, with all of the important studio figures appearing at the railroad station to bid the traveler farewell or welcome him back.

At the Santa Fe station right to left: Louis Mayer, Harry Rapf, Hunt Stromberg, Irving Thalberg, John Gilbert

Mayer recognized at the outset that something would have to be done about the studio commissary. It was being operated by a concessionaire, and the food was so poor that many of the workers were eating elsewhere. This was not only bad for morale, it was bad business as well. The actors had a habit of eating lunch in the better restaurants of Beverly Hills or the speakeasies of nearby Venice or Ocean Park, and they often returned to the sets late or drunk, or both. That wouldn't do.

A man who enjoyed his victuals, especially when prepared by his wife, Mayer hired an expert chef and ordered him to take a thirty-day course in kosher cooking from Mrs. Mayer. The chef then took over the M-G-M commissary and his food proved so tasty and reasonably priced that actors had no reason to leave the lot. The commissary operated at a deficit, but Mayer was pleased with the results in promoting efficiency and in bringing all the studio workers together once a day.

While the studio operation was running smoothly, relations with the Loew's hierarchy of the East had early developed into an uneasy alliance. The Loew's people had come up from nickelodeons and were acutely cost-conscious; they were ever alert against the profligacies of the studio. Mayer and Thalberg realized they couldn't

build a movie empire with penny-pinching methods and were always fighting for more production money. Each faction had a representative in the other's camp. J. Robert Rubin, who served as secretary of Metro-Goldwyn-Mayer, watched out for the Mayer Group's interests in New York. Loew's sent to the studio its own watchdog, Eddie Mannix, a lusty Irishman who had been a bouncer at Palisades Park in New Jersey. In time Mannix succumbed to the lotus-land allures of Hollywood and the charm of Louis Mayer and Irving Thalberg. Mannix became a studio man.

The combination of Mayer and Thalberg became well nigh invincible. Both were tireless in their service to the studio, and they expected others to give the same measure of devotion. Such was the M-G-M spirit that many did. Inspired by the fervor of Mayer and Thalberg, studio aides worked twelve- to fourteen-hour days with the knowledge that the two bosses were working longer. They didn't even rest on the weekends. Mayer's Sunday brunches, with Mrs. Mayer herself preparing a vast array of delectable foods, became weekly occasions at which Mayer and Thalberg completed many business deals.

Hollywood was dazzled by the performance of Irving Thalberg during the formative period of Metro-Goldwyn-Mayer. The handsome young man from Brooklyn seemed unable to do wrong in his decisions about film subjects and stars. He did not cultivate this adulation, but he enjoyed it enormously; it was part of the reward for his earnest effort, just as Henrietta Thalberg's praise had rewarded his special achievements at Boys' High School.

Henrietta had also instilled in him the notion that he should be paid in direct ratio to his contribution. Obviously $650 a week plus a nebulous amount of profit-sharing* was not an adequate compensation for supervising the entire creative program of a huge studio. This inequity was remedied a year after the merger when Mayer secured a new arrangement for his management group. His own salary was raised from $1500 to $2500, Thalberg's from $650 to $2000, and Rubin's from $600 to $1000. In addition, their share of the profits would be no less than $500,000.

* The Mayer Group was to receive 20 percent of Loew's profits on the studio's films, divided thusly: Mayer 53 percent, Rubin 27 percent, Thalberg 20 percent. Rubin's share reflected his initial importance in instrumenting the merger.

Thalberg was not satisfied for long. Within a year he protested to the Loew's executives that he was still not being paid enough for the millions he was providing for the corporation's treasury. After lengthy negotiations, Loew's arrived at a new formula. Thalberg's salary would be raised to $4000 a week with the assurance that his total income, including a share of the profits, would be no less than $400,-000 per year. Now twenty-seven years old, Thalberg was pleased with the arrangement—for a while.

Despite the disagreements over compensation, the partnership with Mayer was functioning amazingly well. The older man remained impressed with his protégé's artistic acumen and seldom intruded on story and casting decisions. Thalberg recognized Mayer's considerable powers as a politician and relied on him to push through policy decisions, particularly in the always difficult relations with New York. As a close associate described the relationship: Thalberg made the bullets and Mayer fired them.

In matters of ego, the two men found an adequate balance. Both had strong ego drives, but they were satisfied in different ways. Thalberg was content with the esteem of his contemporaries in the film industry, as well as the financial rewards that his station brought him. His policy of not putting his own name on the screen was considered by some to be the supreme egotism: he was too important to need such an expression of vanity.

Mayer needed to remind the world that he was no more the little Jewish junk dealer. He lived with great ostentation, traveled like an Oriental prince, dabbled in Republican politics, and made sonorous speeches.

Thalberg was content to let him have the spotlight. The young man shied away from interviews, not because he didn't realize the value of publicity in a business that lived on public acceptance, but because he was fearful of being hurt. In general, he had become calloused to criticism, but he could become profoundly upset over what was said about him in print. This stemmed from his early career when he was constantly referred to as "the boy wonder"—a phrase he learned to abhor. A precisionist, he was disturbed when his utterances were misquoted or used against him. As a result, he learned to deliver the blandest of replies to interviewers' questions, and they generally returned to their typewriters shaking their heads over how to vitalize their stories.

The first important article about Thalberg was printed in *Collier's* shortly after the merger. Written by Frederick L. Collins, it bore the title, "Meet the Boy Wonder of Hollywood." The beginning:

> "Who's the child with Elinor Glyn? Her son?"
> "Elinor's son?" laughed Hollywood's oldest inhabitant. "That's her employer! Her boss! The baby magnate of moviedom! . . . That's Irving Thalberg!"
> "Who's Irving Thalberg?"
> "Twenty-five years old. Fifty thousand a year. Hundred per cent chance to be the biggest man in the picture industry. That's Thalberg."

The speaker continued effusing: "Wherever Irving Thalberg sits is always the head of the table." Collins provided a description of the "infant prodigy":

> He has a good presence, Thalberg; metallic rather than magnetic; clean-cut, direct, not at all flashy; he is well-poised and well-gaited; active without being in a hurry. There is a smiling sadness about his full, sensitive mouth; and incandescent brilliance in his small jetty eyes. His rebellious black hair, forced off his high, broad forehead, tops a set of small, conventionally-placed features, which stand up well under close analysis. He made me think of a beautifully executed miniature—the miniature of a great man.

Collins recounted Thalberg's Brooklyn boyhood and his fast rise in the film industry and produced only one quote from an interview with his subject: "I came to Hollywood as a private secretary. . . . I was fortunate enough to get a job where I saw the business as a whole. Then my chance came to make good while the boss was away. And I worked hard. That's all."

Thalberg became increasingly sensitive of such articles. He was also piqued by a series of short stories by George Randolph Chester in *The Saturday Evening Post*. The tales depicted the adventures of an ambitious young movie man named Izzy Iskovitch, whom the Hollywood crowd took to be Irving Thalberg.

His indisposition to give suitable quotes to interviewers was demonstrated when a woman reporter from a movie magazine began by suggesting he represented the new order in films—"a young man with ideals."

Thalberg interrupted her sharply: "If you mean that I think I'm superior to the so-called cloak and shoe and glove manufacturers who have really given their lives and their pocket-books to this business in order to allow us something to build on—why then—you are wrong. I respect them very much—they had ideals, too." The interviewer slunk away without her story.

In 1927 *Vanity Fair* took cognizance of the "boy wonder" with an article by the iconoclastic Jim Tully. The writer confessed to a personal fondness for Thalberg, but the article left some doubt. Excerpts:

> There is a latent spiritual quality in Thalberg. It even survived a business course in Brooklyn.
>
> Not strong physically, he gives one the impression of a poet. There is about his eyes a twinkle of mirth and sadness. His fingers are long, sensitive and delicate—the fingers of a Richelieu —or a Machiavelli. . . .
>
> I would have considered him a real boy wonder had he curbed with understanding the torrent that was Von Stroheim. For, in that far day, when those who follow us will be able to get a perspective on film history, Stroheim is likely to be considered the first man of genuine and original talent to break his heart against the stone wall of cinema imbecility.
>
> Thalberg is boyish, kindly and intuitive. He has a quick mentality that runs in narrow grooves. If it were deeper and vaster and more profound, he would be a financial failure in the business of films. To Thalberg all life is a soda fountain. He knows how to mix ingredients that will please the herd on a picnic. It is doubtful if such an attribute can be listed among the great talents. It was possessed by Barnum and Bailey. Morris Gest, David Belasco, Aimee Semple McPherson, Billy Sunday and Wayne B. Wheeler also have the same quality.
>
> Thalberg has piled one piece of clay upon another until he has succeeded in building a hill for the commonalty. Upon this hill his co-workers, being lesser people than himself, and more nearsighted, see a mirage which they call genius. It often takes the form of a young man with a sad expression, leading sheep to a withered pasture.
>
> Thalberg is the epic of the common man. . . .

Thalberg was stung by such comments, especially because they came from a man who professed to be a friend. Thalberg believed the attack on himself for merely aiming to please the herd was unwarranted. Several times he had authorized projects that appeared to have little chance for popular acceptance. When King Vidor proposed a film based on man's loss of identity in a pluralistic society, Thalberg encouraged him to go ahead, even though Vidor predicted the film would probably not return a dollar at the box office.

"That's all right," Thalberg replied. "M-G-M can afford to take a loss on an experimental picture now and then. The picture will pave the way for another one like it in two years—when the audience will be ready to accept it."

He not only authorized *The Crowd;* he put no pressure on Vidor to make it quickly. The director fashioned the film with great care, creating huge offices and hospital wards to illustrate how man becomes a cipher in the modern world. Vidor spent much time on location in New York to capture the size and hurry of the city. He employed a hidden camera for a more realistic view; a single cameraman in a packing box was pushed from the Bowery to Times Square without detection. The shooting schedule lasted long enough for the leading lady, Eleanor Boardman, who was also Mrs. Vidor, to leave the film, have a baby and then return to *The Crowd.*

Nor was Thalberg satisfied when the film was completed. *The Crowd* underwent seven previews, and Vidor filmed seven different endings. Both he and Thalberg were in such a dilemma as to how the picture should end that they released it with a happy ending but supplied exhibitors with a reel depicting a sad finish. "Try it either way," they were told.

As Vidor had predicted, *The Crowd* was not a popular success. But many a discerning critic pointed out its value, and Thalberg was satisfied.

Thalberg disliked the implication that he was surrounded by "lesser men" who followed his dictates unquestioningly. He was proud of the associates he gathered about him in the early period of M-G-M. Indeed they were, for Hollywood of that period, a fairly distinguished lot. Compared to the primitive types who surrounded most producers, the Thalberg group resembled the faculty at Caltech.

Too much of a realist to tolerate yes-men about him, Thalberg sought men of refined tastes as his closest collaborators. Although they generally deferred to his instinctive judgment, they were men of more impressive background than he.

Bernard Hyman had been born in Grafton, West Virginia, and educated in the public schools of New York City. He went on to study at Yale before joining Carl Laemmle as a salesman of Universal pictures and later a story editor. Thalberg first met him at Universal, and they became close friends. They had much in common. They were the same height, though Hyman had a stockier build; both were shy and contemplative. Thalberg found pleasure in Hyman's amiable nature and quick wit, and he enlisted Hyman for the new M-G-M production team soon after the merger.

Paul Bern was also Thalberg's size, but an entirely different kind of man. Born in Wandsbeck, Germany, he had come to America at an early age and moved into the theater after training at the American Academy of Dramatic Arts. He drifted into films as a cutter, then screen writer and director. Thalberg was attracted by his polished manner and incisive analysis of story material and employed him as a production assistant. Bern was a strange man whose cerebral qualities contrasted with his fondness for escorting the most tantalizing of Hollywood beauties.

Harry Rapf remained a close associate of Thalberg's, although he oversaw the lower-budget M-G-M films in which Thalberg took scant interest. Rapf was well-suited for his trade, having been schooled in minstrel shows, vaudeville, and other fields of popular entertainment. He was an ebullient man, less polished than others of the Thalberg team and hence often the butt of their jokes. They made sport of Rapf's monumental nose, and even Thalberg was not above an occasional jest. Once the pair were crossing the M-G-M lot when Thalberg stopped and asked, "Do you smell smoke?"

Rapf sniffed the breeze and replied, "No."

"Then there isn't any smoke," Thalberg replied.

Hunt Stromberg had entered films as press agent for the old Goldwyn Company after serving as reporter for the St. Louis *Times*. He came to Hollywood as personal representative of Thomas Ince and indulged in independent production before joining Thalberg in 1925.

The associate who began early with Thalberg and stayed longest was Albert Lewin. He was a strange fish in the Hollywood of the 1920s, having not only graduated from New York University but acquired a master's degree at Harvard. Such a background made him suspect to many of M-G-M's self-made types, including Louis Mayer, who considered him something of a revolutionary.

Actually Thalberg knew that Lewin was revolutionary only in his belief that films should not be made in the same old patterns. Thalberg realized this on their first meeting. Lewin had been a screen writer at Metro during the period of the merger. His first script, an adaptation of Charles Norris's *Bread,* was being filmed when he received a call to report to the production boss of the new company. He was taken aback to meet the youthful, engaging Thalberg.

"I just got back from the merger signing in New York," said the young man. "I took a lot of scripts to read on the train, and one of them was *Bread.*"

Lewin took a deep breath, expecting the worst. But Thalberg commended the script. He made three suggestions which seemed masterful for Lewin. Thalberg added one more concerning an important scene. Lewin didn't think it sounded right, and he argued with Thalberg. After three days, the two men still couldn't agree, and Thalberg finally said, "It's your picture; go ahead the way you want it."

It was an important lesson for both of them: Thalberg learned that Lewin was a man of conviction; Lewin discovered that Thalberg did not want to be yessed.

Bread was a successful film, but Lewin fell victim to the politics involving the changeover to M-G-M and left for a position with Harry Cohn at Columbia. Then Thalberg sent for Lewin and hired him at $300 a week to write screen plays for Bernie Hyman. Later he became head of the story department, then a producer.

In those times none of the Thalberg team had clearly defined duties; all were expected to have a hand in everything—story selection, casting, script writing, cutting, etc. Thalberg held frequent meetings with the entire staff, and he earnestly sought the opinions of his associates. He conducted the meetings in an amiable, constructive way, and all felt a responsibility and pride in the entire studio product.

Thalberg demanded of his associates no less than the effort he devoted to M-G-M, which was considerable. The men close to him grew accustomed to receiving telephone calls at two in the morning from Thalberg, who had an important production detail to discuss. They would also be expected to devote their weekends, if necessary, to script sessions at Thalberg's house, and to spend several evenings a week traveling to a nearby suburb to watch previews of the latest pictures.

When Thalberg transferred from Universal to the Mayer Company, those who were wise in the ways of movie nepotism predicted that the handsome young man would inevitably marry one of Mayer's two daughters. Indeed, Mayer remarked more than once, "If Irving was my son, I couldn't love him more; what a wonderful thing it would be if he married one of my daughters!"

But Irving's illness of 1924 changed that. His doctors had confided to Mayer that Thalberg would probably not live to be thirty. Mayer laid down the ukase to his daughters: "I am not going to cure something; I am going to prevent it. If either of you girls gets any ideas of a romantic nature about Irving, you can forget them. I love Irving, but I love you girls more. I don't want either of you to have the heartbreak of being a young widow."

Both Edith and Irene Mayer were devastated. They were quite naturally infatuated with the dark-eyed young man who often came to the house for dinner. But their father enforced his will. Irving himself knew of Mayer's decision, and he respected it. At Hollywood parties, he danced only once with Irene or Edith and then excused himself, saying, "The old man doesn't like it."

Henrietta Thalberg became convinced that the well-being of her son should not be entrusted to strangers three thousand miles away. She uprooted her obliging husband and their daughter Sylvia, and they went west. William Thalberg opened a real estate office near downtown Los Angeles, and Henrietta devoted herself to Irving. He was delighted. Since moving to California, he had lived first with an aunt, then with various bachelors, but the bother of maintaining a household interfered with his work schedule. He much preferred coming home to a house that was kept in good order by his mother. She understood his desire for simple food, and she forced him to conserve his energy when he was overworking.

It was not all work for the busy young film mogul. He enjoyed a good time as much as anyone in that fun-loving Hollywood era, and he found companions in such blades as Jack Conway, Victor Fleming, and the Hawks brothers, Howard and William. Henrietta registered her strong disapproval of such playboys, but Irving needed the exhilaration and release from his studio duties.

The most notable of Thalberg's early romances in Hollywood was with Peggy Hopkins Joyce, famed for her penchant of collecting husbands and diamonds. The onetime Ziegfeld Girl, who claimed to have exacted three million dollars from the five millionaires she had married, came to Hollywood and had a brief fling with Charlie Chaplin. She dropped him after encountering the slender, dark-eyed young man who was running production at M-G-M. Their romance was a passionate one, and rumors were heard that they would marry. The talk brought shudders to Henrietta Thalberg, who railed to her son against the blonde fortuneseeker. The infatuation passed.

Irving then became enamored of Constance Talmadge, the gayest of the talented Talmadge sisters, and the attachment continued, much to Henrietta's disdain. Nor did she approve of Irving's continued association with Rosabelle Laemmle; despite his departure from Universal, his fondness for Rosabelle continued. One of the few girl-friends of Irving's that Henrietta liked was the actress Marie Prevost. But his interest in her was fleeting.

Then a new girl entered Irving's life.

Norma Shearer, the onetime Miss Lotta Miles, had been progressing well as an M-G-M actress. She had performed ably in the first film made by the studio after the merger, *He Who Gets Slapped*, a circus picture that starred Lon Chaney and John Gilbert. She followed with a less impressive film, *The Snob*, with Gilbert and Conrad Nagel, and her subsequent pictures were equally undistinguished. This caused her to protest to Thalberg, and he listened attentively, but the situation didn't improve. He seemed to take no more interest in her than he did in the dozen other promising young actresses at the studio.

One chilly Christmas Eve, Miss Shearer was working late on a picture that was being finished to meet a deadline. It was after ten when the director finally called "Cut!" and the company disbanded. Miss Shearer went to her dressing room to gather her make-up. When she emerged, the set was empty. The bus had left without her, and she faced a half-mile walk to her room in the actors' building.

She found nothing there to cheer her except a Thermos of hot

John Gilbert and Norma Shearer, The Snob

chocolate her maid had left. The actress sipped the drink as she changed out of her costume. The telephone rang.

"Norma, this is Irving Thalberg," said the warm voice.

"Good evening," she replied.

"I heard you had worked late tonight, and I just wanted to call and wish you a Merry Christmas."

He, too, was working late that Christmas Eve, and from his office he could see the light in her dressing room across the courtyard. Nothing more was said, but Miss Shearer was encouraged. The dark young man she privately adored had taken notice of her.

She was further encouraged a few weeks later when Thalberg's secretary, Vivian Newcom, telephoned to ask if she would like to accompany him to the premiere of *The Gold Rush.* It was not the most romantic way of being asked for a date, but Miss Shearer quickly accepted. They danced after the premiere at the Coconut Grove, and Thalberg seemed to have an enjoyable evening.

It was not a quick romance. Miss Shearer continued to go out with various men-about-town, and Thalberg maintained his interest in Constance Talmadge and Rosabelle Laemmle. But when neither was available, he called Norma.

"I'm Irving's spare tire," she announced delightedly, and she continued her patient waiting.

8

Besides shouldering the responsibility of supplying a feature film every week, Irving Thalberg devoted attention to building up a list of stars who could lend excitement to such an outpouring of product. In this he was extraordinarily gifted. Between him and actors there existed a remarkable empathy. He understood them. He recognized their follies, their outpourings of ego, their fickle nature, but he also realized they were unusual human beings. Most of them were beautiful people, and he had a deep admiration for beauty. Many of them were delightful company, despite their insistence on having everything revolve around them.

Actors liked Thalberg. They admired his own particular style: his handsome assurance, his quiet persuasion, the unstudied elegance with which he conducted his life. They discovered he would listen to their protests about an unfeeling director or a role that wasn't substantial enough. He would not always decide in their favor, but he would listen to them and reason out the problem.

The premiere M-G-M star of the mid-1920s was John Gilbert, of whom Thalberg was personally fond. His lusty spirit had made a profound impression in *The Merry Widow*, and with *The Big Parade* he established himself as an actor of depth and versatility. He became the studio's most serviceable as well as its most popular star, his range extending from tragic romance (*La Bohème*) to swashbuckling adventure (*Bardelys the Magnificent*) to modern drama (*The Snob*).

Thalberg's most unusual star was Lon Chaney, the peculiar genius who had established a standard for the macabre in *The Hunchback of Notre Dame*. Chaney followed Thalberg to M-G-M and, except for a 1925 return to Universal for *The Phantom of the Opera*, made the remainder of his films there. He seemed to have no limit to his versatility. He played a clown in *He Who Gets Slapped*, a ventriloquist and old lady in *The Unholy Three*, a demented scientist in

The Monster, an armless man in *The Unknown*, a Chinese menace in *Mr. Wu*, and various other horrors. Then, to demonstrate that his star was not reliant on mechanics, Thalberg stripped Chaney of make-up for the role of a tough Marine sergeant in *Tell It to the Marines*. It was one of his finest portrayals.

Ramon Novarro continued to be a valuable star following his enormous success in *Ben-Hur*. He carried on the Valentino tradition as a romantic Latin, but he also portrayed a South Sea Islander in *The Pagan* and a Heidelberg cadet in *The Student Prince*.

Lillian Gish was an enormous contribution to M-G-M's prestige in the period following the merger. One of the great figures of the silent screen because of her films with D. W. Griffith, she came to the studio with a six-picture contract and an iron will. Her contract guaranteed that she would have full rehearsals before the start of shooting, as was Griffith's custom. King Vidor, who was to direct her first M-G-M film, *La Boheme*, reluctantly agreed. He provided makeshift scenery to indicate the sets, and Miss Gish was upset when she saw them. Griffith always rehearsed on a bare stage.

William Haines and Lon Chaney, Tell It to the Marines

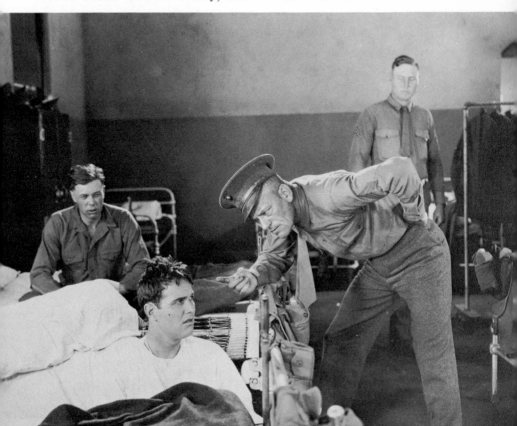

After a day of rehearsal, Miss Gish requested that the company
move outside so she would not be distracted by the scenery. The
entire film was rehearsed on a lawn outside the stage, in full view
of Thalberg's office.

Miss Gish had a virginal concept of the romance between Mimi
and Rudolph, and she argued that her love scenes with Gilbert should
be played with distance between them, so as to build up the emotion.
As always, her will prevailed. But when Thalberg and Mayer saw
La Boheme, they insisted on love scenes of a more intimate nature.
They could not risk the Great Lover reputation of their number-
one star, John Gilbert.

La Boheme was well received in the nation's theaters, as was the
next film starring Miss Gish, *The Scarlet Letter*. She made three
lesser movies before leaving M-G-M.

Marion Davies became an M-G-M star when her Cosmopolitan
Pictures transferred to the new studio from the old Goldwyn Company. Cosmopolitan was an independent company financed and directed by Miss Davies' mentor, William Randolph Hearst, and its
advent to M-G-M was welcomed by Louis Mayer. With his love of

Norma Shearer, Ramon Novarro, Ernst Lubitsch on the set of The Student Prince

power and prestige, Mayer enjoyed the association with Hearst and the attendant publicity for Cosmopolitan films, as well as M-G-M and Mayer himself, which the publisher ordered in his chain of newspapers and magazines.

Mayer relieved Thalberg of the responsibility of dealing with Hearst and the Davies films. That suited Thalberg, because finding vehicles for Miss Davies was an onorous and unrewarding task. A clever comedienne, Miss Davies was often cast, at the insistence of Hearst, in dramatic roles beyond her depth. Despite lavish productions and popular leading men, her films rarely returned much profit. But her presence at M-G-M unquestionably contributed to the studio's prestige. She maintained her headquarters in a magnificent "bungalow," where she and Hearst entertained such visitors as Winston Churchill and George Bernard Shaw. Louis Mayer and Irving Thalberg were always asked to be among the guests on such occasions.

William Haines was a versatile leading man who played drama or comedy with equal skill, specializing in portrayals of breezy young Americans. He had moved over from the Goldwyn Company and made a good impression in *Tower of Lies* with Lon Chaney and

King Vidor and Irving Thalberg gaze at Lillian Gish on the set of La Boheme

Irving Thalberg and Marion Davies pose with visiting French tennis star, Suzanne Lenglen

Norma Shearer. He later delivered a sensitive performance as a Marine recruit in *Tell It to the Marines* with Lon Chaney. Thalberg enjoyed Haines' bright personality and saw much of him, since the actor was a frequent escort of his sister Sylvia. Haines often drove with the Thalbergs, including Henrietta and William, to weekends at Lake Arrowhead.

Buster Keaton was one of the legacies of the Metro Company, and for a time, he was a valuable one. Thalberg had developed no real affinity for comedy, yet every major company needed comedies to fill out its program. Keaton supplied them in bountiful measure with such films as *The Navigator, Seven Chances* and *Go West*, which were produced by Keaton's own unit. The comedian defected to United Artists in 1926 for the classic *The General* and other films, then returned to M-G-M in 1928 for the last five years of his career as a star.

Joan Crawford, the former Lucille LeSueur, came to M-G-M in 1925 after being discovered by Harry Rapf and J. Robert Rubin in a Broadway show, *Innocent Eyes*. Her vitality and ambition were apparent from the start. Paul Bern took her under his wing and advised her in the ways of Hollywood society and studio politics. His tutelage was expert. Within less than a year, she was starring with

Joan Crawford, Our Dancing Daughters

Constance Bennett, Sally O'Neil and William Haines in *Sally, Irene and Mary*. Within two years, she was engaged to filmland's crown prince, Douglas Fairbanks, Junior.

She became one of M-G-M's busiest actresses, appearing in everything from Westerns starring Tim McCoy to *Rose Marie*. Her real glory began in 1928 when she starred in *Our Dancing Daughters* and immediately became the symbol of flaming youth. Such an authority as F. Scott Fitzgerald commented: "Joan Crawford is doubtless the best example of the flapper, the girl you see at smart night clubs, gowned to the apex of sophistication, toying iced glasses with a remote, faintly bitter expression, dancing deliciously, laughing a great deal, with wide, hurt eyes. Young things with a talent for living."

Greta Garbo came to the studio in 1925 as the aftermath of the trip Louis Mayer made to Europe in an attempt to create some order out of the Roman chaos of *Ben-Hur*. Part of the journey was devoted to scouting talent for the new company, and in Berlin Mayer interviewed the Swedish director, Mauritz Stiller, and his protégée, Greta Garbo. Mayer was impressed with the work of both in a Swedish film, *The Story of Gosta Berling*, and engaged them to work in Culver City for M-G-M.

Thalberg's first view of Garbo—Stiller had changed her name from Gustafson—was not entirely favorable. She was tall and athletic-looking and seemed to care little for her appearance. Communication was difficult, since she spoke no English. But Thalberg was intrigued by a report from Albert Lewin, who had watched the unreeling of the German-made film, *The Street of Sorrow*, in the company of the studio's cutters. It was a turgid film about decadence in postwar Vienna, but Lewin noticed that the cutters remained to watch a young actress in a supporting role. Garbo.

Thalberg ordered a test of the new actress from Sweden, and it proved a disappointment. Stiller made another test that captured the magical quality of the twenty-year-old Garbo. Thalberg was impressed. He was preparing *The Torrent*, based on a novel by Vicente Blasco-Ibáñez, to star Ricardo Cortez, and he considered Garbo for the feminine lead. Now Mayer was having misgivings about his discovery, and he argued that it was too big a part for an untried actress. Thalberg replied that Cortez would be able to carry the film despite the new girl's inadequacies. Thalberg's judgment prevailed.

But then Garbo rebelled. When she learned that the film was to be directed by Monte Bell, not Stiller, she refused the role. Stiller held a powerful influence over her, and without him she felt unable to perform in a strange country with a cast and crew whose language she could not understand. Stiller himself persuaded her to make the film without him. A Swedish actor was assigned to interpret the instructions from Bell.

A fortuitous event happened during the filming of *The Torrent*. The cameraman suffered a fall in which he cut off his little finger, and he was replaced by William Daniels, whom Thalberg had brought to M-G-M from Universal. Daniels was accustomed to working with temperament—he had filmed *Greed* and *The Merry Widow* with Von Stroheim—and he recognized the creative power behind Garbo's shyness. Daniels suggested mounting black flats—large, cloth-covered shields—at each side of the set so the lesser workers and occasional visitors would be hidden from her view. The device improved her morale and rid her of the inhibitions she had felt in the presence of strangers.

During the filming of *The Torrent*, Daniels marveled at the ease with which he could photograph her. She had no "good side"; either

Lucien Littlefield and Greta Garbo, The Torrent

half of her face was readily photographable. Nor did she require special lighting, as some actresses did to heighten their beauty; Garbo could look lovely in candlelight. Such faculties allowed directors freedom of movement without concern for cumbersome lighting. Hence her performances had unique mobility.

Thalberg was pleased with Garbo's performance in *The Torrent,* and the critical response was favorable. He next cast her in another Ibáñez drama, *The Temptress,* and this time he heeded her wishes and assigned Mauritz Stiller to direct. The co-star was Antonio Moreno.

Stiller proved erratic and undisciplined. He ordered a hundred extras and then failed to use them. He exposed thousands of feet of film, repeating the same scene over and over again. Thalberg was slow to anger, especially with creative talent, but he would not tolerate lack of professionalism. Finally he snapped, "Is the man mad? Has he ever been behind a camera before?"

At the end of a day's shooting, Thalberg summoned the Swedish director to his office. The two men argued for an hour over the lack of progress on *The Temptress,* and Stiller was adamant; he would continue to direct in his own manner. Thalberg paced up and down his office, using all his powers of persuasion. The scene in the office could be viewed from the studio street, and hiding in the shadows was the angular figure of Greta Garbo. When the interview was over, she would sense from Stiller's air of defeat what had happened.

Fred Niblo replaced him, and Garbo was sullen under the new man's direction. She continued to be under Stiller's spell, and he convinced her *The Temptress* would be no good without him. He vented his feelings in explosive German to Thalberg after the preview, and the bemused Thalberg merely nodded and replied, "*Ja . . . ja . . .*" Stiller complained to a friend afterward, "When I was at Metro, that fellow pretended not to know any German. Now I find he speaks it fluently!"

Despite Stiller's dread predictions, *The Temptress* continued the progress of Greta Garbo's career. For her next picture, Thalberg provided an encounter which would help remove her from the grasp of Mauritz Stiller.

John Gilbert was unimpressed with the studio's new Swedish actress —until he was introduced to her on *The Flesh and the Devil* set by

Greta Garbo and John Gilbert, Flesh and the Devil

the director, Clarence Brown. At this point in his history, Gilbert was between his marriages to Leatrice Joy and Ina Claire.

Garbo herself was reluctant to appear in *The Flesh and the Devil,* even though it meant playing opposite M-G-M's foremost star. Loyal to Stiller, she resisted the assignment for days until she finally gave in to Thalberg's persuasion. And when she met Gilbert, she was immediately impressed with his gaiety and charm. Soon their love scenes had an unmistakable feeling of reality, and they proved as passionate as any seen on the screen before. Gilbert's lightheartedness brought her out of the reclusive life she had led in Hollywood, and she even allowed him to escort her to film premieres.

The Flesh and the Devil established Garbo as an important star, and Thalberg again teamed her with Gilbert in *Love.* Thalberg was delighted with the dramatic range which she displayed, and he was unconcerned with complaints from the publicity department that she was increasingly uncooperative. "Don't force her to do what she doesn't want to do," he instructed, and the Garbo image began to take form.

Arriving for the premiere of Bardelys the Magnificent, *left to right: King Vidor, Eleanor Boardman, Norma Shearer, Irving Thalberg, Greta Garbo, John Gilbert*

9

It was a glorious time to be young and rich and gifted with power. Irving Thalberg enjoyed it all. He was the marvel of the movie world, and he accepted the esteem of his contemporaries with engaging modesty. Even his office was humble, in contrast to the baronial quarters of Louis B. Mayer. The contrast may well have been intended by Thalberg.

His office was located in one of the original studio buildings, facing on Washington Boulevard. It was a wooden structure which had grown quite rickety, with stairs that groaned with every footfall and an elevator noted for its hesitancy. Visitors approached the second-floor executive offices through a waiting room which accommodated about eight persons and was almost certain to be filled during working hours. A Dutch door was half-open to an office with three secretaries. To the right was the office of Eddie Mannix. A corridor on the left led to the offices of Thalberg and Harry Rapf, both rooms of modest size. Outside Thalberg's office was an iron stairway that led to the lot and to the first-floor office of Mayer. Later a passageway was built from Thalberg's office to his projection room across the street; it was called The Bridge of Sighs.

At least once a day, Thalberg went down the stairs to visit the sets. Unlike some studio bosses who traveled with entourages, he usually made his rounds alone. He generally began his tour by stopping at the studio commissary to buy a candy bar, which he munched en route; his doctor had recommended candy for quick energy. He slipped quietly onto the stage, stood in the background for a few minutes to observe what was going on, then departed without ceremony. Occasionally he was asked to come to a set by a director who was having trouble with an unplayable scene or a balky star. It was not unusual for the director to step aside and allow Thalberg to stage the scene himself.

At work Thalberg invariably wore a dark blue suit, a white shirt with soft collar, and a dark tie of undistinguished design. His conservative upbringing in New York caused him to shrink from the gaudy outfits that many film people affected. Besides, he felt that the conservative attire gave him a more dignified air and helped sublimate his youthful appearance.

Charged with the responsibility of overseeing fifty feature films per year, Thalberg had to keep track of an enormous amount of detail. Not only did he need to be acquainted with the films in production and in preparation, he had the responsibility of maintaining relations with all the creative personnel of M-G-M—directors, actors, writers as well as technical workers. His underlings were repeatedly impressed with how Thalberg could leap from an intricate plot situation of a film to the contractual demands of a star in an instant, without sacrificing the complexities of either one.

Thalberg could not remain seated behind his desk for long, and he prowled about the office as he talked with visitors. He was addicted to nervous activities with his hands, and this contributed to the nervousness of those with whom he conferred. One of his favorite activities was flipping a twenty-dollar gold piece into the air, often letting it clatter on the top of his glass-covered desk. This bothered Albert Lewin, boldest of his underlings, because Thalberg performed the trick while he, Lewin, was talking. Lewin tried to enlist his fellow

supervisors to produce their own gold pieces and begin flipping in
unison with the boss. They prudently declined. The next time Thalberg began flipping the coin in a conference, Lewin brought out his
own and bounced it on the glass-topped desk.

Thalberg was startled. He gazed at Lewin, recognizing that his habit
had been distracting to his fellow workers. He said not a word in
response. But he never flipped the gold piece in Lewin's presence
again.

Other habits were substituted. Thalberg wore a chain from which
dangled a pocket knife, and he twirled the knife at great speed. At
other times he constructed enormous lengths of paper-clip chains.

Always Thalberg was in command of a situation. When a young
assistant, Lawrence Weingarten, reported on studio matters, he became
annoyed because Thalberg continued perusing his mail. Weingarten
stopped to get Thalberg's attention, but Thalberg merely said, "Go
on! Go on," and resumed his study of the mail. At the end of the
conference, it was apparent that Thalberg had heard and understood

*The M-G-M Power, left to right: Buster Keaton, Rapf, Thalberg, Schenck,
Mrs. Schenck, Mayer, Mannix, Stromberg*

everything. He explained that he had learned to keep his attention on a number of levels while studying Spanish and stenography in night school.

The situation in Thalberg's waiting room was chaotic almost from the start of the M-G-M experience, and his habit of keeping people waiting was to remain the most controversial aspect of his professional behavior. He had no compunction about requiring the most talented and high-salaried of employees to remain outside his office for hours at a time. Some of them believed that Thalberg enjoyed an almost sadistic delight in keeping such people waiting. Indeed, he once confided to King Vidor, "You know, I get a kick out of looking out there and seeing people like Von Stroheim, Seastrom and Niblo waiting to see me."

Others argued that the congestion in Thalberg's waiting room was merely the result of his attempting too much. As the creative hub of an entertainment empire, he needed to confer intimately with a vast number of persons. He did so with little concern for time, concentrating his complete attention on the matter at hand. Meanwhile the appointments were piling up in the outer office.

In his studio life, Thalberg was closest to those who worked with him in a production capacity: Bernard Hyman, Albert Lewin, Harry Rapf, Hunt Stromberg, Paul Bern. He also formed strong relationships with directors, especially on a social level; his cronies included King Vidor, Jack Conway, and Victor Fleming. But Thalberg relied more and more on writers to supply the creative force he needed to bring new distinction to the screen.

He seemed to take a proprietary attitude toward writers. He believed that their creative forces, indeed their entire lives, should be devoted to the making of better films for M-G-M. His favorite writers learned to expect a motorcycle messenger to arrive at their homes each weekend with a package from Mr. Thalberg. It would contain a script that they were to read and report on on Monday morning. Writers were expected to attend the studio's previews and to see the other studios' product as well. Every Saturday morning Thalberg conducted a meeting in his office, and the writers were asked to comment on the films they had seen during the week. Those who had not done their homework were subjected to cool treatment by Thalberg.

Thalberg sometimes called upon his writers to perform extraordinary duties, as he did one day with Laurence Stallings. Thalberg outlined his problem: "We've got Ramon Novarro under contract for four pictures a year at seventy-five thousand a picture. I don't have a script for him right now, and if I can't convince him I've got one coming up, I've got to pay him the seventy-five thousand. Now I'm going to get Ramon in my office with you and Eddie Mannix, and we'll tell him a story so I won't have to pay him. I'll start the story and then you take over."

Novarro arrived at the office, and Thalberg informed him that a very promising project was in preparation for his next vehicle. "It starts with John meeting Mary," Thalberg began—the leading characters in all his projected pictures were "John" and "Mary." He began spinning a sea story, then he asked Stallings to continue. The writer detailed a plot that excited Novarro's interest.

"That sounds very good," said the actor. "Can I see the script?"

"I could show it to you," Stallings replied, "but it isn't in shape, and I know that a man of your sensitivity would want to see it in its best form."

Novarro departed after agreeing to do the picture. "Where did you get that story?" asked the amazed Thalberg.

"Right off your shelf," Stallings admitted. "It's *All the Brothers Were Valiant* by Ben Ames Williams." Thalberg ordered him to write the script and it was produced as *Across to Singapore*.

Early in his career, Thalberg began the practice of employing women script writers. While he was still at Universal, he became acquainted with Frances Marion when she called one day for an appointment with Carl Laemmle. He was impressed with the books under her arm—she was studying philosophy at the University of Southern California at the time—and after a time they discussed the possibility of making films together. But she began writing for Samüel Goldwyn, from whom Thalberg hired her in 1927.

Lenore Coffee was almost hired by Thalberg at Universal but she accepted a better offer at Metro. When he joined Louis B. Mayer, Thalberg succeeded in employing her as a "title doctor." She had a unique capacity for taking a sick picture and making it successful with new titles which sometimes changed the entire meaning of the action. Her first assignment was to bring new life to *The Dangerous Age*, in which Lewis Stone played a middle-aged man in love with a young woman. One of Miss Coffee's titles was used as part of the exploitation campaign: "When a man of forty falls in love with a girl of twenty it is not her youth he is seeking but his own." Miss Coffee moved over to M-G-M with the merger.

Bess Meredyth, who had been an extra with D. W. Griffith, also accompanied Thalberg from the Mayer Company to M-G-M. She was a skilled constructionist and helped the rebuilding of the *Ben-Hur* script. Before the start of shooting, Thalberg asked her opinion on every film, as he did with Miss Marion and Miss Coffee. He valued their "woman's touch."

Although Thalberg could work in complete harmony with female writers, he seemed incapable of establishing any deep friendships with women. He had known periodic infatuations with Hollywood beauties, and he enjoyed the pleasure of their company on social occasions. But he appeared not to *like* women for themselves. He worked in a world that was intensely masculine, despite his employment of actresses and female writers. That studio world was everything to him, and he was devoted to the men who helped him build and maintain it. They, in turn, almost worshiped him. Despite his heavy demands on their time and allegiance, they responded with a love that transcended any hint of unnatural attraction. All of the men around Thalberg gave every evidence of being completely male; the affection between them and him was unstated but genuine.

The pleasures Thalberg sought were male pleasures. He was too frail to be athletic, but he played tennis and an occasional round of golf. He loved to gamble. Often he indulged in all-night poker sessions at high stakes. Bridge became a passion. He played for hours on the weekend, often with Sam Goldwyn as his partner. Thalberg's bridge skill was better than his poker. On the social level, Thalberg was a prominent member of the Mayfair Club, which organized charity balls for Hollywood society.

Thalberg continued to live with his parents, and the family moved to more impressive houses as Irving's wealth and prominence grew. Always they were rented homes, as Henrietta was unconvinced of the permanence of California. She was a source of great comfort for Irving. She freed him of all domestic responsibilities and ran an efficient household. A warm meal was always ready for him when he came home late from the studio. She sometimes chided him for working too hard, and she did everything possible to guard his strength. If he appeared pale, she made him remain in bed all morning before reporting to the studio. At the slightest sign of a cold, she began filling him with home remedies. He took her and his father along on most social occasions, and Henrietta would glower if Irving danced more than two numbers in a row.

Henrietta wanted her son to marry, but she insisted that his wife must be worthy of him. Such a woman was not easy to find. Henrietta was greatly relieved when the romance with Constance Talmadge came to an end. The actress was entirely too flighty for Irving, Henrietta believed. She was concerned when Irving then concentrated his attention on Rosabelle Laemmle, daughter of his former boss. Henrietta inveighed against Rosabelle, but Irving was not swayed. He even became informally engaged to Rosabelle. Henrietta was aghast. As it turned out, Rosabelle's own strong will ended the engagement.

Rosabelle did not like California. She remained at the Laemmle's Hollywood home as long as her father needed her services as hostess, but when he returned to the East Coast, she was pleased to accompany him. Thalberg often was required to go to New York to confer with Schenck, Rubin, Moskowitz and others of the Eastern hierarchy, and he tried to plan his trips to coincide with Rosabelle's presence there. He enjoyed escorting her to the theater and to the parties that were given to fete the distinguished young production genius from Hollywood.

One night he invited Rosabelle to attend a dinner party in his honor at the home of the J. Robert Rubins. Conferences at the M-G-M offices delayed him, and he instructed his secretary to telephone Miss Laemmle and tell her he would send his chauffeur to her town house. To avoid further delay, he proposed meeting her at the Rubins'.

"No, that won't do," Rosabelle answered firmly.

The apprehensive secretary relayed Rosabelle's reply to Thalberg. His face turned scarlet, the indication by which his intimates had learned to detect his anger. He broke off the meeting and went to his hotel to dress for dinner. When he called for Rosabelle, his attitude was distinctly cool. At the Rubins' party he conducted himself with his usual politeness, but the other guests were aware of the tenseness between him and Rosabelle. When he took her home, the outcome was clear: the engagement was over.

With Constance Talmadge and Rosabelle Laemmle out of the picture, Thalberg turned to his self-styled "spare tire," Norma Shearer.

Thalberg had long idealized Norma. She had been afforded a patrician upbringing in Montreal, and he admired the dignity with which she conducted herself. His associates recognized the respect he held for her. At the time of the merger he was involved in casting *The Great Divide*, which had been a success as a stage play starring Henry Miller and Margaret Anglin and as a 1915 film with House Peters. The remake was to star Conway Tearle and Wallace Beery, and Thalberg was searching for an actress to portray Miss Anglin's original part, a Boston girl who was almost raped in a Western mining camp.

"You have the perfect woman right here under contract," suggested Lenore Coffee.

"And who is that?" Thalberg asked.

"Norma Shearer."

Thalberg rejected the notion immediately. "No one would believe she would allow herself to be raped, no matter what the circumstances," he snapped. "She looks too well able to take care of herself."

A Mayfair Ball. Standing, left to right: Clarence Brown, Robert Z. Leonard, Jack Conway, Irving Thalberg, Adolphe Menjou, King Vidor, Samuel Goldwyn, George Fitzmaurice, Herman Mankiewicz, Dr. Harry Martin, John Gilbert, Lloyd Pantages. Seated: Mona Maris, Mrs. Robert Leonard, Mrs. Jack Conway, Eleanor Boardman, Mrs. Samuel Goldwyn, Marion Davies, Louella Parsons, Mrs. George Fitzmaurice, Mrs. Herman Mankiewicz, Catherine Dale Owen, Aileen Pringle, Hedda Hopper

He continued at length his discussion of why Miss Shearer was unsuited for the role, and concluded by saying, "She makes me feel paternal."

Shortly afterward he cast her in *He Who Gets Slapped*, in which she was well received. She found herself in a position to profit from her success, thanks to the foresight of herself and her shrewd mother. When the merger took place, the contracts of all the Mayer actors had to be renegotiated for the new company. Some of the actors held out for high salaries, and Mayer angrily discharged them. Miss Shearer, with the counsel of her mother, proposed to start at the relatively low figure of a thousand dollars a week, with the salary to increase a thousand each year to a maximum of five thousand a week after five years. Mayer readily agreed to her terms, expecting her option would be dropped long before the maximum figure was reached. But she remained at the studio and ended up with one of the best contracts of any M-G-M star. Contrary to popular belief, it was not because of any influence by Thalberg.

He admired her business acumen, even though it cost the company money and hence reduced his own profit. He also was impressed by the rapport she had established with his mother.

Norma realized early that Henrietta was a power to be respected and cultivated. Whenever Irving brought her to the house, Norma made it a point to discuss homely matters with Henrietta. When the elder Thalbergs accompanied her and Irving to dinners and dances, Norma sat beside Henrietta and made sure she was included in the conversations. Henrietta became genuinely fond of Norma and encouraged her son's interest in the young actress, even though she was a Gentile.

Irving's fondness for Norma deepened into love, and he confided his feelings to Frances Goldwyn. She teased him that he had also thought he was in love with Peggy Hopkins Joyce. "Oh, no!" he replied seriously. "That was sex. This is love."

After three years of being Norma's sometime escort, he reached the moment of decision one night while they were dancing at the Coconut Grove.

"Don't you think it's about time we got married?" he asked.

"If you are proposing, you're not using the right dialogue," she replied. He repeated the proposal in more formal terms.

He presented her with a large diamond ring, and their betrothal was announced by the studio on August 17, 1927. The wedding was to take place at the Thalberg home on September 29.

On the afternoon of the wedding, Laurence Stallings was summoned to the Thalberg home. He reported to Thalberg's bedroom and there he found the studio boss in his striped pants and freshly starched shirt. Henrietta was laboriously trying to fasten the stud through the collar.

"I want to talk to you about those scripts we've been discussing," said Thalberg.

"Now?" asked the surprised Stallings.

"Yes, now," said Thalberg, and he began expounding on the scripts in progress. One wing of his collar sprang loose and the stud flew across the room.

"I'll find it," Thalberg said.

"No, no!" his mother said. "And crease your trousers? *I* will find it."

Both Henrietta and Stallings got down on their hands and knees to hunt for the errant stud while Thalberg continued discussing the scripts. Stallings found the stud behind the rear leg of the dresser, and the conference continued as Henrietta fixed Irving's collar.

The ceremony was unlike the elaborate Hollywood weddings of the period. Norma decided on a simple affair under the arbor in the Thalberg garden, with only a few close friends and members of the family present. Rabbi Edgar F. Magnin officiated; Norma had become a member of the Jewish faith before the wedding.

Louella Parsons provided a description of the bride for the Hearst papers:

> Never has Norma Shearer looked lovelier. Many, many times she has been called upon to play the role of a bride, but yesterday she gave her most realistic performance. Her gown of soft ivory velvet was particularly becoming. The severity of the plain white was relieved by a yoke of hand-made rose point lace studded with pearls and an occasional rhinestone.
>
> Her veil, edged with lace, was thrown back from her face in soft, gathered folds instead of the conventional bridal cap. She carried a bridal bouquet of white and tinted lavender orchids with pale yellow roses. Pinned to the bodice of her dress was a diamond pin—the gift of the bridegroom.

Left to right: William, Irving and Henrietta Thalberg, Norma and Edith Shearer

Left to Right: Edith Mayer, Irene Mayer, Louis Mayer, Sylvia Thalberg, Irving and Norma, Marion Davies, Douglas Shearer, Bernice Ferns

Male ribaldry. Left to right: Lawrence Weingarten, Edward Sutherland, Bernard Hyman, Robert Z. Leonard, Jack Conway, King Vidor, Fred Niblo, Harry Rapf (hoisting the bridegroom's feet)

The solidarity of the Mayer-Thalberg regime was demonstrated by Mayer's position as best man; his daughters served as bridesmaids. The two others were Marion Davies and Bernice Ferns, a friend of Norma's from Montreal. Sylvia Thalberg was maid of honor, and Douglas Shearer gave his sister in marriage. Most of the guests were those who worked most closely with Thalberg.

After the wedding supper, the newlyweds departed for a honeymoon at Del Monte on the Monterey peninsula. When Norma and Irving returned, they moved into the Sunset Boulevard house presided over by Henrietta Thalberg. It was she who ran the household, who sat at the end of the dining table, who received the thanks of parting guests. Norma was content with the arrangement. She realized that any dislocation of Irving's life might be harmful to his health, of which she was now co-caretaker. She knew that Henrietta would be more content with a daughter-in-law who allowed Irving to remain close to his mother. Norma had her own career to manage, and she enjoyed being relieved of the task of overseeing a manorial household. The mode of living suited her perfectly—for a time.

10

As Metro-Goldwyn-Mayer continued to grow in size and importance, it became more monolithic and impregnable to change. At no time was this tendency more evident than during the revolution of sound. M-G-M was not alone in this regard. Except for Warner Brothers, which started talkies with its Vitaphone, and Fox, which soon joined with its Movietone, the major film producers were slow to accept sound. Their reasons were not aesthetic, but economic. The sound installation cost as much as $20,000 per theater. For a company like Loew's with two hundred theaters, this entailed a massive outlay. Many of the theaters were still featuring vaudeville as part of the program; this presented the technical problem of where to situate the amplifying horns, since the area behind the screen was needed for the stage presentation. And Loew's was naturally reluctant to pay its competitors, Warner Brothers and Fox, huge royalties for use of their sound systems.

Irving Thalberg was by no means quick to recognize the importance of sound. In his early statements he indicated that he believed sound would be a useful adjunct to technique but would not replace the

Lionel Barrymore and William Haines, Alias Jimmy Valentine silent film. But if he failed as a seer, he exercised his customary pragmatism in using the new medium to the utmost. He worked closely with his brother-in-law, the brilliant technician Douglas Shearer, to develop new methods to allow M-G-M to catch up and surpass the other studios.

White Shadows of the South Seas was released in August of 1928 with sound effects and a musical score. Then Thalberg ordered *Alias Jimmy Valentine* back into production after its completion as a silent; the final two reels would be filmed with sound. M-G-M did not yet own sound equipment, so Thalberg arranged to rent the facilities at Paramount studio. The stars of the film, William Haines and Lionel Barrymore, repeated their final scenes with dialogue, emoting amid the most distracting of circumstances. Concealed microphones were placed in flower arrangements and under tables.

Alias Jimmy Valentine caught the public's fancy, as did any film with sound, and Thalberg began searching for another subject. He found it in an original story by Edmund Goulding about the travails of a couple of sisters in vaudeville. Norman Houston completed the script, and Thalberg commented, "This is good; let's do it as a half-talkie." As supervisor he assigned young Lawrence Weingarten. Jimmy

Gleason, whose slangy *Is Zat So?* and *The Fall Guy* had been stage successes, was engaged to put the dialogue into Broadway jargon. Thalberg was impressed with the results. "Let's make this an all-talkie," he ordered.

There was no precedent for a movie musical, and M-G-M had to experiment all the way. The studio had no music department, and an orchestra was recruited from musicians all over Los Angeles. After one of the first recording sessions, Thalberg asked Douglas Shearer, "How did it go?"

"We had a lot of problems," Shearer admitted.

"Why?" Thalberg demanded.

"Because there's no system here. Every time we need some music, we have to go out and hire musicians."

Weary at the end of a busy day, Thalberg muttered, "You're talking to me like I was an office boy!"

"You're talking to *me* like *I* was an office boy!" Shearer retorted.

Thalberg lowered his head. "You're right," he admitted wearily. "What do you suggest?"

Shearer proposed telephoning Major Edward Bowes, operator of the Loew's-owned Capitol in New York, and telling him to dispatch the theater's music library to the studio, as well as the arranger, music librarian and conductor. Thalberg picked up the telephone and made the call.

Thalberg wanted hit songs for the picture, and he employed several song writers, including two local boys, Nacio Herb Brown and Arthur Freed, and two New Yorkers, Billy Rose and Fred Fisher. Brown and Freed first composed a number called *Broadway Melody*, and they played and sang it for Thalberg at a piano in a rehearsal hall. Thalberg listened but made little comment.

Billy Rose hired a full orchestra to audition his songs for Thalberg, who listened approvingly. "I don't want to decide until I hear the Brown-Freed songs with an orchestra," he said. Brown and Freed arranged with a local radio station owner, Earle C. Anthony, to have his studio orchestra play their songs, and Thalberg went to KFI for the audition. With Brown at the piano, Freed sang the numbers in his uncertain baritone. The two song writers looked anxiously to Thalberg after they had concluded. He nodded. "I like your songs better," he said. Brown and Freed, who had been hired at $250 a week

Tin Pan Alley scene of Broadway Melody

apiece, were each to earn a half-million dollars from royalties of the movie's songs.

Goulding had called his story *Whoopee,* but Florenz Ziegfeld preempted the title with an Eddie Cantor musical comedy. Thalberg selected one of the Brown-Freed songs, *Broadway Melody,* to title the film. He instructed his staff: "This is an experiment; we don't know whether the audience will accept a musical on film. So we'll have to shoot it as fast and as cheaply as we can. I want quality, but I don't want to spend too much money."

Veteran Harry Beaumont directed the film at a rapid pace, but there were numerous delays for technical reasons. Cameras were stationed in booths to protect the sound track from camera noise.

For recording purposes, the scenes were shot in long takes, placing an added strain on the already nervous performers. For some scenes, two or three cameras were placed in booths on the stage to film the same action from different angles. Added to the problems of pioneering sound was the difficulty of coordinating the singers' voices with off-scene orchestras.

Despite the technical hazards, filming progressed at a satisfactory pace, and Thalberg was encouraged to order the use of color for the production number, *The Wedding of the Painted Doll.* Then he went off to New York for one of his periodic meetings with Nicholas Schenck and other New Yorker executives.

When Thalberg returned, he viewed the *Painted Doll* number on film. "That's not a motion picture," he told his aides afterward. "It's not a movie at all; it's a stage presentation. We'll have to do it all over again. This time arrange the cameras so we can get some different angles, instead of making the audience look at it from the front, as if they were in a legitimate theater."

When Thalberg ordered the return of the orchestra for the retake of the number, Douglas Shearer made a suggestion: "We don't need the orchestra. We've got a perfectly good recording of the music. Why not just play the record and have the dancers go through the number? Then we can combine the film and the sound track in the lab."

"Can you do that?" Thalberg asked.

"I see no reason why we can't," Shearer replied.

"Okay, do it," said Thalberg, inaugurating the playback system by which musicals have since been filmed.

Even with the expensive retake, *Broadway Melody* was completed with the economy Thalberg insisted on; the total cost was $350,000. The film was rushed into release in early 1929 to beat other film musicals to the theaters. *Broadway Melody* played fifty-three weeks at the Astor Theater in New York and long-run engagements in all other cities.

The film also brought Irving Thalberg his first accolade from the Academy of Motion Picture Arts and Sciences. *Broadway Melody* was selected the best picture of 1928–29, the first talkie to win the honor.

"Wedding of the Painted Doll," Broadway Melody

I I

Irving Thalberg performed his functions as a film maker in private, seldom expressing his theories beyond the intimacy of the studio family. But on March 20, 1929, he delivered a rare public statement of his beliefs about the movie medium. The occasion was a lecture at the University of Southern California as part of a course called Introduction to the Photoplay. It was sponsored jointly by the University and the Academy of Motion Picture Arts and Sciences.

He was not yet out of his twenties, yet he was a veteran in films. His remarks reflected his earnest beliefs: that movies were the foremost medium of expression; that film was ephemeral and topical; that the director was the predominant figure in film making. The speech also revealed his sensitivity to criticism of the movie medium. Most of all, he disclosed himself as a complete movie man, one who had an unswerving devotion to films, while maintaining a realistic view of their shortcomings.

The highlights of his speech:

My friends, as you have probably already observed, or as you will know before I am through, I am not a lecturer, but the opportunity of speaking to you and presenting a subject that is as close to my heart as the modern photoplay was one that brought me out of my shell. A lecture with the modern photoplay for its subject is very broad in its scope, and in the short time I have to speak, I can only touch on some of the most vital and fundamental aspects of it.

In order to understand the modern photoplay, in my opinion, which is based on about twelve years of experience during which time I have made fifty or more pictures in each of those years, one must understand the meaning of the word, entertainment, for entertainment is the purpose and end of the photoplay. The definition of the word, entertainment, as given in the dictionary, is that something which engages and holds the attention agreeably. . . . Other arts generally appeal to a selected group, but the motion picture art, and it *is* an art, must have universal appeal. This is fundamental, for the motion picture industry, with its investment of hundreds of millions of dollars, is based on the hope that it will appeal to the people of a nation and of a world, and if it did not have this appeal, it could not have reached its present state of development. . . .

We have seen that motion picture audiences are interested in pictures, movement, and changes in form, but even more important than these is the necessity of having the subject matter of photoplays correspond closely to current thinking—they must be topical. One of my chief functions is to be an observer and sense and feel the moods of the public. When I am asked to pass on the expenditure of huge sums of money and decide whether one kind of picture should be made or another kind, the greatest problem to be settled is that of judging whether or not the subject matter of the story is topical. What is accepted by the public today may not be accepted tomorrow. One of the finest examples I can give you of this is that war pictures in one period and another, in order to be successful, have had to be presented in an entirely different flavor.

During the war, various patriotic pictures were produced with success, showing war as a glorified thing in which no sacrifice was too great to make for your country, and having all the various forms of patriotism that could be gotten into a picture, including titles such as *The Kaiser, The Beast of Berlin.* The people were stirred up and were thinking along those lines, and war pictures were not successful [after the war was over], at least that was the common belief.

However, we produced a picture called *The Big Parade* which to a great extent has made history along the lines of pictures, and the only difference between it and the other war pictures was the different viewpoint taken in the picture. We took a boy whose idea in entering the war was not patriotic. He was swept along by the war spirit around him and entered it but didn't like it. He met a French girl who was intriguing to him, but he wasn't really serious about her. The only time he was interested in fighting was when a friend, who was close to him, was killed. It was human appeal rather than patriotic appeal, and when he reached the German trenches and came face to face with the opportunity to kill, he couldn't do it. In other words, a new thought regarding the war was in the minds of most people, and that was the basis of its appeal . . .

The motion pictures present our customs and our daily life more distinctly than any other medium and, therefore, if we were to come back a thousand years from today and tried to find some form of expression that would more clearly, more perfectly explain how we live today, it would have to be the motion picture, because there is no medium of today that so universally must please as great a number of people. . . .

Right there is another side to this question. I have often been asked, "Do you think that the modern pictures, the great pictures, will endure forever?" While no one can state with any authority what will happen, in my opinion, the modern picture will not live forever as an artistic production, because one of the most important features of pictures is currency—the immediate fitting in with current thought.

Now, of course, there are exceptions and at all times, a great story, a great work of genius will overcome any obstacle. We have the work of a master artist like Emil Jannings. At times he has been successful in overcoming all obstacles of ordinary standards of acceptance by the public. A great director like Ernst Lubitsch, through his cleverness and his genius will and has at times overcome the general lack of acceptance of his type of thinking. In short, I believe that although the modern picture will not live forever as a work of art, except in a few instances, it will be the most effective way of showing posterity how we live today. . . .

The various directors and stars are examples of style and can very easily trace their popularity up and down on the style of the moment. For instance, it is no accident that Clara Bow with her representation of the flapper of today, is a star. If it hadn't been her, it would have been some other girl of exactly her type. The directors, I think, are probably a more interesting group of men in our art than any other group because they have in their command and within their powers, the ability to tell stories and are more responsible, in my opinion again, to tell stories than almost any other group—the writers, the stars, or any one else. . . .

I think it is entirely fitting that I should start with D. W. Griffith, who is certainly a master director and one whom we remember with great awe and appreciation of the many things he accomplished. He was an idealist and his love scenes on the screen were idealistic and things of beauty—nobody could direct such scenes with as much appreciation for them as Griffith. His heroine, Lillian Gish, his heroes, Richard Barthelmess and Henry B. Walthall, and others, were the epitome of everything that was fine, noble, and glorious; but his pictures are not successful today because modern ideas are changing. The idealistic love of a decade ago is not true today. We cannot sit in a theater and see a noble hero and actually picture ourselves as him. William Haines, with his modern salesman attitude to go and get it, is more typical. The other thing becomes abnormal and, therefore, is less interesting.

In contrast to D. W. Griffith is Cecil B. De Mille, who is a very excellent example of a director who is not interested in art for art's sake. I have heard him discussed in various terms by critics, and I know his attempt to appeal to the current thinking of the day, is not haphazard . . .

King Vidor is as much a realist as Griffith is an idealist, and his pictures have been an attempt to mirror life of today as it really is. I have discussed scenes with him many times, and have asked him to do this or that to heighten the dramatic effect, and his worst fear has always been to make any character do anything that wasn't natural for him to do.

There are other directors who have entirely different styles, equally successful, and tell their stories with equal strength. Murnau's *Sunrise, Faust,* and the various pictures he made in Germany certainly were fine achievements, disregardless of their commercial success. He does not mirror life from the moment, but from a mood. If his mood is oppressive, his characters are oppressive, his lighting is oppressive. If a flower were growing in a scene he wants to make oppressive, he would not permit it to be there unless it were drooped over. His whole thought in each scene is to represent a mood.

Lubitsch has the George Bernard Shaw quality, if he doesn't mind the observation, of trying to turn each thing into a point of amusement. He sees life from an amusing standpoint and his whole effort in directing is to turn each situation into a laugh. . . .

You have seen that change in form and change in subject matter are of great importance to the motion picture. Indeed, one may truthfully say that change is the lifeblood of the art and this doesn't only apply to the form, but also to the people employed in the industry. The favorites of yesterday are gone and the favorites of tomorrow come up. Where new material is to come from we do not know, and although we are drawing on the stage, from the writers of literature, and other sources, there are not enough people to make the thing as it should be made. Perhaps we will get some material from this [college] class. At any rate, the field is open because it isn't like the electrical business or the shoe business and cannot get along with any one group of brains that is in it at the moment—it must be supplemented. . . .

There is no greater subject, and that goes for all subjects, than the motion picture. It is the art of arts because there is no other medium that appeals to so many people. There are others who think just as I do and I am going to quote a few lines from an article written by Aaron Horn in *The Educational Review*, under the title, "Teaching Appreciation of the Photoplay":

". . . For the common people, a course in photoplay appreciation is more needed than a course in literature because it is a much larger and interesting factor in the life of the average person than literature is."

I think the University of Southern California is to be congratulated on the making of a course of this kind, and I am very glad of the opportunity to have been here and hope I have made my point clear and have interested you. If I haven't, it is because of myself and not the subject. There never was a subject more worthy of interest than the motion picture.

IV

TRIUMPH 1929–1933

He carried with him the accouterments of an artist; hence he was unique in the Hollywood of that period. I don't know of anyone else who has occupied that position. He was like a young pope.

—Budd Schulberg

I

 T HE DIRE PREDICTIONS proved false, and Irving Thalberg reached
thirty on May 30, 1929. Throughout his adult life he had been faced
with the imminence of death. Once Lenore Coffee came into his
office as he was rolling down his sleeve after an examination for
an insurance policy. He said with a grim smile, "I'm twenty-five,
and I have to pay the premium of a man forty years old." He never
complained of his health to his associates, but they remained aware
of his perilous situation. Sometimes he remarked wistfully, "I'd settle
for another ten years." Because he realized his lifetime was limited,
he became intolerant of the waste of time. Every minute of his studio
day was occupied with story conferences, visits to the sets, interviews with new talent, viewing film, greeting dignitaries. He was
impatient with correspondence and wrote as few letters as possible.
A pile of mail sat on his desk, and he once confided to a secretary,
"If I leave it there long enough, I don't have to answer it." He
listened attentively to the problems of actors, but he could be sharp
with them if they didn't come to the point. Once William Haines
came to him in a pouting mood, and Thalberg said crossly, "Take
the nipple out of your mouth and tell me what's wrong." Haines

stated his grievance: he was being underpaid in comparison to John Gilbert. Thalberg gave Haines a $10,000 bonus, but insisted that he put it into an annuity instead of spending it.

Having passed thirty, Thalberg's health seemed to take a favorable turn. Under the watchful supervision of Henrietta, he continued to conserve his strength whenever possible. He often remained in bed during the morning, making telephone calls to the New York office and reading scripts before he reported to the studio at eleven. Norma also was vigilant over his health. She learned to detect the transparent look his skin acquired when he was overly tired, and she then enforced a rest. Often she changed their sheets twice a night because he was inclined to sweat while asleep. Her work at the studio occupied her days, but the rest of her time remained unencumbered so she could adjust to her husband's plans. She kept their social life as simple as was possible for a man who was a leader of the community. They went to a few of the big parties and dined with the Samuel Goldwyns and other close friends. But Irving's busy schedule of previews precluded many evening plans. For weekends, the Thalbergs sometimes went away to Palm Springs or Agua Caliente. Often they were invited by Marion Davies and William Randolph Hearst to join other Hollywood celebrities in weekends in the mountain fastness of San Simeon. They ate in the medieval dining hall with aristocratic splendor—except for the paper napkins which Hearst decreed. They also complied with their host's bidding and went on overnight horseback treks, dining in the California wilderness on fine china.

In the year following their marriage, Norma and Irving began their journeys to Europe. He liked to keep in touch with what the European film makers were accomplishing, and he and Norma enjoyed sightseeing in such places at Heidelberg. There they visited Mother Ernst, who operated a tavern made famous by *The Student Prince*, one of Norma's most successful films. Thalberg's principal reason for the regular travels to Europe was to take the waters at Bad Nauheim in Germany. He placed himself in the hands of Dr. Franz Groedel, who operated a sanitarium for heart patients. Thalberg drank the mineral waters of the famed resort and underwent therapy, and he found great comfort from the treatment.

Refreshed by his journey, Thalberg plunged himself into work on his return to Culver City. His talent as head producer came into

The Thalbergs on return from their honeymoon

At San Simeon. Back row, left to right: King Vidor, Beatrice Lillie, Richard Barthelmess, Eleanor Boardman. Standing (middle row): Frank Orsatti, E. B. Hatrick, Edmund Goulding, Ma Talmadge, Greta Garbo, Nick Schenck, unidentified, Harry Rapf, Aileen Pringle, J. Robert Rubin, Norma Shearer. Seated: Hal Roach, Natalie Talmadge, Eddie Mannix, Constance Talmadge, Buster Keaton, Paul Bern, Irving Thalberg. Reclining: John Gilbert

full flower in the sound era; all that had gone before seemed only a rehearsal. He had perfected the visual mechanics of film during the silent period; now he was prepared for the vastly more complex challenge of combining dialogue with action, of bringing sophistication and immediacy to the screen.

Thalberg refined his work methods in order to handle the greatly increased demands of preparing and completing sound films. He could no longer concern himself with the day-to-day procedure of filming; it was in the preproduction and postproduction stages that he exerted his peculiar skill. In the beginning he made the choice of material. Unlike most producers, he did not rely on the capsuled accounts of novels and plays prepared by studio readers. He had trained himself to read at an astonishing speed, and he could consume handfuls of books in an evening.

After the material was acquired, Thalberg assigned it to one of his supervisors—Hyman, Lewin, Stromberg, Weingarten, etc.—who began developing it with writers. Supervisors and writers met regularly with Thalberg as the script progressed, and he provided guidance on story line and character development. His associates were repeatedly amazed at how Thalberg solved an impasse by a simple observation or change of action.

Rarely would Thalberg allow a film to begin production without a completed script. Sometimes there was no choice, because a free-lance player was scheduled to begin salary and was available for a specified term. But Thalberg was developing more and more stars and featured players who were under contract to M-G-M and thus were able to work whenever he assigned them.

Thalberg seldom concerned himself with the progress of the actual filming unless serious problems arose. A day's volume of rushes was too time-consuming for him to review. He preferred to reserve his judgment until the film was completed and assembled. Then he contributed what many of his co-workers considered to be his greatest talent as a film maker.

"Movies aren't made; they're remade," he declared.

He carried out his belief by perfecting the system of audience testing. The Thalberg preview became almost ritualistic in form. His close associates and other studio officials, plus the director and cutter of the film, assembled at dusk near the Pacific Electric tracks which ran just outside the studio. Thalberg was usually the last to arrive, and he hurried out of his office and boarded the big red streetcar that had been hired for the evening. The others followed, and the trolley began the trip to San Bernardino, Riverside, San Pedro, or some other city on the Pacific Electric route. As the trolley clanged through Southern California suburbs, the movie men ate delicatessen sandwiches, drank soda pop—no liquor was allowed— and discussed the day's events at the studio. Thalberg invariably played bridge.

The trip home from the preview demonstrated how well the picture had performed in the outlying community. If Thalberg settled down cheerfully to his game of bridge, his associates knew that the preview had been a success. But if he neglected the cards, the men realized that the picture had gone awry and they would be subjected to intense questioning on the streetcar that night and in Thalberg's office the following morning. Curiously, there was no fear involved, for Thalberg never attempted to fix blame. Nor was he glum or pessimistic in his attitude. A bad preview merely presented a challenge which he met with the question: "What can we do to make the picture better?" Usually he himself provided the answer.

Thalberg came closest to a reprimand at the preview of *The Great Meadow*, which had been supervised by Hunt Stromberg. There was a scene in the early part of the picture which showed Johnny Mack Brown returning to his wife after a two-year absence. A baby's cry was heard in the next room, and Brown said lovingly to his wife, "Oh, darling!"

The preview audience roared with laughter. Thalberg said nothing. He merely turned around and stared at Stromberg, who was seated behind him. "Sorry," said the abashed Stromberg. Thalberg made no reply; he merely kept staring at Stromberg.

Thalberg continued to stare as Stromberg sputtered, "I said I was sorry, Irving . . . Please turn around! . . . I'll never do it again, Irving." After long minutes, Thalberg turned around to watch the rest of the picture, his point having been made.

Retake Valley was the name applied to M-G-M by local jesters. The cognomen didn't upset Thalberg at all. He had demonstrated time after time, from *The Big Parade* to *The Broadway Melody*, that retakes could change a bad picture into a good one, and a good one into a triumph.

"Take a man in the oil business," he reasoned. "Supposing he drills a thousand feet and he starts producing four hundred barrels a day. But the experts tell him if he drills another thousand feet he might well get a thousand barrels a day. Would he be a wise man to be satisfied with four hundred barrels?"

Thalberg demonstrated his theory in an early talkie, *The Big House*. Frances Marion had written a strong story about prison life, with an important message for prison reform. Thalberg took a gamble in casting two of the leads: Wallace Beery, a film veteran who was in a decline after being dropped from his Paramount contract, and

En route to Europe with the Hal Roaches

With Mother Ernst at Heidelberg

Robert Montgomery, an M-G-M newcomer from the Broadway stage who had played college boys and socialites in his early films. After years of playing second leads, Beery seemed an unlikely candidate for a starring role, and Montgomery appeared out of place in a tough prison film. Yet both performed ably under the direction of George Hill, as did Chester Morris. Thalberg believed that he had a potent attraction.

The Pacific Electric trolley trundled to San Bernardino for the preview of *The Big House*. Thalberg played no bridge on the return trip. He was stunned by the cool reception to the film. His associates offered suggestions, but he discarded them all.

"There's something wrong in the picture, but I can't put my finger on it," he said.

He took *The Big House* to another theater, but this time he went alone. He shifted his seat from one part of the house to another,

Chester Morris and Leila Hyams, The Big House

trying to fathom the reason for the audience's failure to accept the film.

At his staff conference the following day, he announced: "I think I found out what's wrong. When Morris gets out of prison, he goes to see Montgomery's wife and gets into a romance with her. Women flinch at that; they don't like it. Now supposing we make the girl Montgomery's sister instead—"

The change was made, and when Thalberg previewed the new version of *The Big House*, the audience acclaimed the film. Beery was established as a star in the characterization which would serve him handsomely for the next twenty years—as the rough-edged, endearing mug. Montgomery demonstrated his qualities as a distinctive actor, not merely a callow juvenile. And *The Big House* was the first important crime picture of the talkie period, beginning the wave that brought *Little Caesar, Public Enemy, Scarface* and hundreds of lesser films.

The prison yard of The Big House

No retake was too large or too small for Thalberg. When he became dissatisfied with Mauritz Stiller's work on *The Temptress* and replaced him with Fred Niblo, Thalberg ordered all of Stiller's footage scrapped. His reason was twofold: Greta Garbo had proved a promising star in her first American picture and he didn't want her seen in film he didn't approve of; Fred Niblo was an important director and should not be placed in the position of completing another man's picture.

When *Tugboat Annie* was previewed with an excellent response from the audience, Thalberg remained unsatisfied. He said to the director, Mervyn LeRoy: "You know that scene where Beery walks down the aisle at the assembly in the girls' home?"

"Yes," said LeRoy.

"Wouldn't it be funny if his shoes squeaked?"

"Yes," the director replied. "But that set has already been struck. It would cost thirty-five to forty thousand dollars to shoot a retake of that scene."

"I didn't ask you what it would cost. I asked you if it would improve the picture."

"Well—of course it would."

"Then we'll do it."

Retakes rescued many an M-G-M film from abject failure at the box office; in his years as production chief Thalberg never had a monumental flop of the kind that could ruin a corporation's financial statement for the year. Yet he placed no blind reliance on the system. At the conclusion of one important film, the M-G-M College of Cardinals, as the executive staff was sometimes called, gathered around Thalberg to make a variety of suggestions for the film, which had not been enthusiastically received by the audience. Thalberg ended the discussion by remarking, "I don't think this picture could survive a lot of improvement." The implication was clear: production values and plot reworkings would not enhance a film which was by its nature limited in scope and appeal. The picture was released without changes.

The Thalberg system of-retakes was economically feasible in an era when most of the important players in a film were under contract to the studio. They could easily be called in for additional scenes, or borrowed from a subsequent production for a few days. Whenever possible, Thalberg ordered key sets to remain standing until he had determined after the previews that they would not be needed again.

The system had its opponents and its adherents. Some argued that by taking a film to a relatively unsophisticated city like San Bernardino, Thalberg was aiming at the lowest denominator of the audience. He replied that the people of San Bernardino *were* his audience, typical of the vast numbers who supported movies across the land. That did not necessarily mean that he catered to lower tastes. He told his aides, "Always remember, there's nothing too good for the audience." Throughout the Thalberg era, M-G-M pictures possessed a higher degree of sophistication than did those of any other studio. Thalberg used the preview to determine if the average audience comprehended what the film makers were striving to attain; it was his method of eliminating elements that were unclear, disturbing or ineffectual.

Sometimes he did follow too blindly the desires of the audience; many of his films were marred by synthetic, tacked-on happy endings, because he believed Americans were by nature optimistic and preferred events to turn out nicely in the end. But in other instances he defied the public's response.

2

William Haines described the coming of sound to M-G-M: "It was the night of the *Titanic* all over again, with women grabbing the wrong children and Louis B. singing *Nearer My God to Thee.*"

Amid the chaos stood the slender figure of Irving Thalberg, exhilarated by change, making rapid decisions on matters for which there was no previous experience. Some of his judgments proved remarkably apt, some went awry. The percentage of correct ones was high. He once explained his policy: "Under the law of averages one will always make mistakes, but I can take a long time and still be wrong. If I take a short time to make the decision, I am not costing the studio a lot of money while I'm making up my mind."

Among the many problems brought on by sound was the question of what to do about the foreign market. The silent film had spoken an international language; the only requirement for distribution overseas was the inexpensive one of reprinting the titles in German, Spanish, Chinese, etc. The addition of dialogue brought complications. Dubbing was unknown. How would foreign audiences react to hearing movies in an unfamiliar language?

Thalberg met the issue by filming complete foreign versions of the important pictures. He placed Albert Lewin in charge of creating a stock company of foreign performers. Some were recruited in Hollywood; many were imported from abroad. When the English-language film had finished production, a German cast and German-speaking director moved into the sets and filmed the same story. Then a French company. Then a Spanish company.

In some instances, stars appeared in more than one version. Ramon

Novarro performed in the English-language version of *The Call of the Flesh* with Dorothy Jordan, then played it in Spanish with Conchita Montenegro and in French with Suzy Vernon, directing the latter two versions himself. Novarro was studying for the German version when Thalberg relieved him of the assignment. "It's too much work for what we can get out of it," Thalberg explained.

Buster Keaton appeared in four different versions of his early talkie comedies. The chore was eased by the fact that many of his scenes were in pantomime. For the dialogue scenes he learned the French, German and Spanish lines phonetically, calculating that any errors he committed would add to the comic effect. His lines were written on cue cards and held up to his view off-camera.

Eventually the policy of foreign-language versions was discarded. The system had too many drawbacks: the expense was too great for the money received; production was slowed because sets had to remain standing for a long period; the creative talents of stars were tied up on two or more versions of the same film; foreign audiences preferred seeing their American favorites in Hollywood-made films. The process of dubbing was soon perfected, making the foreign-language versions unnecessary.

During the early days of talkies, the studios competed fiercely to capitalize on the public's consuming interest in the new medium, and Thalberg conducted his campaign with the aid of M-G-M's impressive list of stars. The studio's biggest names were put into the first talkies, and the results brought triumph—and disaster.

In the case of Norma Shearer, the result was triumphant. Thalberg chose to star his wife in M-G-M's first all-talking drama, *The Trial of Mary Dugan*. The choice of material was sagacious on two counts: it had been a sure-fire play on Broadway, and the confinement of most of the action to one courtroom set made it an easy subject for the immobile sound camera.

Thalberg left little to chance. He hired the author of the play, Bayard Veiller. The entire cast was rehearsed in the script for two weeks, and the play was performed before an audience at the studio before filming started. Norma was coached on voice by the famed actress, Mrs. Leslie Carter; fortunately Norma's voice was already well-pitched and cultured.

Norma Shearer, Lewis Stone and H. B. Warner, The Trial of Mary Dugan

The filming of *The Trial of Mary Dugan* was a nightmare. For some of the courtroom scenes, six cameras were placed before the set in outhouse-like enclosures. The walls of the stage were heavily padded, and a refrigerator-style door was placed at the entrance. Still, the noise of trucks passing on Washington Boulevard invaded the sound track, causing much waste of time and film. Because the intercutting of sound film had not been fully developed, scenes often ran as long as ten minutes. Actors grew nervous toward the end of the scene and misread their lines. The studio workers found themselves at the mercy of the sound technicians who had been brought from New York; whatever the new men decreed had to be followed.

Irving Thalberg and inventor Lee De Forest with a reel of Romance, *which introduced M-G-M's new process of automatic volume control*

The film was finally completed, and it was rushed into the theaters. Although critics complained that *The Trial of Mary Dugan* was little more than a filmed stage play, it enjoyed great success. Most important to Irving Thalberg, the film proved that the talking Norma Shearer was just as appealing as the silent one.

Other stars were not so fortunate. Both William Haines and John Gilbert were the victims of unperfected methods of sound recording that turned their not-unpleasant voices into piping tones. With Haines the results were not immediately felt; he had specialized in playing breezy characters, and his screen voice was not too jarring. The real tragedy was Gilbert. For years American women had imagined the romance of his voice as he made love to a succession of actresses in silent films. A combination of poor recording, his own clipped diction and his understandable nervousness produced a voice that was high-pitched and ludicrously unrelated to his romantic figure. His love scenes with Renée Adorée in *His Glorious Night* brought guffaws from audiences in New York. *Redemption*, his next film, proved even worse.

Hollywood's foreign-born stars presented a formidable problem for talkies, and many of the personalities—Emil Jannings, Pola Negri, Vilma Banky, etc.—could not bridge the transition to sound. Fortunately for screen history, Thalberg understood the problem and chose not to rush his exotic star, Greta Garbo, into a talkie.

Thalberg urged Garbo to undergo coaching to relieve the heaviness of her Swedish accent. When he felt that she had made sufficient progress, he began searching for a vehicle for her talkie debut. He found it in *Anna Christie*, Eugene O'Neill's Pulitzer Prize play which had previously been filmed in 1923 with Blanche Sweet in the title role created on the stage by Pauline Lord.

For director Thalberg chose Clarence Brown, who had established a good rapport with Garbo on *Flesh and the Devil* and *A Woman of Affairs*. Thalberg took no chances; he ordered two weeks of rehearsals before shooting began. Garbo didn't like to rehearse, but she acquiesced. One thing she did insist on: a five o'clock quitting time. At that hour every afternoon, her maid brought her a glass of water. That was the signal for Garbo to leave the set.

The filming of *Anna Christie* went with surprising ease. Two cameras were employed for many of the scenes, affording closeups and medium shots at the same time. After each take, the sound was played back on the record disc. Garbo was startled when she heard her own dialogue for the first time. "My God," she exclaimed, "is that my voice?" After finishing the film, she made it once again in a German-language version.

Thalberg previewed *Anna Christie* in San Bernardino. He was so pleased with the results that he went directly from the theater to the Santa Fe station and boarded the *Chief* with the cans of film. He continued on to New York to show Garbo's first talkie to the M-G-M Eastern executives.

Anna Christie was a triumph on two counts: it provided Garbo's safe passage to talkies, and it gave Thalberg another new star.

Marie Dressler had known fame in her early and middle years and neglect in her later life. She had starred in films with Charlie Chaplin in *Tillie's Punctured Romance* and on the Broadway stage with Weber and Fields. But at the age of fifty-five she found no producer wanted to hire a dumpy old lady with a face like a mud fence. It had been nine years since she had enjoyed her last comeback, and in 1927 she seemed to have reached the close of her career. She contemplated an offer as a housekeeper at a Long Island estate. There she might have ended out her years except for a chance encounter during her stage heyday.

Frances Marion, a sixteen-year-old reporter for the San Francisco *Examiner*, had been assigned one day to get an interview from the visiting star, Marie Dressler. The young reporter hurried to the theater and told her mission at the stage door. Miss Dressler, who held a grudge against the Hearst press, sent a blunt reply: "Any reporter from a Hearst paper gets kicked off the stage." Miss Marion was not dissuaded. She waited until the actress emerged from the theater and pleaded: "If you don't give me an interview, I'll lose my job." Miss Dressler took the girl by the hand and led her to the dressing room. "I'm going to give you the best interview I've ever given," she promised.

The two women became friends over the years, then Miss Dressler dropped out of sight. One day in 1927, Miss Marion, now a successful screen writer, received a letter from a mutual friend who described the actress's plight. Miss Marion devised a plan. She fashioned a screen play from an M-G-M property called *The Callahans and the Murphys* and presented it to Irving Thalberg.

Greta Garbo, Marie Dressler, Charles Bickford, Anna Christie

"It's good," he commented after he had read the script. "Who do you suggest for the leads?"

Miss Marion mentioned the clever comedienne, Polly Moran, for Mrs. Murphy, and added, "I want Marie Dressler for the role of Ma Callahan. I had her in mind when I wrote it."

"Those big Broadway stars want all the money in the world," Thalberg protested. "She won't come out here for what we could give her for the part."

"I can get her," Miss Marion replied confidently. "I think she'll come if we give her two thousand a week."

Thalberg agreed to $1500, and Miss Marion sent her old friend the money to make the train trip to California.

The Callahans and the Murphys proved to be an amusing film, but it was bedeviled by protests of the Irish, who believed that Irish womanhood had been libeled by the blowzy portrayals by Moran and Dressler. After a number of stink-bomb throwings in theaters, the film was withdrawn by M-G-M.

Thalberg co-starred the pair in another film which had only middling success. For almost two years Miss Dressler remained idle and lived on the charity of friends.

Frances Marion didn't give up. When Thalberg assigned her to write Garbo's first talkie, the writer built up the part of Marty, intending it for Marie Dressler.

"Marie Dressler!" exclaimed the director, Clarence Brown.

"Yes, she's the one actress who can play the part," Miss Marion insisted.

"Look, I know you're friends with her, Frances," said Brown. "But she's a Mack Sennett comic!"

Miss Marion persuaded Brown to make a test of the actress in the role of the aging waterfront barfly. Thalberg was impressed and assigned her to the picture. Miss Dressler's brief scenes in *Anna Christie* provided that rare happening in films, when a performer makes a magical transference of humanity from screen to audience. Critics and audiences alike recognized Marie Dressler for what she had always been: a star.

To Irving Thalberg's great fortune, another M-G-M performer was emerging from years of neglect at the same time: Wallace Beery. The confluence of these two stars provided one of the great combinations of films. They teamed in only two films—*Min and Bill* and *Tugboat Annie*—but the combin'ng of their weather-worn faces and their sentimental bluster made an indelible impression on audiences.

3

The uneasy alliance that was Metro-Goldwyn-Mayer came apart one cataclysmic day in 1929. On March 3 William Fox, the aggressive founder of the Fox Film Corporation, announced at a press conference that he had acquired control of Loew's, Inc., by purchase of a considerable amount of common stock. Nicholas Schenck, who had succeeded to the presidency of Loew's after the death of Marcus

Wallace Beery and Marie Dressler, Min and Bill

Loew in 1927, sat beside Fox to give the announcement official sanction.

The news struck the movie world with earthquake force. There had been rumors that Fox might try to buy control of Loew's, but he was already overextended by the acquisition of theater chains, as well as the operation of a studio. Everyone in the film industry was stunned by the Fox announcement, especially Louis Mayer and Irving Thalberg. They had no inkling that Schenck was negotiating to sell out Loew's, nor did their Eastern representative, J. Robert Rubin. All the backstage maneuvering had been kept secret from him.

The feelings of Mayer and Thalberg quickly turned to fury.

Ever since the merger, five years before, they had been devoting all their energies to building M-G-M into the number-one studio of Hollywood, and to a degree they had succeeded. Now they learned that Nick Schenck had been scheming behind their backs to wipe out their efforts so he could collect millions for negotiating the sale to Fox. Mayer and Thalberg considered it a betrayal, and they told Schenck so in a fiery confrontation in New York. Schenck, who had learned the rough and tumble as operator of Palisades Park, remained defiant.

"You haven't heard the last of this," Mayer said ominously. "I have friends in Washington. They don't like the idea of big corporations swallowing up other ones. They might like to look into this particular deal." His was no idle bluff. Mayer had just come from Washington, where he had slept in the White House and attended the inauguration of his good friend, Herbert Hoover.

Fox and Schenck were not intimidated. They went ahead with the financial arrangements for the purchase and considered it to be a *fait accompli*. Thalberg was infuriated when department heads from Fox studio arrived at the M-G-M lot "to look over the facilities" in preparation for the take-over. He was disheartened to see the plummetting morale at the studio he and Mayer had built.

Three happenings changed the situation to favor Mayer and Thalberg. William Fox was seriously hurt in an automobile accident and was unable to pursue the purchase with his customary zeal. Then came the October 29, 1929, stock market crash, hurling his affairs into disarray. Finally, Mayer's dire prediction came true: the government filed anti-trust proceedings against Fox.

The threat of the acquisition by Fox was over. But the distrust between the Mayer Group and the Loew's hierarchy would continue.

Money helped to salve the wounds. Schenck attempted to conciliate Mayer, Thalberg and Rubin with an indemnity in the hundreds of thousands of dollars. Mayer and Rubin were content with the settlement; Thalberg was not. His mother's lesson—that he should be compensated according to his contribution—continued to nag at him, and everyone in the film industry agreed that his contribution to M-G-M was enormous. He wanted more money.

Mayer realized that Schenck could not ask the stockholders to approve a bigger salary for Thalberg, who already was earning

$4000 a week. There was only one other way to give the young man added compensation; Mayer had to supply it from his own share of M-G-M profits. In December 1929 he agreed to lower his percentage from 53 to 43 and raise Thalberg's from 20 to 30. Rubin's share remained at 27 percent.

The beginnings of discontent were being sown, but the three members of the Mayer Group remained a powerful combination. Thalberg was the production genius; he conceived the films, selected the talent and followed the creative process to the end. Mayer provided the business acumen permitting Thalberg to realize his dreams. Mayer took charge of the studio staff and was constantly striving to make it the best in Hollywood. He wrote contracts, swung deals and fought the studio's battles with the Loew's hierarchy. The urbane Rubin maintained contact with the literary and theatrical worlds, scouting material and talent for the studio; he also served as watchdog for the Mayer Group's interests in the New York office.

Mayer fully realized the value of Thalberg to M-G-M, and he deferred to the younger man in most matters. Mayer rarely made an important decision unilaterally. When a business proposal was made to him in his office, he generally said, "Wait a minute—I'll see what Irving thinks," and he discussed the matter on the intercom.

Yet minor stresses were beginning to show. Inevitably, both men developed their own coteries, and some of their followers and social friends sought favor by appeals to the ego. Thalberg was told that he alone was responsible for M-G-M's spectacular rise, that Mayer was merely a boorish, meddlesome and untalented man. Mayer was told that he deserved equal credit for the studio's success, that M-G-M would go broke if he hadn't curbed Thalberg's uneconomical ways. Neither man was swayed, but the insinuations continued.

Money proved to be the most effective wedge between the two men, and the issue was kept alive by Thalberg's periodic requests for a bigger share of the company's profits. This worked to the advantage of Nick Schenck, who realized that by dividing the two studio partners, his own power would be increased. Schenck continued to maintain the best of relations with Thalberg while his dealings with Mayer became more and more acrimonious. The near-betrayal by Schenck in the Fox merger remained a vivid memory to Mayer; he could no longer fully trust Schenck again.

4

Trader Horn proved to be one of Thalberg's biggest problems of the early sound period. M-G-M had bought the rights to the best-selling book about a real-life African adventurer, and Thalberg proposed filming it entirely in Africa. Mayer agreed, and Wallace Beery was asked to play the title role. He refused; the rigors of an African location held no charm for him. Thalberg decided on Harry Carey, who had appeared in *The Trail of '98* for M-G-M in 1927.

Thalberg was in New York when he learned Carey was playing in vaudeville in East Hampton; the actor had lost his $750,000 ranch in the St. Francis Dam break in California and needed funds. Thalberg sent for him, and he arrived at the New York offices of M-G-M with his wife Olive, who advised him on career matters.

"Do you want to go to Africa and make *Trader Horn?*" Thalberg asked.

"Yes—if I can take Ollie and the kids," Carey replied.

"I think that can be arranged. I'm prepared to offer you six hundred dollars a week."

The actor was stunned. "But you know damn well I got twenty-five hundred for *Trail of '98!*"

"That's as high as I can go—six hundred. This is going to be an expensive picture, and we've got to hold down expenses wherever possible. Why don't you talk it over with Olive and let me know?"

The Careys were unable to decide about the offer, so they went to ask their friend Will Rogers. Rogers said to see his wife, who made *his* business decisions. Mrs. Rogers counseled that since *Trader Horn* would be a million-dollar picture and since Carey had no better offer, he should take it.

On March 29, 1929, the *Trader Horn* troupe left from New York. Included were Carey and his family; Duncan Renaldo, a handsome actor; Edwina Booth, an unknown actress who had been selected in a publicity search for a girl to play the White Goddess; and W. S. (Woody) Van Dyke, a dashing, eccentric director noted for his swiftness in filming.

The expedition landed in East Africa on May 1 and plunged into the interior. The disaster that followed was signaled by one of the early events: the sound truck fell into the water at Mombasa. Tropical diseases, accidents, insects, balky natives, contrary beasts and other afflictions plagued the company, but Van Dyke continued exposing tens of thousands of feet of film. He finally decided that enough location scenes had been filmed, and the interiors would be completed in Culver City.

But when the actors docked in New York at year's end, they were told *Trader Horn* had been scrapped and they were fired.

Mayer had looked at the film Van Dyke sent back from Africa and concluded that it was hopeless. Thalberg agreed. The sound was impossible, the story lacked cohesion, and there was none of the excitement that he had hoped would come from the African location. The project was shelved.

Bernie Hyman viewed the footage and believed it could be salvaged. He and Paul Bern talked Thalberg into investing more time and money in the project, and the performers were summoned to the

studio. Before Harry Carey had his appointment with Thalberg, he lunched in the M-G-M commissary with his old friend, Lon Chaney.

"Listen, Carey, you got 'em over a barrel," Chaney counseled. "I knocked 'em for five thousand a week to talk [in his only sound film, *The Unholy Three*]. They fired you, now they need you. Sock 'em for all you can get."

"No," said Carey, "I set out to make it for six hundred and I'll finish it at six hundred."

He held to his word, much to Thalberg's surprise. Olive Carey was not as compliant. She had played the brief role of a lady missionary during the African location; Thalberg planned to replace her with Marjorie Rambeau. But then he discovered another actress would not match the longshots filmed in Africa, so he offered to pay Mrs. Carey $300—her total fee on location—to do the role again in Culver City.

"No, thanks," she replied. "How much were you going to pay Rambeau?"

"I won't tell you," Thalberg replied.

"I found out—it was a thousand dollars a day. That's what I want."

"I won't pay that!" Thalberg insisted.

"Oh, yes, you will," she said. She earned $5000 for five days' work.

Trader Horn continued filming in Culver City, in nearby locations that could double for Africa, and in Mexico, for almost a year. Thalberg permitted no publicity on the shooting, reasoning that it would detract from the value of the first made-in-Africa talkie. Much of the African footage was retained, but the majority of the dramatic scenes were staged at the studio. The ferocious lion-kill was photographed in Mexico, beyond the reach of humane societies. The non-African sequences were staged with such skill that they went unnoticed by the general public, and *Trader Horn* proved to be one of M-G-M's biggest hits of the early sound era.

5

Following the immense success of *Broadway Melody*, Thalberg employed many of M-G-M's important names in a plotless extravaganza, *Hollywood Revue of 1929*. It featured everything from Marie Dressler

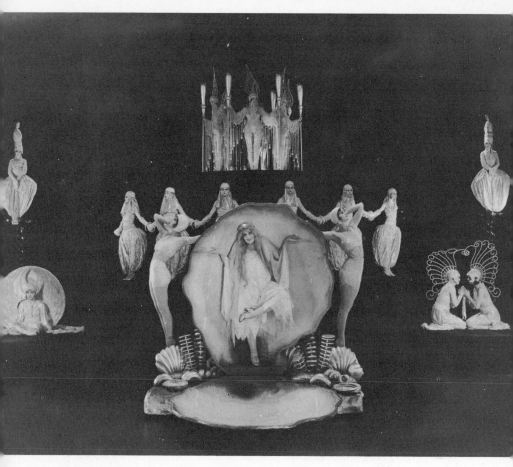

Marie Dressler, Hollywood Revue of 1929

in an underwater ballet to Norma Shearer and John Gilbert in the balcony scene from *Romeo and Juliet*. Jack Benny and Conrad Nagel performed as masters of ceremony, and for a finale Buster Keaton, Marion Davies, Joan Crawford, George K. Arthur and others appeared in yellow slickers—the film was in color—to sing the revue's hit song, *Singin' in the Rain*. The aim of the film was purely commercial, and it succeeded in its purpose.

Thalberg was not solely concerned with making money with the talkies. For his first sound film, King Vidor wanted to do a story about the simple life of rural Negroes in the South. He had been nurturing the idea for three years; now the addition of sound would permit him to use the Negro music as an added dimension. Thalberg favored the project, but neither he nor Vidor could win Schenck's approval. "It's not practical," said the Loew's president. "A picture like that will attract too many Negroes to the theaters, and the whites will stay away."

Vidor resorted to a proposal that won Schenck over: "I'll put my salary into the picture's cost, dollar for dollar with everything you spend. I'm willing to gamble my money with yours."

The offer was accepted, and Thalberg gave Vidor complete freedom in making *Hallelujah*, including a lengthy location in Tennessee. After Vidor had finished shooting, Thalberg kept the cast under salary for another six months while he mulled whether retakes would be necessary. An Irving Berlin song number was added; otherwise the film was released as Vidor had made it.

Hallelujah drew splendid reviews from serious critics and did strong business in a few big-city theaters. But elsewhere it was as Schenck

King Vidor adjusts microphone on the Hallelujah *set*

had predicted. Theater owners were reluctant to book the film for fear of alienating their white customers. *Hallelujah* had run up a cost of almost $600,000 and it produced a sizable deficit. "M-G-M can afford it," Thalberg remarked with unconcern. He realized the need to forge into new areas of film content and to satisfy the creative urges of a gifted film maker like Vidor. Besides, after each experiment Vidor agreed to expiate himself by directing a Marion Davies film.

For Thalberg the most personally satisfying development of the early sound era was the emergence of Norma Shearer as an actress of wide appeal. He continued to choose her vehicles with care. After *The Trial of Mary Dugan*, he cast her in *The Last of Mrs. Cheney*, another well-constructed stage success. She followed with *Their Own Desire*, in which she again played a society girl. Thalberg could see her in no other kind of role; he clung to his idealistic view of her.

Norma pleaded for a change. "Irving, the public is getting tired of me being the lady in every picture," she said. "I've *got* to play something more daring!"

Thalberg was shocked at the proposal, and he declined to discuss it. But he admitted to Bernie Hyman one night as they were driving from the studio to the Thalberg house: "Well, after all, Norma is a very strong-minded girl and she knows what she wants. Not only does she usually get it; she is usually right."

Bowing to her wishes, he selected for her next role an Ursula Parrott novel, *Ex-Wife*, about a divorced woman who believed in sexual freedom. Norma was surrounded by three handsome men—Robert Montgomery, Chester Morris and Conrad Nagel—and gowned in ravishing style by Gilbert Adrian, who had come to M-G-M with the Cecil B. De Mille unit and stayed on after De Mille's departure. The film was directed by Robert Z. Leonard and titled *The Divorcee*. It justified Norma's judgment, drawing excellent returns in the theaters and winning her the Academy award for best actress of 1929–30.

The award brought great joy to Irving Thalberg, since it displayed to the world that Norma was an honored performer who achieved her position not merely because she was the wife of the studio boss. He had reason for even greater joy: during the filming of *The Divorcee*, Norma was pregnant with their first child.

Irving Grant Thalberg, Junior, was born on August 25, 1930. The

Tyler Brooke, Robert Montgomery, Chester Morris, Norma Shearer, Florence Eldridge, Robert Elliott, Mary Doran, The Divorcee

arrival provided Norma with the occasion to make her move. Now that they had their own family, she told her husband, it was time they had a home of their own. He reluctantly agreed, and the news was broken to Henrietta Thalberg. Predictably, she protested. What was wrong, she wanted to know, with the very comfortable arrangement with the Thalbergs all under one roof? Her son explained as gently as possible that as a mother Norma should now be mistress of her own home.

Henrietta remained concerned about Irving. For most of his thirty-one years, she had devoted herself to the meticulous care of his health, cautioning him against overexertion, applying her remedies at the slightest sign of illness. Norma promised she would be just as vigilant. With grave misgivings, Henrietta allowed Irving to leave.

Norma and Irving chose their home to be at the foot of the Santa Monica palisades, along the same stretch of shore that boasted the mansions of Louis Mayer and Marion Davies. The Thalberg house lacked their ostentation, being tastefully designed in French provincial style. The house sat on the sand several yards from the Pacific, but visitors had no sensation of being close to the ocean. Thalberg slept poorly, and the noise of the surf was shut out by soundproof walls and double windows. Because the ocean air was considered bad for his heart condition, the entire house was air-conditioned by a primitive system that blew air over cakes of ice. Between the house and the beach was a swimming pool in which Thalberg never swam.

The Thalbergs were delighted with their first home, and Norma fulfilled her promise to Henrietta. Everything possible was done to make Irving's home life restful. She established no regular dinner hour, realizing he might feel guilty if he missed it; dinner was ready whenever he returned from the studio, which was normally after she had finished her day's work. She mixed him the weak Scotch-and-water which he enjoyed at the end of the day, and she listened to the problems that faced him. In a community not noted for marital permanence, it was a good marriage.

6

At the age of thirty-two, Irving Grant Thalberg had been an important figure in the film world for a dozen years. William Clark Gable, only two years younger, seemed to have accomplished nothing.

The desire was there. Gable had long hoped for an acting career in the movies; as early as 1925, he was playing an extra in *The Merry Widow* and observing with envy the eminence of John Gilbert. But Gable seemed too compliant to achieve success in the movies. He lacked the self-promotional qualities that appeared necessary to gain attention. He went away for five years of touring the West in stock companies.

When he returned to Hollywood in 1930, his chances seemed unimproved. Producers immediately noticed his outsized ears and were blind to his more obvious merits. They were also blind to the new kind of leading man that talkies demanded.

Lacking the reality of dialogue, the silent film was essentially

Norma receives her Oscar from Conrad Nagel

The Thalberg house at Santa Monica

fantasy-like in tone, and the heroes were idealized conceptions. The talkies, which arrived with that destroyer of illusions, the Depression, required a more fallible male, one whose profile was less than classic and whose manner lacked polish. Clark Gable was such a man. The years in make-up had not obliterated his beginnings as a lumberjack and oil rigger. His crackling voice and take-over style bespoke masculinity. Not the least of his attributes was a sturdy physique that permitted him to wear clothes magnificently well.

Lionel Barrymore provided the bridge for Gable's entrance to M-G-M. Thalberg had hired Barrymore not only as an actor, but as the director of such early talkies as *The Rogue Song* with Lawrence Tibbett and *Madame X* with Ruth Chatterton. Barrymore also directed tests of newcomers, and he made one of Gable, who had appeared with him in the Los Angeles company of *The Copperhead* in 1927. The choice of scene was unfortunate. Barrymore was scheduled to direct a South Seas picture, and he posed Gable in a native costume with hibiscus behind his ears. Thalberg saw the test and was unimpressed.

Gable's agent, Minna Wallis, had found him a role in an RKO Western, *The Painted Desert*, and she had begun negotiations for a term contract with RKO. Learning that Gable was sought by another studio, Thalberg had a change of heart and offered the actor a contract starting at $650 a week. The astonished Gable accepted.

His first film was *The Easiest Way*, and he was billed after Constance Bennett, Adolphe Menjou, Robert Montgomery, Anita Page, Marjorie Rambeau, J. Farrell MacDonald and Clara Blandick. Despite the smallness of the role, Gable drew special attention from the preview audience. Thalberg made note of this, and he later observed that Gable received an inordinate amount of fan mail following the picture's release.

One of the first to realize Gable's potential was Thalberg's most reliable screen writer, Frances Marion. Thalberg cast Gable in a small role in one of Miss Marion's scripts, *The Secret Six*, which had Wallace Beery, Lewis Stone, John Mack Brown and Jean Harlow as the leading performers. As the filming progressed, Miss Marion injected new scenes for Gable, and he ended up with a role three times the size of the original script.

Thalberg then assigned Gable to *Laughing Sinners* opposite Joan

Clark Gable, Wallace Beery, Jean Harlow, Lewis Stone, The Secret Six

Crawford, an M-G-M star who had made the transition to sound with great ease. The casting reflected Thalberg's technique of building new stars by combining them with well-established players.

Next came Gable's biggest challenge: *A Free Soul.*

He found himself in the fast company of such stellar performers as Norma Shearer, Lionel Barrymore and Leslie Howard. Gable was apprehensive about his chances of meeting the challenge. "I don't know what I'll do if Brown stops me in the middle of a speech," he said to a co-worker (the director was Clarence Brown). "I've got a photographic memory, and I think of everything in one piece—that's my stock company training. If I'm stopped, I'll have to go back to the beginning again." But he managed to avoid such pitfalls. The script was carefully fashioned to give Gable dynamic scenes, notably the one in which he pushed Norma into a chair when she tried to end their shady romance. The effect on audiences was electric. A lady had never been treated that way on the screen before.

Gable treats Norma roughly in A Free Soul

Thalberg soon realized he had created a new style of screen lover. The romantic heroes of the silent films—Rudolph Valentino, John Gilbert, Ramon Novarro, Antonio Moreno, etc.—had been adored by the nation's women, but resented by the men. Along came Gable, who shoved his sweethearts around and made them like it. Men envied and admired such technique, and they saw in Gable something more than a ladies' man. Thalberg encouraged Howard Strickling, M-G-M's publicity director, in his plan to build up Gable's rugged image. The actor spent hours on the bridle trails of Griffith Park learning to ride horseback. He took up hunting and fishing, and he drove high-powered automobiles. Fortunately, he enjoyed such activities, and they became natural aspects of his personality.

A Free Soul was the making of Clark Gable. When he next appeared with Joan Crawford in *Possessed* and with Greta Garbo in *Susan Lenox, Her Fall and Rise*, he was a full and equal star.

7

Helen Hayes had known one brief adventure into silent films, and the experience had proven to her that the stage was her medium. And so, when the Hollywood studios were looting the theater of stars, directors, playwrights, song writers and other craftsmen during the talkie period, she resisted the lure. She was perfectly content to remain on Broadway, where her fresh beauty and insouciant charm had brightened one hit play after another.

Her resolve to resist films was destroyed by the fact that she had fallen madly in love with Charles MacArthur, the brilliant, erratic playwright and former newspaperman. After their marriage, MacArthur hired himself to the studios and came under the aegis of Irving Thalberg. The writer's magical knack for dialogue and his ability to doctor ailing scripts were valued highly by Thalberg, who also enjoyed his amiable wit. But Thalberg recognized that the writer was restless to return to his wife. Thalberg realized the only way to keep his prized scenarist in California was to bring Miss Hayes to M-G-M.

At first she refused to entertain such a proposal, but her husband entreated her by long-distance telephone to consider the offer. She agreed to a conference with J. Robert Rubin in the New York head-

1931—Two more Oscars for M-G-M stars: Marie Dressler, Min and Bill, and Lionel Barrymore, A Free Soul. With them are the previous year's winners, George Arliss and Norma Shearer

quarters of M-G-M. When he mentioned the salary that M-G-M was willing to pay her, she replied, "But that's half what I'm getting on the stage!"

"Yes, Miss Hayes," Rubin replied, "but you're known in the theater. Your name means nothing in the movies."

"I'm still an actress," she protested.

"That isn't important. We'll have to spend a lot of money to build you up in pictures. We can't afford to pay you any more."

The meeting ended unsatisfactorily, and when MacArthur telephoned that evening, his wife told him, "No, I won't go!" He
related the encounter with Rubin to Thalberg, who called Miss Hayes
and said, "Disregard your dealings with M-G-M. I'll handle your contract personally." The conditions were more to her liking, and, after
more pleas from her husband, Miss Hayes agreed to go to Culver City.

Thalberg assigned her to *Lullaby*, a potboiler that had starred
Florence Reed on Broadway. It was a turgid and unlikely tale of a
French whore who was hounded by the memory of the illegitimate
child she had abandoned in his infancy. MacArthur was appalled
when he learned of the assignment; he was further disturbed to learn
the film had been entrusted to Harry Rapf, who supervised the lesser
productions of M-G-M. MacArthur found the script to be lifeless
and cliché-ridden.

"You can't do this to Helen!" he protested to Thalberg.

"What is the matter?" Thalberg asked.

"That script! It's God-awful!"

"Then you fix it."

Thalberg was leaving for one of his pilgrimages to Bad Nauheim,
and he left MacArthur in charge of improving *Lullaby*. The writer
worked late each night to produce scenes for the next day's filming,
but his efforts could not cure the story's basic malaise. Edgar Selwyn
directed the film in plodding style, and Miss Hayes was beset with
doubts of the wisdom of her leaving the theater.

Lullaby was completed and previewed, and all agreed that it was
a disaster. Rapf decided that the film was too hopeless to release,
and Mayer concurred. MacArthur, noting his wife's eagerness to return to New York, did not give up. As soon as Thalberg arrived
back from Europe, MacArthur implored him to do something about
Lullaby.

"Helen is fine," Thalberg remarked after viewing the film, "but
she didn't get the protection she needs. She is a stage actress, not a
motion picture actress, and she must be directed with care."

"But what about the picture?" MacArthur asked. "Can anything
be done with it?"

"Certainly," Thalberg replied. "There is more than two-thirds of
a picture here. All we have to do is supply the other third."

He outlined to MacArthur the changes that were needed: "You've

Madelon Claudet (Helen Hayes) meets her son (Robert Young)

got to have a scene that takes place at the birth of a child, a scene that will motivate her actions for the rest of the picture. She must decide that she is going to fight fate, life—even God—to see that her child has a good life."

Instead of the mawkish happy ending, Thalberg suggested a new one in which the woman's son, now an eminent doctor, examined his mother without knowing her identity. Thalberg also suggested that the story would acquire more significance if told in flashback. He and MacArthur invented the device of having a kindly old doctor, Jean Hersholt, tell of the mother's sacrifice to the son's wife, who was preparing to leave him because of neglect.

Miss Hayes had received an offer to appear opposite Ronald Colman in *Arrowsmith* for Samuel Goldwyn, and she was in the midst of filming when it came time for the *Lullaby* retakes. The scenes were filmed at M-G-M on Sundays—until Goldwyn found out about it and made her stop. As soon as she finished *Arrowsmith*,

she reported back to M-G-M and completed the film, which was now titled *The Sin of Madelon Claudet*. Thalberg took it out for another preview and was pleased to note the tears it evoked. The picture proved to be one of M-G-M's biggest moneymakers of 1931.

The flipflop of *Madelon Claudet* encouraged Miss Hayes to remain in Hollywood. This delighted her husband and pleased Thalberg, who was assured of the services and companionship of his favorite writer. Thalberg was especially proud at the next Academy awards when Miss Hayes won the Oscar as the best actress of the year for her performance in *The Sin of Madelon Claudet*. After the presentation at the Ambassador Hotel's Coconut Grove, he invited the MacArthurs to join him and Norma for a small celebration at the beach house.

MacArthur proudly drove the Academy award winner to the Thalbergs' house in his little sports roadster, and he proposed many toasts to the glorious victory. It was early morning when the MacArthurs finally returned home. Later Miss Hayes reported sleepily to Paramount, where she was starring in *A Farewell to Arms*. Her co-star, Gary Cooper, asked to see the Oscar.

"The Oscar!" she exclaimed. "My God, I have no idea where it is!" She hurried to a telephone and called her husband.

"Charlie, have you got the Oscar?" she asked.

"Hmmmm, I don't think so," he replied. "Don't you have it?"

"No."

"Well, I'll call Irving; he'll know where it is."

MacArthur placed a call to Thalberg, who had no idea of the Oscar's whereabouts. MacArthur began a search and finally found the statuette—in the trunk of the roadster.

Despite her honors, Miss Hayes remained a puzzle to many of the executives of M-G-M, including Louis Mayer. She lacked the more obvious attributes to be a movie star, and Mayer could not conceive how she could fit into the M-G-M programing. One day he sent for her and he said: "We don't know what to do with you. To be a success in pictures, an actress must have sex appeal. But I don't know whether you have any sex appeal or not."

"Mr. Mayer, I don't know, either," she admitted.

"I've decided to find out," he continued. "I'm going to have a

Louis Mayer presents the Oscar to Helen Hayes

white satin gown made for you, like the one that Norma wore in
A Free Soul."

Miss Hayes was astonished. "That wasn't a dress; that was an
invitation!"

Mayer ignored the comment. "Now I'm going to have that dress
made for you by one of the best designers in town, and I'm going
to pay for it myself."

"Mr. Mayer," she said, "I'm going to save you a lot of money.
I can tell you right now there won't be anything under that dress."

Mayer sighed defeatedly. "Well, I guess we'll just have to keep you
acting every minute."

Miss Hayes was kept busy in vehicles that were not especially to
her liking. Thalberg knew of her feelings—she never complained
to him at the studio, but he learned of them on social occasions.
Trying to please her, he planned a film version of *What Every
Woman Knows,* the James Barrie play which had been one of her
Broadway hits.

The preview was held in Huntington Park, an industrial district
south of Los Angeles, and the MacArthurs and Thalbergs drove to it
in high spirits. They were plunged into depression on the drive home.
The Barrie charm had been wasted on the working-class audience
of Huntington Park.

"It's so awful," Miss Hayes exclaimed. "I look like the devil in the
picture. I change appearance three times." Midway in the filming, the
cameraman had been changed because Constance Bennett had returned to the studio and demanded him.

Thalberg would not be panicked. "That performance was perfectly
fine," he insisted. "Your change of appearance is no more important
than a fly walking across the screen. The audience will never notice
it."

But he realized that changes had to be made to appeal to the
general audience. A few days later, Miss Hayes reported for retakes.
She was aghast when she read the added scenes; they were filled with
Scotsman jokes of the Joe Miller variety.

"Oh, Greg, you can't do this," she protested to the director,
Gregory La Cava.

"Listen, baby," he answered, "Barrie laid an egg in Huntington
Park. Forget Barrie."

Miss Hayes went through with the scenes, but she expressed her disapproval to Thalberg. "Helen," he said gently, "it isn't what you'd like or what I'd like, but it will please those people in Huntington Park and get them to watch the rest of the picture, which we know is good. We've got to have something for everyone."

His instinct proved correct. *What Every Woman Knows* was another Hayes triumph.

8

Thalberg sought other Broadway stars to lend distinction to M-G-M's talkies, and he proposed filming *The Guardsman* with the couple who had made it a Broadway hit, Alfred Lunt and Lynn Fontanne. By coincidence, they were in Chicago playing *Elizabeth the Queen* in April of 1931 when Thalberg was there for an M-G-M sales convention. He invited them to come to his hotel at the only time he had available—seven in the morning. It was a forbidding hour for stage performers, but the Lunts agreed to meet with him.

Norma had accompanied Thalberg to Chicago—they were on their way to Europe—and Miss Fontanne said to her, "My dear, I have something to tell you. I recently saw you in one of your comedies, and I would like to give you some advice: You must not laugh at your lines after you deliver them." Norma accepted the advice graciously, and Thalberg was charming in his proposal that the Lunts come to work for M-G-M.

"If we do," Miss Fontanne said firmly, "Alfred and I will not do any swimming, high diving, fast horseback riding or any of those other things that you do out there in movies."

Thalberg smiled indulgently. "Miss Fontanne, I can assure you that motion pictures have progressed beyond such things," he said.

At that moment Lunt and Miss Fontanne were startled to see a man enter the room with a medium-sized lion on a leash. As the pair recoiled, Thalberg explained, "Oh, they're having an M-G-M sales convention here, and the lion is part of it. Don't give it a thought."

Despite some forebodings, the Lunts agreed to their joint film debut in *The Guardsman*. Sidney Franklin was assigned to direct, and he came to see them in Minneapolis, where they were continuing their tour of *Elizabeth the Queen*. He was so impressed with the play that he proposed injecting a portion of it at the beginning of the film.

The Lunts arrived in Hollywood still unconvinced of the wisdom of their decision. Their doubts seemed to be confirmed when they reported to the studio in the 1927 Ford sedan they had bought. The gateman eyed them suspiciously, demanded a pass, and refused to allow them to enter when they said they had none. The pair turned around and went back to their rented home. Sidney Franklin was apologetic and personally escorted them to the studio.

Many things about film making perplexed the Lunts. They were distracted by the primitive sound equipment and the number of takes that were ruined by noises outside the stage. Miss Fontanne was amazed that there were no bathrooms on the stage; she had to call a car in order to use one. "What a mistake!" she exclaimed to Franklin. "You could save hundreds of dollars simply by having a toilet on the stage."

One day Franklin was complaining that the studio didn't supply him with the kind of pillows he wanted. "Well, Sidney, why don't you simply call up Mr. Meyers and tell him exactly what you want?"

She noticed that her remark evoked laughter from electricians in the catwalks above the set.

"Mr. who?" the director asked.

"Mr. Meyers," she said. "You know—the head of the studio." Franklin educated her on the identity of Louis B. Mayer.

One of the scenes called for Miss Fontanne to receive a telephone call in the bathtub, and Franklin positioned her with back to the camera, since she was nude from the waist up. He called for the shot to begin, and the telephone bell sounded. The actress turned directly toward the camera.

"Cut," said the embarrassed director. "We can't use that, Lynn. Don't you understand you can't turn toward the camera when you have nothing on?"

"But the telephone bell sounded from that direction," she replied. "Naturally I would turn in the direction from which it came." Franklin solved the situation by putting the bell at the back of the set.

The Guardsman was filmed in twenty-one days, which was surprisingly swift in view of the technical delays for sound. Having performed the play hundreds of times, the Lunts were familiar with their roles and always arrived with their lines memorized letter-perfect. After the footage had been assembled, Thalberg returned from Europe and saw the finished film. He made an appointment to see the Lunts and Franklin in his office at 10:30 one morning.

The Lunts appeared in Franklin's office with time to spare for the 10:30 date. But word came that Mr. Thalberg could not see them yet. The trio waited until eleven and no word came. When 11:45 arrived, Miss Fontanne rose and said, "He said he wanted to see us, so we'll just go up to his office."

Franklin was alarmed. "No, you can't do that with Irving," he warned. "You have to wait until he's ready for you."

"Nonsense," she replied, and she led the march to Thalberg's headquarters. To Franklin's astonishment, Miss Fontanne swept through the offices and into Thalberg's office. He gave no indication that the invasion upset him. He praised the Lunts' work in the film and remarked that only one retake was needed. When he outlined what he wanted, Lunt protested.

"But that's entirely out of keeping with the characters," he said.

Thalberg insisted that they go through with the retake, and it was scheduled for nine o'clock in the evening. The Lunts performed it with good grace, but when Thalberg viewed the retakes, he was startled to see that Lunt's eyes did not match.

"You did it on purpose to ruin the retakes," he accused.

"I can assure you that I cannot make my eye roll out if I wanted it to," Lunt replied. "It always happens when I am fatigued." Thalberg gave up on the retake. Just in case Thalberg had any other notions about tinkering with the finished film, the actor had his hair cut so it wouldn't match the character he had played.

The Guardsman was previewed in San Bernardino, and Thalberg was disappointed to discover that the film's humor was entirely too sophisticated for the audience. On the following day, he displayed some of the deprecatory cards that had been filled out by the audience.

"But these are all written by children!" Miss Fontanne protested. "This is not a picture for children. This is a sophisticated comedy about adultery. Children shouldn't know about such things."

Thalberg gestured toward the cards. "This is our audience," he observed.

"Not any longer," Miss Fontanne replied.

Lynn Fontanne, Zasu Pitts and Alfred Lunt on the set of The Guardsman

The Guardsman drew critical acclaim, and both its stars won Academy nominations for their performances. But the San Bernardino reception had been a portent of the film's popular appeal; *The Guardsman* was not a commercial success.

Thalberg was not discouraged. He realized that the cinematic art could progress only with distinguished performers like the Lunts. He offered them a contract for a series of films at a combined salary of almost a million dollars. They attracted headlines by turning the munificent offer down during the depths of the Depression. They refused because the contract did not give them approval of vehicles.

9

Irving Thalberg's attitude toward writers was that of a Renaissance prince with a vast patronage of artists. He was tolerant of their human frailties. He allowed them to perform their mystical functions without unnecessary interference. He appreciated their indispensable contribution to the film making process and paid them handsomely. He could form intellectual relationships with writers, but not personal ones. Always he was friendly, even cordial, but he was personally aloof. He rarely revealed himself in his dealings with writers.

At times he seemed to hate his very dependence on writers and his frustration that he could not perform their functions. During one heated script session he said almost contemptuously, "What's all this business about being a writer? It's just putting one word after another."

Lenore Coffee corrected him: "Pardon me, Mr. Thalberg; it's putting one *right* word after another."

Despite such raillery and his attitude of aloofness, most writers who worked intimately with him maintained vast admiration for Thalberg. He could be maddening, as when he would enforce the rewriting of the same scene a half-dozen times with an earnest, "You can do better than that—I know that you can." Usually they could.

Writers could not have failed to appreciate Thalberg after encounters with other studio heads and producers. Nearly all of them were primitives who didn't know Henry Fielding from W. C. Fields. Thalberg could discuss literature without pretense. More importantly, he had superb command of the literature of the screen. No one in Hollywood had a greater knowledge of script construction. Time after time he could produce a simple solution to a plot problem over which writers had agonized for weeks.

"I feel like an idiot," George S. Kaufman confessed after an encounter with Thalberg. "That man has never written a word, and yet he can tell me exactly what to do with a story."

Thalberg was tireless in his search for the best possible scripts. Important projects sometimes remained in the scripting process for a year or two before he was satisfied. One of these was the 1931 Garbo film, *Susan Lenox, Her Fall and Rise*. Four previous writers

had worked on the script when the assignment befell authoress Mildred
Cram. For weeks she conferred with Paul Bern, who was supervising
the film, and King Vidor, who was to direct it,* in an effort to bring
life to the turgid novel by David Graham Phillips. After two months
they arrived at a script and they presented their effort one night
to Thalberg. He seemed to be studying papers and letters on his desk
as they recounted the story line. When they had finished, he said,
"No, you've missed it. Entirely. The formula we're after is this:
love conquers in the end! We're not interested in defeat—no one is!
You've got this girl *down*, but there's no *rise*. Try again." Ten more
writers labored on the story before Thalberg considered it ready for
filming.

While working with writers, Thalberg rarely made a criticism without offering a suggestion for improvement. Yet he did not expect
blind acquiescence to his proposals. After long arguments with
Frances Marion, he often said, "All right, try it your way." She did
so, and sometimes she proved herself right, sometimes not. Thalberg
took no pride in proving her wrong. All he cared about was the best
possible script.

Thalberg paid high prices for screen properties, but he wasn't
profligate with M-G-M's money; he bargained whenever possible.
After reading *A Free Soul* by Adela Rogers St. Johns, he wanted it as
a vehicle for Norma and sent for the author. She said that Hearst
had an option on the story until after the second installment had
appeared in *Cosmopolitan*.

"I can arrange it with Mr. Hearst to clear the rights before the
second installment," Thalberg said. "How much do you want for it?"
Mrs. St. Johns said bravely, "Forty thousand dollars."

"That's ridiculous!" Thalberg exclaimed. "I can't pay you half
that."

"I'll have to think it over," she replied. The next day she received
a telephone call from her banker who said that Thalberg had inquired how much money she had in her account. She herself didn't
know, and the banker told her: $10.85.

When she returned to see Thalberg, he placed a check on his desk.
It was for $25,000. She shook her head.

"Now, Adela, don't be ridiculous!" he chided. His arguments made

* Robert Z. Leonard was later assigned to direct.

no headway. Then he took another check out of his drawer and handed it to her. It was for $40,000.

He was no pinch-penny studio man. On another occasion he gave Mrs. St. Johns a script about a newspaperwoman and asked her to rewrite it. She read the material and returned to tell Thalberg she could not accept the assignment.

"Why not?" he demanded.

"Because the story is idiotic," she replied.

He paused. "Between you and me," he said, "tell me what's wrong with it. Where does the story go to pieces?"

She analyzed the script in ten pages of criticism which she sent to Thalberg. She received a check for six weeks' salary and a note from him saying: "You deserve this. You could have taken the script and worked on it for weeks. Then I would have made the picture, but it still would have been wrong. You saved me several hundred thousand dollars by telling me what you did."

With the coming of sound, Thalberg's relationships with writers intensified. The exigencies of dialogue called for more careful preparation of scripts; no longer could areas of action remain vague, to be interpreted by the director as he saw fit. Now the writer was ascendant, and the position of the director at M-G-M declined. Thalberg rarely employed directors with a unique flair, except for his gifted friend, King Vidor. Thalberg's early experiences with Von Stroheim had demonstrated the pitfalls of placing too much power in the hands of a director.* Now Thalberg aimed to present directors with compact, explicit scripts. He expected them to put the story on film in a straight-

---

* Another example of M-G-M's incapacity to accommodate film makers of rare, if undisciplined talent: In 1927, Thalberg engaged Robert J. Flaherty to co-direct *White Shadows of the South Seas* with studio man W. S. Van Dyke. Flaherty, who had earned distinction with the real-life beauty of his *Nanook of the North* and *Moana of the South Seas*, accepted with the hope that he could portray real Polynesian life in a commercial film. He was disappointed to learn on his arrival in Hollywood that Thalberg had bought the Frederick O'Brien book only for its intriguing title. Flaherty was further discouraged when he observed the concocting of a typical South Seas script and when the film's supervisor remarked to his aides after a showing of *Moana*: "Boys, I've got a great idea! Let's fill the screen with tits!" A Mexican actress, Raquel Torres, and a part-Indian, Monte Blue, were assigned to play the leads. After a few weeks of filming with Van Dyke in Tahiti, the disheartened Flaherty resigned.

186

forward manner, without fancy camera angles or other frills. And Thalberg did most of the important cutting himself—first, in the script, and then in the final editing before and after previews. As a result, most of the M-G-M directors were highly accomplished journeymen, but seldom more than that.

The sound era brought a flood of writing talent to Culver City. From the theater and the New York literary scene came George S. Kaufman, Moss Hart, Dorothy Parker, Donald Ogden Stewart, Ben Hecht, Charles MacArthur, John Van Druten, George Kelly, Elliott Nugent, Sidney Howard, Anita Loos, F. Scott Fitzgerald. From London came the playwright Frederick Lonsdale. The writers' building overflowed with more than a hundred persons, many of them earning a thousand or two thousand dollars a week.

Thalberg had reasons for employing so much talent. He needed writers to be readily available; when a movie went wrong, he wanted to avoid the delay of borrowing a script doctor from another studio. Moreover, he was under constant pressure from the Eastern office to continue pouring out product. He couldn't afford to let a Clark Gable or a Marie Dressler remain idle because a script had not been prepared. So he had five different writers working on Gable and Dressler scripts; one of the five might produce the next vehicle for the star.

The multiplicity of writers inevitably led to damaged egos. Writers sometimes met over coffee to discuss their current projects and were shocked to discover both had been assigned by Thalberg to the same story. Thalberg made no excuse for this practice. In a deadline situation he often sought the inspiration of two or more writers. He reasoned that he couldn't afford to wait for one writer to come up with a solution he sorely needed.

Thalberg preferred to use previously published works as the source material for screenplays; novels, plays, short stories and biographies were purchased in large numbers. His preference was novels, which afforded the depth of character and intricacy of plot that gave more substance to a film, and the Thalberg films were generally novelistic in form. But the publishing world could not supply enough material to satisfy the never-ending need for screen entertainment, and Thalberg also relied on original stories. He often outlined to the writer what was needed.

In need of a vehicle for Greta Garbo, he summoned Willis Gold-

Irving Thalberg welcomes a new M-G-M writer, Frederick Lonsdale

beck and instructed him: "Write me a story on the same lines of *Blind Husbands*." The formula: a husband and wife travel to an exotic land and one of them strays from the marriage with a fascinating native. Goldbeck used a John Colton story to fashion a film plot about a plantation owner who takes his young wife to the Orient, where she becomes enamored with a Javanese prince. It was filmed as *Wild Orchids* with Miss Garbo, Lewis Stone and Nils Asther.

In 1931, Thalberg was impressed by the success Universal had enjoyed with horror pictures. He told Willis Goldbeck: "I want you to give me something even more horrible than *Frankenstein*." Starting with a story by Tod Robbins, Goldbeck produced a script about bizarre happenings among freaks of a circus sideshow. After Thalberg read the script, he placed his head in his hands. "I asked for something horrifying," he muttered to Goldbeck, "and I got it." Despite the heated opposition of Mayer and other studio officials, Thalberg allowed Tod Browning to film *Freaks* in compromising style. Browning, who had directed *Dracula* and some of Lon Chaney's best films, assembled a collection of real circus freaks and exploited their abnormalities. The result was a Grand Guignol classic, but it proved to be too much for movie audiences to stomach.

The greatest source of irritation for writers in their dealings with Thalberg was the waiting.

With his jam-packed daily schedule, Thalberg was eternally behind in his appointments. In his waiting room was the famous "million-dollar bench," where waited some of the most famous names in America—stars, directors, supervisors as well as writers. But it was the writers who complained most. Many of them were like Adela Rogers St. Johns, who thrived on the enthusiasm of the moment; she found the long wait for Thalberg deadened her inspiration. Despite the resentment, those who had waited hours, sometimes weeks to see Thalberg were inevitably softened when they finally gained admittance. He had the faculty for making each conference seem to be the most important of his day. His charm, his intense interest in what the visitor had to say wiped away the anger and frustration of the long wait.

Many of the town's wits had sport with the institution of Waiting for Irving. George S. Kaufman, who served his time on the million-dollar bench, originated the lines: "On a clear day you can see Thalberg."

Dorothy Parker was not gifted with patience, and she suffered from the interminable delays in her appointments with Thalberg. On one occasion she had completed her work on a script and was told to stand by until Thalberg sent for her. The period of waiting extended for days, and her impatience grew. At the time she was infatuated with a gentleman who lived in Santa Barbara, and she recklessly departed from the studio for a rendezvous with him. After her departure, the call came from Thalberg's office. But Miss Parker was not there to receive it.

Thalberg was not easily upset. One thing he did not like was for studio employees to be unavailable when he needed them. He dictated a curt letter to his secretary:

Dear Miss Parker,

On March 5 at 5 p.m., my secretary placed a call to your office to inform you of a meeting on the script in progress. She was told that you were not at the studio. A call was placed to your residence and there was no response. The meeting had to be cancelled because of your unavailability. I would like to have an explanation of your absence.

Sincerely,
Irving G. Thalberg

Thalberg received this reply to his letter:

Dear Mr. Thalberg,

Yours of March 6 received and its contents duly noted. In reply to your query as to my inability to attend the script meeting, I can only offer the explanation that I was too ———ing busy and vice versa.

Sincerely,
Dorothy Parker

10

Many writers produced their own legends about their waits for Thalberg. Among the most noted was S. J. Perelman's story, "And Did You Once See Irving Plain":

On a sunny November afternoon in 1936, the Japanese gardener pruning the bougainvillaea that entwined Villa 12 at the Garden of Allah in Hollywood inadvertently glanced into its bedroom window and saw a sight that caused him to drop his shears. Sprawled on the bed, my eyeballs extruded like Catawba grapes, I lay snuffing uncontrollably into the counterpane. A 130-page manuscript labeled *Greenwich Village* had just fallen from my nerveless hand, and the realization that hunger might compel me and my wife to distill from it a vehicle for Joan Crawford contorted my face with a despair only Hieronymus Bosch could depict.

The circumstances underlying our plight were all too prosaic. Of the small bundle of loot we had accumulated the previous winter in Hollywood there remained only a frayed elastic band, and by mid-September my wife and I were again back on the Coast, feverishly importuning our agent for an assignment. The latter, a frog-faced individual named Kolodny, clad entirely in suede even down to his underthings, assured us there was nothing to worry about. The studios were crying for writers, he declared buoyantly; in a week or two at the utmost, he would have us established, at a princely salary, with one of the titans of the industry. The week had grown into nine, and the manager of the hotel bubbled like a percolator every time he saw us, when Kolodny phoned in a lather. Irving Thalberg, a producer whose name was uttered only in cathedral whispers, universally acknowledged the top genius of celluloid, had expressed interest in us and was sending over a story for our inspection. True, the *quid pro quo* was paltry but, Kolodny added quickly, the luster of associating with Thalberg, the patina we would gain in his orbit, would cinch our position forever in Hollywood.

My wife's reaction to *Greenwich Village*, if somewhat less volcanic than mine, was one of vast incredulity. "He *can't* be in earnest about this," she said after thumbing through it. "Why, it's pure parody, all these roistering poets, the painters in their picturesque smocks, that motherly old bag in the boardinghouse with the capacious bosom and the heart of gold. They'll hoot it out of the theaters. What made him pick us to work on it?"

"Our background, it seems," I said. "Kolodny told him we lived near Washington Square once. I gather he described us as dead ringers for e. e. cummings and Edna Millay."

"Well, there's no sense fighting our custard," she declared with brisk feminine acumen. "God knows it isn't Flaubert, but it's better than picking lettuce in the Imperial Valley. How fast can we get on the pay roll?"

The answer to her query was soon forthcoming. Before the sun gilded the steeples of the Pacific Finance Company, the agent had transmitted our conviction that the property was a bewitching blend of *Trilby* and *La Bohème*, and we were ordered to report for duty at M-G-M the next morning. Kolodny was jubilant. Henceforth, he announced, we belonged to the aristocracy of filmdom. In a burst of clairvoyance, he foresaw us occupying *palazzos* in Coldwater Canyon, lolling in Bentleys, hobnobbing with the elite at Palm Springs. The story editor at Metro next day, while not quite so rapturous, expatiated similarly on our good fortune.

"I hope you appreciate the break you're getting," he said, as he led us to the structure, colloquially known as the Triangle Shirtwaist Factory, where writers were housed. "I know people in this town who'd give half of their salary to work under the aegis of Irving Thalberg."

"You're looking at two of them, Jack," I confided.

"Well, just wait till you meet him," he said. "I've dealt with some pretty brainy men in my time, from L. B. Mayer down, but between you and me, Thalberg is the greatest intellect we have. And cheek by jowl with it goes a wonderful candid humility which reminds you of Abe Lincoln. The most simple, unaffected person you can imagine."

"Gee, that's swell," said my wife. "Listen, if it isn't violating any secret, how much did they pay for this—this original we're supposed to adapt?"

"Somewhere in the neighborhood of seventy-five grand," he replied. "A humdinger, isn't it?"

"A peachamaroot," she agreed. She looked around the gloomy little lazaret we were to occupy, furnished with a worm-eaten desk, two gumwood chairs and a spavined divan. It was a pity, she observed mildly, that the studio's prodigality did not extend to its decor.

Our cicerone, nettled, retorted that the office had harbored a series of distinguished authors, none of whom had voiced any complaints. The most recent, it appeared, was a celebrated lady playwright much in vogue then, who had spent the past fourteen months there in vain, had added, since nobody had come up with a story worthy of her stature. Curious to learn how she had beguiled the time, I made a quick inventory of the desk the moment the door closed behind him. The only memento of her tenancy was a pair of highly intricate doilies, created by braiding together narrow strips of yellow typewriting paper. Assuming she had received fifteen hundred dollars a week—a modest estimate for anyone of her attainments—it followed that the mats had cost the corporation roughly forty-two thousand dollars apiece: a heartwarming example of craftsmanship adequately rewarded.

From the air of immediacy surrounding our project, we figured it would be all of noontime before Thalberg summoned us to impart his hopes and dreams for the script. When three days elapsed with no manifestation, however, I grew restive and phoned. His secretary reassured me at length. Our picture was high on the agenda, but Mr. T. had two in production and was working around the clock; she would advise us the instant he was free. Since it was fatuous to proceed without some clue to what he wanted, we settled down resignedly to wait. Inside of a week, the tedium was well-nigh claustrophobic. Even by reading the trade papers, Louella Parsons' column and Dostoievsky's prison memoirs, we barely got through the mornings, and the antlike industry of our colleagues discouraged fraternization. Possibly the most consecrated was a writer just across the hall, whose creative habits seemed to derive from science fiction, He customarily wore on his head, while dictating into the mouthpiece of an Ediphone, a scalp vibrator resembling a metal cocktail shaker, which oscillated so busily that you wondered what his dialogue would sound like when transcribed. I subsequently saw the movie he worked on and can testify that I left the theater deeply shaken.

Languishing through our fourth week, I again rang up Thalberg's office and again was counseled patience; the audience was just around the corner. Our agent Kolodny, who checked us at intervals like a lobsterman visiting his pots, scolded me roundly for fidgeting. He besought us to lie doggo, collect the weekly stipend and thank our lucky stars that we were eating. That night, on our way home from the jute mill, my wife stopped off in Westwood and bought an ambitious needlepoint design and a dozen hanks of yarn. I ransacked the stores for a narwhal tusk or a bit of whalebone wherewith to execute some scrimshaw work, but none being available, compromised on a set of Boswell and a handbook of chess problems.

Some two weeks later as I was emerging from the studio commissary, I ran into a Broadway acquaintance named Reifsneider. At our last encounter five years before, he had been the choreographer of some thimblerig musical I was embroiled in. Now transformed into a scenario writer for no visible reason, he drew me into the oubliette where he had been laboring the past fifteen months on a screenplay of *Edwin Drood* and began recounting his woes.

"It's a witch," he lamented. "I can't seem to figure out an ending for it." I remarked consolingly that Dickens hadn't been able to think of a finish, either, and to cheer him up, told him of our impasse. He emitted a cluck of pity at my naïveté. Nobody, even the most eminent of playwrights, had ever succeeded in conferring with Thalberg, he asserted, and went on to relate the chronicle of George Kelly. Imported at an astronomical fee from the East, the author of *The Show Off* and *Craig's Wife* had been shown every courtesy, installed in a luxurious office and left to await Thalberg's convenience. After two months of futile telephoning, Kelly sent the producer word that he was departing for New York in twenty-four hours unless he was given an interview. He was put off with fervent promises, and finally, embittered, shook the dust of Culver City from his feet. About six weeks later, though, other business recalled him to Hollywood and he drove out to M-G-M to pick up his mail.

Neatly crisscrossed on his desk were six envelopes containing salary checks for the period of his absence. In a rather somnambulistic state, Kelly pocketed the checks and withdrew. Just as he was rounding a sound stage, he came face to face with Thalberg. The producer, his face remorseful, caught his sleeve.

"Forgive me, old boy," Thalberg apologized. "I know I've been neglecting you, but this time you have my word as a gentleman. I'll see you tomorrow—tomorrow afternoon. Four o'clock at the very latest."

As another ten days dragged by, my wife and I seriously began to question whether Thalberg even existed, whether he might not be a solar myth or a deity concocted by the front office to garner prestige. If few had ever actually beheld the man, however, there was no lack of legends about his idiosyncrasies. One of the more memorable, vouched for by Ivan Lebedeff, the actor, concerned a Russian officer he knew. A veteran of the Foreign Legion with a brilliant record in the North African campaigns, Major Peshkov had written a book around his exploits called *The Bugle Sounds* and was promptly hustled to California by Thalberg to translate it to film. Meeting each other one day at Metro, the fellow countrymen beheld a joyous reunion over a stoup of borsch, and Lebedeff asked how his friend's venture was progressing.

"To tell the truth, I'm a little worried," Peshkov admitted. "I've been trying to discuss the story the last two months, but Mr. Thalberg always puts me off. Mind you, he's been the soul of courtesy—gave me a fine office, a lovely blonde secretary—"

With cynicism born of long experience, Lebedeff allayed his fears. This was standard Hollywood conduct, he explained. Thalberg would eventually materialize; meanwhile, there was the steady honorarium, an excellent commissary and, above all, the beautiful blonde. At their next meeting, a month or two later, Peshkov betrayed distinct agitation. He announced that a man of his temperament, accustomed to the Sahara, could not brook such inactivity and confinement. If Thalberg persisted in avoiding him, he said through his teeth . . . Lebedeff urged self-control, reminded him of the discipline and fortitude he had shown in his arduous military career. The wars with the Bedouin, retorted Peshkov darkly, had been child's play compared to what he was undergoing in Culver City. He would hang on a little longer, but only because he hesitated to reflect dishonor on the Legion. It was a good ten weeks afterward that Lebedeff saw him again, and he instantly detected a change in the other's bearing, a new air of decision.

"The die is cast," declared Peshkov. "I am returning to Morocco tomorrow and nothing on earth can dissuade me. I have just wired Mr. Thalberg that I shall call on him at four today to settle our accounts."

The nature of the interview puzzled Lebedeff until he heard it from his friend's own lips in Paris several years later. On the stroke of four, Peshkov had entered Thalberg's suite, brushed aside his secretary and invaded the sanctum. Tersely introducing himself, he sought indulgence for bungling his mission, adding that had he done so in the Legion, he would have been shot.

"But look here," said Thalberg, perplexed. "You couldn't be more mistaken. We're completely satisfied with you—in fact, we're picking up your option. You and I'll sit down together one of these days—"

"No, no," said Peshkov. "It's too late." He withdrew an itemized list and laid it on the desk. "I believe you will find this accurate," he said. "My salary for eight months at $750 a week—$24,000. Steamship, rail and hotel charges en route from Morocco—$915. Incidentals, $360. And here," he continued, extending a slip of paper, "is my check for the total. I can only ask you to forgive me for abusing your trust."

Thalberg stared at him uncomprehending for a few moments, and then, with a shrug, flicked up the key of his Dictograph. "Suit yourself, Major," he said. "I don't know what your game is, but if you won't talk to me, you'll talk to Loophole, my attorney. Good afternoon, sir."

It may have been the unsettling effect of such stories or merely slow attrition, but three weeks later my wife and I decided we had reached the breaking point, and spitting on each other's hands, began work on the screenplay of *Greenwich Village*. After all, we reasoned, we could hardly be accused of insubordination when we'd waited so long in vain for orders. We were waistdeep in clichés one morning, portraying Joan Crawford's anguish at the onslaught of a lecherous etcher, when Thalberg's secretary phoned: we were to present ourselves instanter at his bungalow. Thunderstruck and wrangling over how best to comport ourselves, we hastened toward the Palladian stucco edifice that contained his unit. Cooling their heels in the anteroom were a dozen literary artisans of note like Sidney Howard and Robert Sherwood, George S. Kaufman, Marc Connelly, S. N. Behrman and Donald Ogden Stewart. The epigrams inspired by such a galaxy may well be imagined, but by winnowing them, I discovered that everybody there had been seeking Thalberg's ear without success and was seething. In a few moments, the door of his lair opened, someone of the caliber of Pirandello or Molnar emerged, and to our intense surprise, the secretary waved us in. The resulting epigrams may well be imagined. I forget what they were, but they made my cheeks flame at the time.

The room in which we found ourselves was very long, bathed in shadow and reminiscent of an advertisement for Duo-Art Pianos. Picked out in a single beam of light at the far end was a frail gentleman with intense eyes which he kept fixed unwinkingly on us during our trip to his desk, barely a matter of two minutes. After routine salutations, he inquired if we saw any possibilities in *Greenwich Village*. I replied that they were limitless and that we were already busily at work on the screenplay.

"Oh, you are, are you?" said Thalberg with marked displeasure. "Well, you can stop right now. I don't want a word on paper—I repeat, not a single word—until we've found the answer to the question."

"The question?" I repeated uncertainly.

"That's right," he said. "The all-important question your story raises—namely, should a woman tell?"

There was a short, pregnant silence, approximately long enough to consume a slice of poppyseed strudel, and my wife leaned forward. "Should a woman tell what?" she asked with almost Japanese delicacy.

"Why, the truth about her past," returned Thalberg, like one addressing a child. "In short, should a beautiful, sophisticated woman confess her premarital indiscretions to her fiancé?"

Before the beautiful, sophisticated woman beside me could confess that this was her first inkling of any such problem in the story, she was saved by the Dictograph. Some Olympian personality, whose voice contained enough gravel to pave the Cahuenga Pass, was calling to borrow a cupful of proxies, and halfway through his plea, word arrived from Miss Garbo that Western civilization would collapse unless Thalberg hastened on the double to Stage 9. The next my wife and I knew, we were blinking in the sunlight outside the building, the same suspicion burgeoning in our breasts. Neither of us put it into words, but we were both right. At suppertime that evening, Kolodny phoned to say that we could sleep as late as we wished the following morning. *Greenwich Village* had been shelved and we were back on the auction block. I toyed with the idea of driving over to pick up the needlepoint and the set of Boswell, and then, on due reflection, abandoned it. I also abandoned, even more speedily, the notion of emulating Peshkov and returning the loot. Strong as was my sense of *noblesse oblige*, I had enough headaches without the honor of the Foreign Legion.

I I

Irving Thalberg considered actors to be charming, vital and beautiful children. Like children, actors were to be enjoyed and admired for their ingenuous qualities and to be tolerated when their behavior seemed abnormal. They were, after all, exceptionally emotional persons, since the very nature of their work required trafficking in human feelings. So they were to be forgiven their tantrums, their errratic behavior, as long as they caused no unreasonable interruption of the making of movies, which was Thalberg's consuming occupation.

He also believed that actors, like children, should not be allowed to make major decisions about their own destinies.

Thalberg rarely consulted stars about their vehicles. Normally he handed them a script and said, "Here's your next picture." He considered the casting a *fait accompli*. Occasionally a star complained about the size or nature of a role; Thalberg generally calmed such doubts with his cool logic and earnest charm. There was no such thing as suspension of an M-G-M actor for refusing a role. "I have never forced an actor to play a role against his will," Thalberg said proudly.

Greta Garbo was reluctant to accept *Flesh and the Devil* until Thalberg convinced her that the film would be good for her career. Thereafter she never questioned Thalberg's judgment. All of her studio dealings were conducted with him.

Actors placed utter confidence in Thalberg, and with good reason. He was deeply concerned about their careers, not merely on a picture-to-picture basis, but from a long-term view. No one understood the magic of the star system better than he. No one perfected it to such a high degree. He realized that actors became stars only by arousing the emotions—love, hate, admiration, amusement—of the individual members of the audience. For that reason, the Thalberg films were heavy with emotion. They might have lacked the action and the hilarity of other studios' product, but they reached more readily to the heart.

"We make pictures for people to see; Thalberg makes pictures for people to feel," said one despairing competitor.

This was not accomplished haphazardly. Thalberg had an unfailing instinct for the motivation of characters and how to combine motivations for the utmost dramatic effect. For that reason, the M-G-M scripts contained great scenes. The best of the Thalberg-produced films—*A Free Soul, Grand Hotel, Camille, The Good Earth*—progress from one eminently playable scene to another.

Actors realized this. They knew that careers could be built—and Academy awards won—by magnificent scenes. Hence an M-G-M contract became the most highly regarded in Hollywood.

Those who qualified for an M-G-M acting contract were assured the most proficient publicity buildup in Hollywood. First under the leadership of Pete Smith and then of Howard Strickling, the publicity department operated with precision smoothness in bringing personalities to public attention and protecting them from elements that could damage or destroy careers. The department had learned a stern lesson from its early attempts to publicize Greta Garbo; she had been persuaded to pose in track togs with college runners, and the indignity helped make her a recluse. Now the M-G-M accent was on dignity, with each personality receiving a specially tailored campaign. A staff of a hundred publicists and photographers, many of them the most expert in their field, contributed their services.

The actors were expected to give something in return. Thalberg made it clear to new contract players that the studio required their utmost cooperation. Movie fans expected to share the lives of their favorites, and that meant a certain sacrifice of privacy. After the success of *Trader Horn,* Thalberg wanted to sign Harry Carey to a contract that would have assured him of starring roles and an impressive salary. The proposal sounded attractive to Carey until Thalberg added his stipulation: that the actor live in Hollywood so he would be available for publicity. Carey, who liked to retire to his Saugus ranch between pictures, declined the contract. "I don't want anyone telling me where to live," he said.

Being engaged in the most unstable of professions, most actors need constant reassurance, and Thalberg had exceptional powers to inspire self-confidence. Rosalind Russell, in her early twenties and newly signed by M-G-M, was summoned to the Thalberg bungalow.

After being admitted to the cathedral-like office, she saw the small figure seated behind a desk in the half-light. She was fascinated by the deep, sad eyes that concentrated on her alone, not looking through her, but seeming to summarize what they saw.

"You have a tremendous future in this business," he told her. "But you must be careful what you work in." Miss Russell, who had been loaned to other studios for her first assignments, was greatly encouraged.

Myrna Loy had been the victim of type-casting because of a series of portrayals of slinky Orientals. But Thalberg saw her in an Occidental role in *Skyline* with Thomas Meighan at Fox, and he perceived her potential as a versatile actress. She was signed to an M-G-M contract.

Directors were puzzled about what to do with Miss Loy, but Thalberg remained confident. Several times he called her to his office to discuss her future. On one occasion, he swiveled his chair as he talked to her and concentrated his attention on the activities outside the window.

"Mr. Thalberg, would you mind turning around?" she asked.

He swung back to her with a startled look.

"I was brought up to believe that a person should look at the person he is talking to," she said.

He was amused at her candor, and he continued discussing her career. He assured her that she was beautiful enough for success in films, which was something she herself had doubted. He added that she had made good progress at M-G-M, and he analyzed her performances.

"But there is something holding you back," he continued. "I don't know what it is, but there seems to be a veil between you and the audience. You've got to cut through that veil. You must reach out there and grab them!"

The lecture had an effect on Miss Loy. She left the protective care of her mother, and she strove to overcome her basic shyness. As she did so, Thalberg gave her stronger roles in such films as *The Wet Parade* and *Emma*. Later came the pairing with William Powell in *The Thin Man*, produced by Hunt Stromberg.

Late in his career, Thalberg befriended a young Englishman, David Niven. Edmund Goulding had arranged an interview, and Thalberg was impressed by Niven's handsome appearance.

Rosalind Russell, China Seas

"What have you done in pictures?" Thalberg inquired.

"Nothing," Niven admitted.

"But you must have done something."

"No, nothing at all. I've been in the Army for the last five years."

Niven expected to be dismissed, but instead Thalberg questioned him intently about his regiment and his experiences. At the end of the conversation, Thalberg ordered a screen test to be made of the young man.

The test failed to impress other producers on the M-G-M lot, and Thalberg had no immediate roles for Niven. But Thalberg kept in touch with Niven, who was living nearby in a beach shack he rented from Carmel Myers. Niven kept his dress suit pressed, hoping that he would be called to fill in as an extra man at Thalberg dinner parties. Very often the call came late on Saturday afternoon, and Niven was assured of an elegant meal instead of his own frugal fare.

Finally Thalberg decided to cast Niven in a minor role in *Mutiny on the Bounty*. One night at a party attended by other studio moguls, he announced, "I'm going to sign David Niven to a contract tomorrow." On the following morning, Niven had contract offers from Warner Brothers, Paramount and Samuel Goldwyn; he chose Goldwyn.

On occasion, Thalberg encountered actors who would not accept his will. In 1929, he hired the stage actor, Edward G. Robinson, to appear opposite Vilma Banky in a talkie version of Sidney Howard's Pulitzer Prize play *They Knew What They Wanted*, released under the title *A Lady to Love*. The film was to prove the last for Miss Banky, who could not survive the transition to sound, but it revealed Robinson as an actor of power and appeal.

Thalberg sent for Robinson and his agent, Milton Bren, and he offered the actor a five-year contract that would have amounted to a million dollars.

"Look, Mr. Thalberg," said Robinson, "I'm essentially a stage actor; that's where my loyalties are. Couldn't we settle for a six-month contract? You see, I don't want to be away from the theater any longer than that."

"No, I couldn't do that, Mr. Robinson," said Thalberg. "We don't operate that way at M-G-M. If we're going to build you into a star, we want to enjoy the cumulative benefits. And I might add that the benefits to you will be considerable, too."

Robinson resisted the lure, much to the exasperation of his agent,

Myrna Loy, The Wet Parade

Bren. The experience was upsetting to the actor, too; after he descended the stairs from Thalberg's office, Robinson promptly threw up. He returned to New York and experienced a series of flop plays. Convinced that the theater was less loyal to him than he was to it, he signed a contract with Warner Brothers and became a star with *Little Caesar*. Thalberg did not forget that the actor refused a million-dollar contract. Robinson never again worked in a Thalberg film.

Thalberg could be a hard bargainer in negotiating actors' contracts, but he could also be swayed by caprice. In 1932, he wanted to add Lee Tracy to the M-G-M list of star performers. He sent an assistant to negotiate with the actor, who had recently left a contract at Universal. The underling used all his powers of persuasion to convince Tracy to accept a contract at $1500 a week. Tracy was adamant in his decision to accept no less than $2000. The negotiation was fruitless.

Tracy was summoned to the office of Irving Thalberg. When he arrived, he found Joan Crawford seated in the waiting room. The secretary told Tracy that Mr. Thalberg would see him, but he replied, "No, let Miss Crawford go in first; she's been waiting longer."

The actress was impressed by his courtesy, and so was Thalberg. He made an effort to convince Tracy to sign for $1500, but settled for $2000. Tracy was convinced that his gesture to Miss Crawford won him the higher figure.

Stars were rarely released by M-G-M; most of them left the studio only when they died, as in the cases of Lon Chaney and Marie Dressler, or when they became impossible to manage. It is probable that Mayer and Thalberg would have kept John Gilbert under contract despite the loss of his following during the talkies; both recognized Gilbert's immense contribution to M-G-M's success in its early years. But the humiliation of being laughed at because of his voice proved too much for the actor to bear. He became sullen and secretive, entering the studio by the back gate so he would avoid the possibility of being ridiculed. He drank heavily and became unprofessional in his demeanor on the set. The warm friendship between him and Thalberg faded into bitterness. At $250,000 a picture—he had demanded such terms just before talkies—he became too expensive for M-G-M. At the age of thirty-four, he was burned out.*

---

* Gilbert returned to M-G-M in 1933 when Greta Garbo, out of loyalty, insisted that he play opposite her in *Queen Christina*. Laurence Olivier had previously been assigned to the role. The film failed to revive Gilbert's career.

Edward G. Robinson, A Lady to Love

Another problem was Buster Keaton. After his separation from Natalie Talmadge, the comedian was devastated, and he showed up drunk or not at all for his third co-starring film with Jimmy Durante, *What! No Beer?*

After the film was finally completed, Mayer requested Keaton to appear one Saturday to perform a mock scene for visiting conventioneers; it was a common studio practice for film makers to go through the motions of doing a scene to provide entertainment for visitors. Keaton said he couldn't appear because he had been invited to act as mascot for the St. Mary's football team in their game against UCLA in the Los Angeles Coliseum. Mayer repeated the instructions. Keaton kept his date at the football game.

On the following Monday, he received a notice: "Your services at Metro-Goldwyn-Mayer Studios are no longer required. Signed, Louis B. Mayer, General Manager and Vice President."

Thalberg tried to save the comedian's career at M-G-M. Keaton had proposed a comic version of the studio's hit *Grand Hotel*. He proposed calling it *Grand Mills Hotel* after a New York flophouse and casting himself in the Lionel Barrymore role, Marie Dressler as an aging ballerina, Jimmy Durante as a bogus count, Oliver Hardy as a hard-driving industrialist, Stan Laurel as a collar-button manufacturer, Polly Moran as a secretary and Henry Armetta as hotel clerk and expectant father. After Keaton had been fired, Thalberg sent word that he wanted to make the travesty. But Keaton was too depleted to consider the film, and he made no effort to answer Thalberg. The comedian's career as a starring performer came to an end.

Thalberg formed close friendships with no actors; it was significant that only producers and directors attended his wedding to Norma. The closest he came to personal relationships with actors came in the early M-G-M period with John Gilbert and in his last years with Charles Laughton.

Thalberg and Laughton enjoyed a close professional relationship, and the two men walked for hours along the Santa Monica beach as Thalberg outlined plans for the actor's career. Laughton, who had trepidations about coming to Hollywood, was greatly impressed by Thalberg's grasp of the medium, and he placed his future in the producer's hands.

Only one star occupied Thalberg's complete and abiding interest and that was Norma Shearer. His concern for her stirred resentment

The home brew overflows in What! No Beer? *Left to right: Jimmy Durante, unidentified, Buster Keaton, Roscoe Ates, Henry Armetta*

among other actresses at M-G-M, particularly Joan Crawford. "How can I compete with Norma when she sleeps with the boss?" Miss Crawford wailed. She experienced sorrowing evidence of Norma's power on more than one occasion. Adela Rogers St. Johns had written *A Free Soul* with Joan in mind, and she petitioned Thalberg to let Joan play it. The actress herself pleaded for the role. But Norma wanted *A Free Soul* for herself, and she got it.

Norma was strong-willed in many things, particularly her clothes. She was particularly fond of white satin evening dresses, and in almost every picture she found an excuse to wear one; Adrian, who had the chore of designing the dresses, called them "Norma's Nightgowns."

Her will did not always prevail. During one film she arrived on the set wearing a dress that did not strike the fancy of the director, Sidney Franklin. He asked her to change the dress, and she refused. "I like it," she insisted. Franklin pointed out that his contract granted him approval of costumes. The pair reached an impasse.

Later that day, Franklin was asked to report to Thalberg's office. There he found a peevish Norma wearing the controversial dress.

"Norma says she wants to wear the dress, Sidney," Thalberg said. "Why don't you like it?"

"It looks like something her maid would wear," the director answered. "I just don't like it, Irving, that's all there is to it."

"Well, let's see how it looks on the screen," said Thalberg. "We'll get the tests out."

The trio went to the projection room and watched the brief test in which Norma displayed the dress. "I see nothing wrong with it, Sidney," said Thalberg.

Franklin remained firm. "I still don't like it," he said.

Thalberg sighed. "All right, Norma, take it off," he said. "Sidney doesn't like it."

Thalberg was by no means compliant to his wife's will, nor was she ordinarily demanding. Theirs was a creative partnership in which the principal concern was the making of good pictures, not the satisfaction of an actress's ego. He expected the best effort from her and would settle for no less.

Ordinarily Thalberg viewed the rushes of only Shearer and Garbo; his duties as production chief precluded overseeing the day-to-day production of other films. Whenever he found flaws in Norma's performances, he told her so in plain terms.

"You can do better than this," he once chastised her after seeing the rushes with other members of the film company. "You're a damned fine actress, but you don't show it in those scenes. Now tomorrow I want you to do them again and show me how good you can be."

The dual position as production boss and husband of one of the studio's top stars was a perilous one, fraught with the dangers of resentment from other performers and complaints of nepotism from stockholders. That Irving Thalberg and Norma Shearer could generally avoid such perils was due to their immaculate behavior and to the fact that she could achieve the challenges he gave her.

12

Thalberg continued his relentless quest for stars, realizing that only by adding to the galaxy could he maintain M-G-M's boast of "more stars than there are in the heavens." Jean Harlow came to the studio in 1931, when the white-hot flash of her career seemed to have burned out. She had been a Howard Hughes discovery, and he exploited her raw sensuality to good results in *Hell's Angels*. Then he loaned her to M-G-M for *The Secret Six*, to Universal for *Iron Man*, to Warner Brothers for *Public Enemy*, to Fox for *Goldie* and to Columbia for *Platinum Blonde* and *Three Wise Girls*. The move from one studio to another helped destroy her wavering confidence, and the series of desultory performances threatened to end her career.

After being borrowed by M-G-M once more for *The Beast of the City*, Harlow rebelled. She sought a release from her contract, and Hughes gave it to her. Louis Mayer signed her to a contract with M-G-M.

Jean Harlow seemed an illogical choice for stardom at M-G-M. She had specialized in playing tramps, sometimes with, sometimes without a heart of gold. M-G-M heroines, due in large part to Mayer's reverence for womanhood, nearly always remained ladies, even when they stumbled into the pitfalls of sinfulness. Around the Culver City lot there were wonder and doubt that Harlow would be able to fit into the M-G-M programing.

Paul Bern became her valuable ally. It was he who first saw in her something beyond the platinum-haired gangster's moll. He was quite obviously infatuated with her.

That had happened before with Paul Bern. Time after time he had proclaimed himself in love, usually with a beautiful and voluptuous actress. The romances never ended in marriage, although he did propose matrimony to the vivacious Barbara LaMarr. When she spurned him for a cowboy actor, his grief prompted him to attempt suicide by drowning himself in a toilet bowl. He succeeded only in getting his head stuck in the seat.

Bern found solace in the company of other lovely actresses, and his contemporaries considered him one of the ablest romancers in

Hollywood. Indeed, he had a remarkable manner with women. He had a way of making them feel like unmatched beauties, and he showered them with gifts, sometimes enough roses to fill a limousine, sometimes a mink wrap or a pearl necklace. But beyond praising their beauty, he could convince the women that he was interested in them as thinking, feeling individuals. He expounded to them on literature and the arts, he read them poetry and played them classical music. Some of the girls were puzzled by his approach, and puzzled further when he made none of the advances that an actress learned to expect from a studio executive.

The Bern method found a receptive subject in Jean Harlow. She had known endless overtures for sex in the hurly-burly of studio life, and she was both relieved and flattered to find a man who didn't want to race her into bed. She was amazed that he earnestly sought to help her career, with nothing demanded in return except her friendship. He wanted to give her some of the polish he knew she would need to succeed at M-G-M.

"My God, he wants to take me to the opera!" she exclaimed, and she went along happily. She was thrilled when he escorted her to dinners at homes to which she had never been invited before—including the home of Norma Shearer and Irving Thalberg.

No one was closer to Thalberg than Paul Bern. Thalberg relied on Bern for intellectual stimulation, for counsel in matters regarding sophistication and taste. So great was Thalberg's regard for him that Bern was entrusted with supervision of the Garbo pictures.

Bern made persistent pleas for Thalberg to cast Jean in *Red-Headed Woman*, which was being adapted from the Katharine Brush novel. Thalberg listened, but he continued to test actress after actress for the role. The volume of tests became such a studio joke that Marie Dressler slapped on a red wig and posed for a photograph as one of the nominees. Thalberg almost decided on Joan Crawford for the role. Then he agreed to Bern's suggestion. Thalberg himself had seen possibilities in combining Harlow's sensuality with humor. He had been unimpressed with her attempts at drama, but he remembered the wry manner with which she delivered her famed line in *Hell's Angels:* "Pardon me while I slip into something more comfortable."

The script of *Red-Headed Woman* was written by Anita Loos after F. Scott Fitzgerald's unsuccessful attempt. The novel had been a

Jean Harlow and Chester Morris, Red-Headed Woman

straight-faced account of how a pretty girl made her way to society's heights by sleeping with the right men. Thalberg reasoned that vitality could be injected into the saga only by applying humor, and Miss Loos was ideally qualified to provide it. She submitted a script that amused Thalberg, but not the director he had chosen for it, Jack Conway.

"You can say what you want, Irving," the director argued, "but people aren't going to laugh at this. I know. I've been in situations like this, and it's no laughing matter. This woman busts up the whole goddam family."

"But look at the family!" Miss Loos replied. "They deserve busting up."

Thalberg was not swayed by Conway's arguments. "Shoot it as it is," he instructed. "And if you get in trouble, send for Anita."

Conway followed the script to the letter, but he complained that he was unable to direct a merry-go-round scene. "Anita, go out and direct it," said Thalberg, and she did.

Red-Headed Woman was a stylish hit, establishing a whole new

career for Jean Harlow as a sophisticated comedienne. The picture
also had a side effect which Thalberg didn't anticipate. Moralists
were outraged because after all her wrongdoing the Harlow character
ended up happily ensconced as the mistress of a French nobleman,
with her favorite lover (Charles Boyer, before stardom) as her
chauffeur.

So great was the outcry over the film that Will Hays was prompted
to enforce the film industry's self-censorship Production Code which
laid down rigid- rules for film makers. Among them: "Adultery,
sometimes necessary plot material, must not be explicitly treated,
or justified, or presented attractively."

Thalberg immediately cast Jean Harlow with Clark Gable in *Red
Dust*, and the combination proved explosive. It was the first of five
co-starrings for the pair, and all the films were successful.

Although Thalberg was pleased to have another potent star for
M-G-M, he displayed no fondness for her as a performer or as
a person. After the first preview of *Red-Headed Woman*, he was
asked by an aide, "How was Jean Harlow?" Thalberg thought for
a moment and replied, "Well, you know that girl's so bad she might
just be good." On the personal level, Harlow was much too earthy
for his taste; she had none of the refinement that he admired in
Norma. And he was increasingly concerned over Paul Bern's infatuation with Jean. Thalberg did not approve.

13

Irving Thalberg was at the height of his powers in 1932. While
other studios were troubled by the falling movie market in Depression
America, M-G-M flourished as never before. Thalberg set a furious
pace for the other studios to follow. In three years he had achieved
a mastery of the sound film and was pushing it to new challenges.
He remained in active command of M-G-M's entire product, and he
seemed to thrive under the rigors of the immense responsibility.
He was calmly confident at all times; unlike his competitors, he
didn't require constant reassurance to sustain his ego. He was the
best and he knew it.

The M-G-M machinery was well constructed and operating
smoothly. Thalberg's assistants were attuned to his mode of operation—they had dropped the unimpressive title of supervisors and were

Donald Crisp, Gene Raymond, Clark Gable, Mary Astor, Jean Harlow, Tully Marshall (back to camera), Red Dust

now associate producers, a somewhat more impressive designation. There were a few signs that they might be restive under their subservience to Thalberg, but to outer appearances their loyalty appeared constant. Thalberg seemed to cast them for films with the same care with which he assigned the M-G-M stars. Hunt Stromberg specialized in the sexier subjects such as *Our Dancing Daughters* and *Red Dust;* he also assumed command of the Joan Crawford vehicles in an effort to remove Thalberg from involvement in the Crawford-Shearer competition for properties. The learned Albert Lewin looked after films of a literary quality, such as *The Guardsman, Smilin' Through* and *Private Lives.* Lawrence Weingarten who had become the boss's brother-in-law by marrying Sylvia Thalberg, oversaw the comedies. Harry Rapf specialized in the tear-jerkers like *The Champ, The Sin of Madelon Claudet,* as well as supervising the

B pictures. The sensitive Paul Bern took charge of the Garbo films, and Bernard Hyman handled outdoor adventures like *Trader Horn* and the new Tarzan series starring Johnny Weissmuller.

The films had a look about them that was unmistakably M-G-M. Mayer and Thalberg had assembled a staff of stylists who gave each production a distinctive mounting. The female stars were gorgeously outfitted by Adrian, whose simple, flowing creations set the standard for sophistication; his square-shoulder suits for Joan Crawford and satin gowns for Greta Garbo were coveted by women everywhere. The sets and furnishings designed by Cedric Gibbons were in advance of their time and had a profound influence on styles of the 1930s. The sound, supervised by Douglas Shearer, was the best in Hollywood, and the photography had unusual clarity; Thalberg had eliminated the soft focus that earlier film makers had considered to be artistic.

At the wedding of Sylvia Thalberg and Lawrence Weingarten: Irving, Norma, William Thalberg, the bride and bridegroom

No other studio could match M-G-M's collection of contract players. This was the list in 1932 (stardom was accorded only to those with special distinction or proven box-office appeal):

STARS—Ethel Barrymore, John Barrymore, Lionel Barrymore, Wallace Beery, Jackie Cooper, Joan Crawford, Marion Davies, Marie Dressler, Clark Gable, John Gilbert, Buster Keaton, Robert Montgomery, Ramon Novarro, Norma Shearer.

FEATURED PLAYERS—Tad Alexander, Nils Asther, Mary Carlisle, Virginia Cherrill, Claire Du Brey, James Durante, Madge Evans, Muriel Evans, W. B. Gilbert, C. Henry Gordon, Lawrence Grant, Nora Gregor, William Haines, Louise Closser Hale, Jean Harlow, Helen Hayes, Jean Hersholt, Phillips Holmes, Hedda Hopper, Walter Huston, Dorothy Jordan, Anthony Jowett, Muriel Kirkland, Pearl Shibita Long, Myrna Loy, Una Merkel, John Miljan, Polly Moran, Colleen Moore, Karen Morley, Conrad Nagel, David Newell, Bert Nolson, Maureen O'Sullivan, Anita Page, Jean Parker, May Robson, Joseph Sauers, Ruth Selwyn, Katya Sergeiva, Martha Sleeper, Lewis Stone, Charlotte Suse, Verree Teasdale, Franchot Tone, Ray Wise, Johnny Weissmuller, Robert Young.

With such a formidable list, it was no wonder that preview audiences began applauding as soon as they saw the M-G-M trademark of Leo the Lion.

Although he was scarcely known outside the industry except as Norma Shearer's husband, all of Hollywood realized that Irving Thalberg was the man responsible for M-G-M's lofty position. He made the selection of story material. He assigned his associates to supervise the myriad of details necessary to put a movie before the cameras. He retained the responsibility for selecting the writers and directors. He thrashed out the scripts with the writers, repeatedly offering his own original solutions to narrative problems. He cast the films and approved the costumes and sets. He made himself available for problems that arose during shooting. After the picture was assembled, he often made important changes in the cutting. He previewed the film and ordered extensive retakes if the public's reception was not favorable. He even oversaw the publicity and advertising campaign.

A convergence of the M-G-M power structure: Paul Bern, Mrs. Nicholas Schenck, Schenck, Norma Shearer, Irving Thalberg, Mrs. J. Robert Rubin, Albert Lewin, Rubin, David Bernstein (Loew's treasurer) at Grand Central Station, New York

He was neither a director, writer, actor, editor, designer, composer nor any other craftsman ordinarily associated with film making. He came closest to being a producer, yet he was not like today's producer, who follows a single film from beginning to end, then commences another one. Thalberg fulfilled the functions of a dozen producers.

The pictures had a mark that was unmistakably Thalberg's. They were generally about civilized people—or at any rate, they were civilized looks at the human situation. There was little or nothing that was lowbrow or vulgar; Thalberg did not care to cater to lower tastes. He believed that the movie public constantly sought better entertainment. The emphasis was on entertainment; he wanted the pictures to please. He liked to bring great literature to the screen—

and more than any other studio, the M-G-M product had a literary quality. But the literature had to bring entertainment as well as enlightenment to the mass audience. M-G-M pictures seldom preached. Perhaps because of the conservative politics of both Mayer and Thalberg, the films avoided social messages (notable exceptions: *The Big House*, about penal conditions; *The Wet Parade*, the evils of drink).

The Thalberg achievements were unknown to the general public because of his unconcern for personal publicity. But he received unusual attention in an article about M-G-M in the December 1932 issue of *Fortune*. The magazine stated that, "For the past five years, Metro-Goldwyn-Mayer has made the best and most successful movie pictures in the U.S." The credit was laid at the feet of Irving Thalberg. He was depicted as the guiding force behind the studio's twenty-million-dollar annual production program, while Mayer's activities were described as "personal connections, intrigues and affiliations."

Fortune described Thalberg's arrival at his office:

"He enters—a small, finely-made Jew of about thirty-three, changeable as the chameleon industry in which he labors. He is five and one-half feet tall, and weighs 122 pounds after a good night's sleep. This lightness, in calm moments, is all feline grace and poise. In frantic moments he appears as a pale and flimsy bag of bones held together by concealed bits of string and the furious ambition to make the best movies in the world. He seats himself, in his *moderne*, beaverboard office, at a massive, shiny desk, in front of a Dictograph which looks like a small pipe organ and partially hides a row of medicine bottles. Before him are huge boxes of cigarettes, which he never opens, and plates of apples and dates into which he sometimes dips a transparent hand. Squirming with nervous fervor in the midst of his elaborate apparatus, he speaks with a curiously calm, soft voice as if his words were a sort of poetry. He describes parabolas with one hand and scratches his knee with the other. Rising, he paces his office with stooped shoulders and hands clasped behind him. This reflective promenading he learned from Carl Laemmle, Sr., who discovered Irving Thalberg when, recently released from a Brooklyn high school, he was an office boy in the Broadway shop of Universal Pictures."

Thalberg at thirty-three occupied a unique position in Hollywood. The prestige that surrounded him was awesome. On important matters concerning the Academy of Motion Picture Arts and Sciences or the Motion Picture Producers Association, industry leaders were careful to enlist the support of Thalberg. His advocacy of the proposal could assure its success. When things went wrong—as often happened in the Depression years—the leaders said, "We'd better talk to Irving."

His counsel was sought on both an industry and a personal basis. Hollywood's power elite became alarmed because it was feared that two of the town's scions had been contaminated by communism. Budd Schulberg, son of B.P., and Maurice Rapf, son of Harry, had taken a trip to Soviet Russia, and they came back with praise for what they had seen. Both boys were seventeen, and their elders suspected that their impressionable minds had been swayed by the Red propaganda.

"Send them to Irving; he'll straighten them out," someone suggested.

The two boys dutifully reported to Thalberg's office at M-G-M. They were ushered into his solemn presence, and he urged them to be seated. He began pacing the floor and delivering his message: "Every young man is a socialist when he is young. Even I was full

of idealism as a boy and wanted to change the social order. Walter Lippmann was a socialist when he attended Harvard. But as we mature, we see things in a different light. We become more conservative."

Thalberg continued with a brief history of communism—a remarkably informed account for a man who was a confirmed capitalist—and he closed with his advice: "Now keep your wits about you. Don't be overly swayed by what you saw in Russia. Go on to college and study all you can. I know that as you grow older and more informed, you will come to the conclusion, as I have, that our way of life is best."

Anything that furthered the prestige of the motion picture drew Thalberg's whole-hearted support. He agreed to Louis Mayer's suggestion to form the Academy, and he attended all the formative meetings. He was an enthusiastic supporter of Conrad Nagel's proposal that the Academy should present annual awards. As early as 1927 he took part in the forming of a self-censorship program as part of a three-man committee which issued what became known as "Don'ts and Be Carefuls." The Don'ts: "Pointed profanity—by either title or lip; any licentious or suggestive nudity—in fact or in silhouette, and any lecherous or licentious notice thereof by other characters in the picture; the illegal traffic in drugs; any inference of sex perversion; white slavery; miscegenation; sex hygiene and venereal diseases; scenes of actual childbirth; children's sex organs; ridicule of the clergy; willful offense to any nation, race or creed."

The Be Carefuls included: "The use of the Flag; international relations (avoid picturizing in an unfavorable light another country's religion, history, institutions, prominent people and citizenry); arson, theft, robbery, safe-cracking and dynamiting of trains, mines, buildings, etc. (having in mind the effect which a too-detailed description of these may have upon the moron); brutality and possible gruesomeness; technique of committing murder by whatever method; sympathy for criminals; sedition; branding of people or animals; the sale of women, or of a woman selling her virtue; rape or attempted rape; first night scenes; man and woman in bed together; excessive or lustful kissing, particularly when one character or the other is a 'heavy.'"

Such Don'ts and Be Carefuls were entirely voluntary, and Will

Thalberg's desk

Hays, president of the Producers Association, became worried when film makers failed to heed them. He became more concerned with the coming of sound, which brought the added hazard of racy dialogue. Thalberg was appointed chairman of another committee to consider a code proposed by Martin Quigley, trade paper editor and a Catholic, and the Reverend Daniel A. Lord, a Jesuit priest. Thalberg and his committee worked with the pair to produce the Production Code, which was adopted by the Producers Association on February 17, 1930. Not until after *Red-Headed Woman* in 1932 was it seriously enforced.

Few things rankled Thalberg more than to read highbrow pronouncements that movies were merely a popular entertainment and could never be considered an art. He was irritated by the way movies were shrugged off by newspapers and magazines as being unworthy of serious consideration. He believed that films were worthy of the same critical appraisal that was accorded plays and books.

"Look at the space they give us," he said one day, spreading the theatrical section of the Los Angeles *Times* on his desk. Turning the pages, he added, "And look what they give sports—page after page. People go to the movies more than they go to baseball games. Why don't the papers give us the same coverage?"

In his relations with his fellow workers at M-G-M, Thalberg was inevitably cool and reserved. His attitude was not so much one of aloofness as it was of unaffected dignity. The years of striving to appear older than his age had created an air of solemnity that few persons attempted to disturb. One exception was Jimmy Durante, whose irrepressible behavior was enjoyed by Thalberg. Durante was one of the few who was allowed to burst into the Thalberg office unannounced.

Once Durante invaded the Thalberg sanctum to find the auto magnate, Walter Chrysler, as his guest. "Ya gotta great invention in that new car of yours, Mr. Chrysler," said the comedian. "I put the top up and the bottom fell out!"

Thalberg on most occasions exhibited an almost royal reserve, and his attitude precluded the clutching and kissing that characterizes personal relationships among show people. Like most hypochondriacs —in his case, he had reason for constant concern with his health— he tried to avoid physical contact with other people. One of the few times when his person was violated came at a costume party given by Marion Davies. Irving and Norma arrived dressed alike as West Point cadets, and the puckish William Haines saw in the situation a chance for one of his practical jokes. When Thalberg was standing alone, Haines walked up stealthily and goosed him.

Thalberg leaped into the air and turned around in outrage. "Oh, pardon me, Irving," said Haines. "I thought you were Norma."

While he was reserved, Thalberg made no pretense of being saintly. He was perfectly capable of employing the vulgar language that was customary in the highest circles of Hollywood, though he generally used more polite terms. Rarely did he engage in off-color remarks. On one occasion, an aide suggested that a proposed project was too trashy for M-G-M. "Well, let's face it," Thalberg commented, "we win Academy awards with crap like *The Sin of Madelon Claudet.*"

At the beginning of one story conference, he was handed a few pages of a new scene that had been written by Bayard Veiller and Lenore Coffee. Thalberg excused himself for a moment, explaining that he would read the scene in his private toilet.

"Oh, Irving, not in there," pleaded Veiller.

Thalberg grinned and said, "Don't worry—I'll bring it all back."

Thalberg seldom deviated from his glacial calm. Even when a grievous wrong had been committed at the studio, his strongest statement was: "I don't want this ever to happen again. I mean this. I won't mention this again." His associates recognized the tight-lipped manner with which the comment was made and guarded against a repetition of the misdeed. One thing Thalberg could not tolerate: being lied to. He had no use for the half-truths and outright lies that underlings employed to ingratiate themselves to studio heads.

One day Thalberg instructed his secretary to summon a producer to his office. The reply came that the producer was unavailable because he was "on the lot." Thalberg realized that this wasn't true, and he muttered, "Why do grown men have to teach their secretaries to lie?"

Once a year Thalberg would unbend with his employees at the studio's Christmas party, which centered in his office. Everyone from star to janitor was privileged to drop in and pour a drink from Thalberg's ample supply. He watched amusedly as longtime antago-

When youthful fantasies
were being lived . . .

In those times. . . .

They enjoyed dressing up like children (Joan Crawford, Douglas Fairbanks, Jr., Clark Gable, Marion Davies, Norma Shearer, Irving Thalberg)

nisms were vented amid the boozy atmosphere and incipient romances were sparked. He was delighted when little Albert Lewin, who had a fondness for tall girls, stood on a chair to converse with a statuesque beauty. It was a time when anyone could voice his complaints, and many did, after the courage of a few drinks. Thalberg listened with care and later made an effort to redress the grievances.

The M-G-M table at industry dinners was always the center of attention, and Mayer and Thalberg presided with a lordly air, surrounding themselves with their most distinguished stars and visiting dignitaries. On such occasions, Thalberg was genial but dignified. Even when he dressed up in a child's costume for a Marion Davies party, he managed to appear solemn.

His passion for film making transcended all. He expected everyone in the company to extend the same measure of devotion as he did, and he thought nothing of telephoning his underlings at any hour to discuss story matters. On one occasion, Howard Dietz, the East Coast director of M-G-M publicity and advertising, was summoned to the telephone as he was attending the Baer-Braddock championship boxing match at Madison Square Garden. Irving Thalberg was calling from Hollywood to discuss an advertising campaign.

Thalberg was devoted to college football, and he attended the University of Southern California games at the Los Angeles Coliseum every Saturday afternoon in the fall. During the games he made frequent notes about studio matters in a small loose-leaf notebook he carried with him, and he went to the telephone several times to make calls about things he considered important.

Outside of the football season, Saturday remained a full working day for him, and he expected his underlings to remain at work with him. One Saturday morning he noted that Hunt Stromberg was repeatedly glancing at his watch during a story conference.

"Are you going somewhere, Hunt?" Thalberg asked.

"Well, I was hoping to get out to Santa Anita this afternoon," Stromberg admitted.

"What for?" Thalberg asked.

"To see the races. And I was hoping to make a few bucks on some tips I have."

"Look—I don't want to lose our train of thought now that we're getting this script licked," said Thalberg. "You tell me what bets you were going to make, and I'll cover them for you." Stromberg gave him a list of his wagers for the day, and the story conference continued. When the race results were tallied, Thalberg had earned $2000 from Stromberg.

One day King Vidor was summoned to Thalberg's office to discuss a forthcoming project. Before the conference could begin, Thalberg said, "Come along to the Santa Fe station with me."

Vidor joined Thalberg in the studio limousine, and on the ride to downtown Los Angeles Thalberg talked about other matters besides the film. When they arrived at the station, Vidor followed him onto the train.

"Where are you going?" Vidor asked.

"To New York," Thalberg replied.

"But you haven't told me what you thought about the next picture," said Vidor. He had to ride the train all the way to Albuquerque to find out.

Vidor and Laurence Stallings waited in Thalberg's outer office for a conference one day, only to be instructed by the secretary that Mr. Thalberg wished them to join him in the studio car outside. There they found Thalberg and Eddie Mannix waiting in the back seat. As the four men were driven away from the studio, Thalberg asked what progress had been made on the *Billy the Kid* script. Vidor began outlining the desperado's homicidal career while the limousine sped toward Los Angeles.

The car stopped before what was unmistakably a funeral parlor. Numerous people in black garb milled outside, and Mannix and Thalberg stepped out to join them. Vidor and Stallings were reluctant to follow since they wore white flannel pants and sweaters and neither had the vaguest notion of whose funeral it was. But there seemed no other course but to follow Thalberg and Mannix.

Inside the chapel, Vidor noted the mass of floral displays about the casket. He also saw a large number of the most noted figures in Hollywood—Charlie Chaplin, Marie Dressler, Lew Cody, Ben Turpin, Mack Swain, Mack Sennett, Harry Langdon, Buster Keaton, Chester Conklin—all of the great clowns weeping profusely. Vidor sent a note to Mannix asking, "*Who is it?*"

Mannix sent back the message: "*Mabel Normand. Don't you read the papers?*"

Vidor was shocked. He had been so engrossed in his script problems that he hadn't heard of the passing of the lovely comedienne. As he contemplated the untimely death of Miss Normand, Thalberg leaned across Mannix and whispered to Vidor, "Too many murders."

Vidor looked at him in astonishment. "The public won't accept it," Thalberg added, and the director realized he was talking about *Billy the Kid*.

The funeral was concluded, and the famous mourners returned to their cars and departed. As the M-G-M limousine began its drive back to Culver City, Thalberg inquired, "Was Sheriff Pat Garrett his friend during the time of the last five murders?" The story conference continued all the way back to the studio. Thalberg emerged from the car and hurried up the steps to his office. "I'll call you," he said to Vidor and Stallings.

Thalberg's absorption with the film-making process was demonstrated one evening as he was leaving the studio at seven o'clock, having promised Norma to be home early for dinner. As he was passing the line of offices known as Directors' Row, he heard angry and profane shouting coming from one of the rooms. He went inside and found a director, Chuck Reisner, and gag man Robert Hopkins embroiled in a heated argument over a Marie Dressler-Polly Moran script.

"Boys, boys!" Thalberg chided. "You've got to tone down your language. We've got girl cutters working here at night. Now what is this all about?"

Reisner and Hopkins began outlining their dispute over the movie plot. Thalberg became so engrossed he thrashed out the problem with them for three hours.

14

Thalberg's great attraction of 1932 was *Grand Hotel*, with which he inaugurated the era of the all-star cast. Until that time, studios had rarely placed more than two of its important stars in a single picture. Thalberg reasoned that the Depression-struck box office needed a jolt with a cast full of stars, and Vicki Baum's multi-character novel and play provided the ideal vehicle.

Everyone anticipated fireworks with such diverse temperaments

Lionel Barrymore, Joan Crawford, Edmund Goulding, Lewis Stone, John Barrymore, Wallace Beery, between scenes of Grand Hotel as Greta Garbo, the Barrymore brothers, Joan Crawford and Wallace Beery working in the same picture, but none developed. The stars seemed anxious to outdo each other in cooperation and cordiality. John Barrymore was on his best behavior and he charmed Garbo. When they were introduced by the director, Edmund Goulding, Barrymore kissed her hand in courtly style and said, "My wife and I think you the loveliest woman in the world."

After a particularly difficult scene, Garbo surprised the crew by impulsively kissing Barrymore and announcing to all, "You have no idea what it means to me to play opposite so perfect an artist."

Garbo even dropped her reserve to say to Miss Crawford: "I'm so sorry we are not working together. What a pity, eh? Our first picture together and not one scene."

Grand Hotel won the Academy award for best picture of 1931–32 and performed admirably at the box office. Its total cost, including distribution charges, was $700,000, and it returned rentals of $2,594,-000. The film was another superb achievement for Irving Thalberg,

contributing anew to his desire for a bigger share of the profits he was providing. Nick Schenck balked at providing any more money from Loew's, and he turned the matter over to Mayer.

Mayer tried to reason with Thalberg, but the younger man was adamant; he wanted more money. Once again Mayer was forced to shave his own share of his group's 20 percent cut of the M-G-M profits. This time he made a concession that put him and Irving on an equal basis: both would receive 37½ percent. Mayer was extremely vexed; "That boy is money-mad," he grumbled.

But Mayer still prized Thalberg's unparalleled talent as head of production and did what he could to help him. In one instance, Mayer's help was of enormous value.

Thalberg had trusted a business agent to prepare his income tax, and the agent by some mistaken reasoning had failed to report as income a substantial share of Thalberg's share of the M-G-M's profits. The fault was not Thalberg's but he bore the legal responsibility. The Internal Revenue service made an investigation and recommended prosecution.

Thalberg was thunderstruck. He felt morally innocent of the charges, but the government had the facts to convict him and send him to prison. Through his trust in the business agent he had placed himself in the position where his entire career and reputation could be wiped out.

He confessed his plight to Mayer. The older man was shaken by the enormity of the consequences. But once before—in the threatened merger with Fox—Mayer had proved that his dabbling in Republican politics had not been wasted. Perhaps he could make it work again.

Mayer secured an appointment with President Hoover at the White House. Mayer outlined the circumstances and pleaded: "Mr. President, this boy did wrong, and he admits it. But he didn't mean to. Putting him in prison would mean endless shame for his beautiful family. If he were gone, his loss would be a serious blow to our studio, which is the biggest in the industry. The government would lose, too, because he pays one of the biggest income taxes in the country. I beg of you, Mr. President, spare this boy. He is willing to pay all the penalties the government demands. And by sparing him you will assure him a productive life for himself and for M-G-M and the entire industry. He deserves this. He is one of the fine, upstanding leaders of our

Thalberg collects his second best-picture award, for Grand Hotel. *With him: Harry Rapf, Lionel Barrymore, Mary Pickford*

community, and putting him in prison would be a tremendous shock to Hollywood and the nation."

As was generally the case, the Mayer persuasion worked. President Hoover directed Internal Revenue to settle the Thalberg case without prosecution and without publicity.

15

The brothers Barrymore did not always perform together with amiability. Thalberg first teamed them in *Arsene Lupin*, in which John played the wily French thief and Lionel was his detective nemesis. John was inevitably letter-perfect in his dialogue, but Lionel had difficulty remembering his. John enjoyed teasing his brother with a comment: "Well, I've learned my lines, Lionel, now you can learn yours." This served to make the older brother more irritated and forgetful, and the director, Jack Conway, complained, "Is there any law against two Barrymores knowing their lines at the same time?" Sometimes Lionel wandered from the written dialogue during a scene, and John was forced to alter his lines in order to maintain a dialogue.

"He's changing his lines!" Lionel roared. "He's giving me the wrong cues!" John never disclosed that he had done so to cover up for his brother.

The fortuitous coupling of the two Barrymores in *Arsene Lupin* and *Grand Hotel* prompted Thalberg to the showmanly move of combining them with their sister Ethel for the first time in their careers. He telephoned Miss Barrymore in New York, where she was playing *The Twelve Pound Look* in vaudeville. Would she be interested in appearing with her brothers in a film based on Rasputin's evil influence on the Russian rulers, Nicholas and Alexandra? The actress said she would, provided she could finish the picture in time to return to Broadway for a play in the fall.

The task of fashioning the script to fit three bravura players befell Thalberg's favorite trouble-shooter, Charles MacArthur. He was hampered from the start. Thalberg insisted on a sympathetic treatment of the royal couple, to be played by Ralph Morgan and Miss Barrymore.

"But how can you do that, Irving?" MacArthur demanded. "The Romanoffs kicked your people around for three hundred years. Now you're trying to make a hero out of that stupid Nicholas."

"The czarina was the granddaughter of Queen Victoria," said Thalberg in a matter-of-fact tone, "and fifty percent of our foreign receipts come from England. I am not going to risk harming our English market because I'm a Jew. It wouldn't be fair to the stockholders."

MacArthur followed instructions and portrayed Nicholas as a weak but well-meaning ruler and Alexandra as a kindly woman who fell under the sway of Rasputin because of his miraculous cure of her son. John Barrymore became Prince Chegodieff, a disguised version of the real-life slayer of Rasputin, Prince Felix Yousepoff.* Rasputin was presented as his rascally, debauched self, and hence Lionel drew the best role in the film.

Everyone expected fireworks to result when the three Barrymores joined in a mutual enterprise, and Lionel himself supplied the ominous note in his inquiry: "What poor unlucky and benighted individual is to direct this opus in which all three of us are to act together?"

John provided another notable quote when he met his sister at the Pasadena railroad station. Reporters asked Ethel if she expected to be nervous while working with two such veteran scene stealers. "You need not worry about Mrs. Colt," John interjected. "Our sister Ethel will be standing right before the camera—in front of us."

The predictions of trouble were borne out. Charles Brabin began directing *Rasputin*, but his pace of shooting was so slow that Thalberg removed him. The new director was Richard Boleslavsky, a Pole who had acted at the Moscow Art Theater in Imperial times. Because of Ethel's deadline, the film had started without a finished script, and MacArthur supplied new pages as the shooting progressed. This irritated the Barrymores, especially Lionel, who was slow to learn his lines. Despite Thalberg's decorous attitude toward the Romanoffs, Miss Barrymore objected to the portrayal of the Empress and reminded him, "I knew Her Majesty personally."

John realized that his brother had the showier role, and he strived to keep up with Lionel by any means possible. At the conclusion of one of Lionel's meaty scenes, John put his hand on Lionel's arm, an ancient technique for an actor to summon attention to himself. Lionel knew what his younger brother was attempting, and he tried to shrug off the grasp, but to no avail. Lionel excused himself from the scene and went to a telephone outside the stage. He called the *Rasputin* set and asked for Boleslavsky.

"Will you kindly instruct Mr. John Barrymore to keep his hands off me lest at the close of this scene I be tempted to lay one on him," said Lionel.

Boleslavsky made a tactful suggestion to John, who smiled and continued the scene. *Rasputin and the Empress,* as it was finally called, was finished in four months at a cost of a million dollars. The

* The disguise was not sufficient to prevent Yousepoff and his wife from winning a costly libel settlement from M-G-M.

On the Rasputin *set: John and Ethel Barrymore and Ralph Morgan (back to camera)*

difficulties in its filming were reflected in its critical and popular reception. The reviews were less than cordial, and the film produced a slight loss. But Thalberg considered it a worthy risk, and he had no regrets.

16

For three years Irving Thalberg had lavished his energies on the creation of a new art form—the sound motion picture—ignoring intimations of his own mortality. Then on Labor Day of 1932 came the event that shattered his calm by bringing death as close to him as it had ever come.

He had not approved of Paul Bern's marriage to Jean Harlow, yet he did not interfere; his natural reserve would not permit him to dictate the personal life of an associate, even one as intimate as Bern. Thalberg was too engrossed in the never-ending problems of M-G-M to consider the possible consequences of the strange union between his intellectual adviser and the studio's sexiest star. Nor did Thalberg pause to inquire into the motives of the pair. For Bern, marrying Jean Harlow meant a public proclamation of the role he had long played: the wooer of voluptuous women. To Harlow, marriage meant an escape from her grasping stepfather and the stifling presence of her mother. Jean remained profoundly touched by Bern's devotion to her. When a friend told her that Bern had been praising her spiritual qualities, she exulted, "You mean he loves me for something else? Thank God! I'm sick of sex."

They were married in July of 1932, a month after the release of *Red-Headed Woman* had assured Jean's future in films. Norma and Irving attended the ceremony and posed smilingly with Paul and Jean and her parents at the wedding cake. News accounts noted that at forty-two, Bern was exactly twice as old as his bride.

A month after the marriage, Jean learned for the first time why Paul had made no overtures to sex: he had a physical deficiency that made intercourse impossible. It was a secret that he had successfully kept from his closest friends; the only person who knew was the studio doctor, who had told him that treatment of his condition would have been unavailing. It was a frightful blow to Jean, yet it did not immediately destroy the marriage. In fact, they continued to live together in Bern's neo-Gothic house in Benedict Canyon and to outward appearances they were completely happy.

And yet, his friends recalled afterward, Bern seemed to have been giving indications of what was to follow. Once he told Willis Goldbeck that his brothers had committed suicide, and he added, "If the time ever comes when I'm no longer useful, I'd do it, too." One day he remarked to Albert Lewin, "I never believed it possible that Jean could be so good to me. If I died tomorrow, I would die happy."

Three days later, Norma and Irving were entertaining Sam and Frances Goldwyn and Minna Wallis for a holiday brunch beside the pool at the Santa Monica house. It was a hot September morning, and crowds were beginning to fill the beach outside the Thalberg wall. The butler emerged from the house and announced that Mr. Thalberg was wanted on the telephone. Mr. Mayer was calling.

When Irving returned to his guests, his face was white.

"My God! Paul Bern is dead!" he declared.

Thalberg instructed Norma to locate Howard Strickling, the studio's publicity chief, and tell him to hurry to the Bern house. Thalberg drove to Benedict Canyon with Mayer, who lived a short distance down the beach.

Norma telephoned Strickling, and he raced to the honeymoon home of Paul and Jean. En route he passed the limousine of Mayer, who stopped and told Strickling what had happened: Bern's butler had discovered the nude body in the bathroom that morning. Bern had been shot in the head, and the pistol lay at his side. Jean was not in the house; she had spent the night at her mother's. Mayer declared that he had commandeered the suicide note lest it bring scandal to the studio family. Strickling convinced him of the error of withholding evidence, and they returned to the Bern house to hand the police the note. It read:

Dearest dear:
  Unfortunately this is the only way to make good the frightful wrong I have done you and to wipe out my abject humiliation. You understand that last night was only a comedy.
            Paul

Thalberg seemed oddly unemotional as he watched the mounting turmoil at the Bern house. Police and reporters were swarming about

Newlyweds Jean Harlow and Paul Bern at the cake with the Thalbergs and her mother and stepfather

and at one point the suicide note disappeared again—into the pocket of a *Herald-Express* reporter; Strickling retrieved it once more. Thalberg drew Strickling aside and told him: "Paul can't be helped now; Jean is the one who needs protection."

Strickling hurried to the home of Jean's mother and her stepfather, Marino Bello. The publicity chief found reporters already stationed outside the home. Inside, he discovered Jean huddled frightenedly on a bed; her mother was on another bed next to her. He told Jean he could help her only if she told him everything she knew. She poured out the story of Bern's impotence, but declared that she had still loved him deeply. He had given no indication of suicide, she said, and she had come to her mother's house for the weekend only because her stepfather had gone on a fishing trip with Clark Gable.

Now Strickling had another urgent concern. He realized what a scandal was brewing and how the newspapers would pounce upon the fact that Jean's co-star, the great Gable, had been friendly enough to go fishing with her stepfather. Even though a Gable-Harlow romance had not developed during the recent filming of *Red Dust*, reporters could easily have made the inference and introduced Gable's name into the case. That had to be prevented.

The holiday had scattered M-G-M's publicity personnel, and Strickling was unable to reach any of his aides by telephone. Finally he located a pair of sisters who worked in the department, and he assigned them to the two intersections by which the Bello home could be reached. Their instructions were to keep a vigil for the car bearing Gable and Bello; if the two men arrived, Gable was to be warned not to accompany Jean's stepfather to the house.

The stakeout produced results. The fishermen returned from their journey and were prevented from blundering into the mass of reporters outside the Bello house. Gable returned to his own home, and Bello climbed his back fence to enter the house without detection. But the excitable Bello became incensed when he realized that his valuable stepdaughter might be accused of wrongdoing in connection with Bern's suicide. He stormed outside and delivered an oration to the eager reporters, denouncing innuendo against Jean that had not yet been printed.

This added more material to Hollywood's biggest scandal in years. The faint air of mystery concerning Bern's past was exploited to a vast degree, and Jean's hard road to success was reviewed again and again. Comments were sought from everyone associated with the pair.

"Everyone's talking too much," said Thalberg concernedly. "Let Howard do the talking."

But even with Strickling as the official spokesman for the studio, the headlines continued. The coroner's inquest called most of the M-G-M executives to testify, among them Thalberg. He said that he knew of no other note besides the one that had been found, that he was privy to nothing in the marital affairs of Bern and his famous wife that might have caused the suicide.

The scandal continued, and although nothing was uncovered to implicate Jean, it appeared that her career was in real danger. To both Mayer and Thalberg, the memory was still fresh of how Fatty

Irving Thalberg testifies at the coroner's inquest into the death of Paul Bern

Arbuckle had been destroyed in films by rape-death charges, even though he was eventually acquitted.

A meeting was called. Mayer and Thalberg were joined by Bernie Hyman, Frances Marion, Adela Rogers St. Johns and Howard Strickling. They discussed how Jean Harlow might be presented in a better light to the public. All agreed that it should be done by a series of articles Mrs. St. Johns would write for the Hearst press. William Randolph Hearst still sponsored the films of Marion Davies at M-G-M, and he could be counted as an ally in the campaign to save Jean Harlow from destruction. The need was urgent. *Red Dust* was scheduled for release in a couple of months, and it represented a large investment for the studio. In addition, Harlow's future value to the studio was incalculable.

Mayer and Thalberg decided to take their problem to Hearst himself. When they met with him, he offered his own solution in his high-pitched voice: "Shut up! Everybody shut up! If you shut up, nobody will have anything to say about this case, and it will blow away."

His advice was heeded, and the St. Johns articles were canceled. With the news sources dried up, the scandal abated, and the reading public turned attention to the Hoover-Roosevelt presidential campaign, the Lindbergh kidnaping and other news stories.

During the early period of the scandal, Thalberg's attitude seemed to be one of cold concern for the future of Harlow's career. But at Paul Bern's funeral, the enormity of his loss finally struck him. Thalberg wept throughout the ceremony. Not only had he lost his intellectual mentor. He had been reminded with piercing abruptness of the time limit that had been placed on his own life.

17

Irving Thalberg suffered moods of depression in the weeks following Paul Bern's death. It was a rare and dangerous mood for Thalberg, whose glowing optimism had propelled him through the exhilarating years of the talkies. Now he paused for introspection, and the pragmatism of his early years could not rouse him from black despair.

"What's it all for?" he muttered to one of his closest associates. "Why the hell am I killing myself so Mayer and Schenck can get rich and fat?"

The associate was greatly concerned, because Thalberg had never before revealed himself so darkly. As part of an industry-wide campaign to restore prosperity to the studios, he had taken a cut of 35 percent in salary, and he noted that those with big holdings of Loew's stock did not make similar sacrifices. Thalberg spent days brooding over his situation, and at length he arrived at his decision. He told Mayer he was sick and wanted to be relieved of his position as head of production.

The hierarchy of Loew's was thunderstruck. There had never been an M-G-M without Irving Thalberg as its creative head; he was as much a symbol of the studio's prestige as Leo the Lion. If Thalberg were to defect to another company—and any studio would pay him royally to do so—M-G-M would suffer a damaging blow.

Nicholas Schenck hurried to California. Mayer told him that he believed Thalberg had grown big-headed from the years of praise.

Whatever the cause, Thalberg was firm: he wanted to be released from his contract so he could go away for a year and contemplate his future. Schenck was equally firm: Thalberg had a contract that extended five more years and he would be held to it.

It became a clash of two indomitable wills: Nick Schenck, the iron-hard commander of the Loew's empire, a man accustomed to enforcing his decisions; Irving Thalberg, the frail, doomed production genius whose only support for his arguments was the fact that he alone had supplied the spark for M-G-M's greatness. The two men became violent in their tirades against each other, and threats filled the air of Thalberg's bedroom.

"Oh, it was hell!" Louis Mayer recalled later. The exchanges became so vituperative that he and Rubin left the room.

When Schenck threatened a law suit, Thalberg merely laughed. Obviously he wasn't bluffing. After lengthy conferences, Schenck arrived at a formula to placate Thalberg. Thalberg was to be allowed to purchase over a period of years one hundred thousand shares of Loew's stock at a cost far lower than the market price. Mayer was granted the right to buy eighty thousand shares under the same terms.

Thalberg was satisfied. His share of the stock, plus his salary and share of the profits, would assure millions for himself and his family. Norma and his parents and his son Irving, now a healthy one-year-old, would be able to live comfortably if he should die.

Louis Mayer was not as content. It was true that Irving's recalcitrance had resulted in a windfall for Mayer—eighty thousand shares of Loew's stock at a bargain rate. But the terms of the settlement damaged Mayer's ego. For the first time in his dealings with Loew's, he had drawn lesser terms than his young protégé. That was an unacceptable position for Mayer, who remained Thalberg's superior.

Their relationship had deteriorated during the heated wrangles. More than once the younger man had directed his scorn at Mayer, accusing him of being a mere figurehead, a man who knew nothing of the intricacies of producing film entertainment. Mayer was deeply hurt. He had long maintained a fatherly attitude toward the youth he had hired on Mission Road. Now, in the flush of his enormous success, Thalberg had turned on him and reviled him. The deed was all the more painful because it had been done in the presence of Nick Schenck. Mayer now viewed Thalberg in a different light. Mayer

considered him to be an ungrateful young man who thought more of amassing riches than of furthering the glory of Metro-Goldwyn-Mayer. Irving had won this time, because of his blind stubbornness. But Mayer knew his own strength, and he was certain that his time would come.

It came sooner than he expected. Content with his new terms, Thalberg returned to his duties at M-G-M. But the intensity of the recent clash had taken its toll, and in late December of 1932, he collapsed. Not since 1924 had he been so gravely ill, and he feared the end had

come. Doctors disclosed that his weak heart had been further damaged.

Once again Nick Schenck rushed to California at Mayer's urging.
They tried to see Irving but were told he could not be disturbed.
Now Schenck and Mayer were faced with the issue that had long
caused them great concern: what to do if Thalberg were removed
from M-G-M. Mayer offered a partial solution: Why not hire David
O. Selznick?

Mayer had not always been so fond of Selznick. When Thalberg
hired Selznick as a two-hundred-dollar-a-week assistant story editor
in 1924, Mayer objected. He detested David's father, the pioneering
Lewis J. Selznick, and wanted no competitor's son at his studio. But
Thalberg prevailed, and Selznick became a busy, energetic production
assistant. His consuming ambition brought him in conflict with the
substructure of M-G-M power. In an argument during the filming
of *White Shadows of the South Seas*, Hunt Stromberg considered
himself insulted by young Selznick. Thalberg instructed Selznick:
"Either apologize to Hunt or—" "I'm packed," replied Selznick.

Three years younger than Thalberg, Selznick went on to Paramount
and RKO and became a prodigy himself. As vice-president in charge
of RKO production, he was responsible for such films as *A Bill of
Divorcement, King Kong, Lost Squadron, What Price Hollywood?*
and *Of Human Bondage*. Meanwhile he had married Irene Mayer.

At first Mayer did not approve of the union. But the marriage
reconciled him to Lewis J. Selznick, and the two patriarchs rejoiced
in the birth of a grandchild in 1932. Mayer was proud of his son-
in-law's accomplishments at RKO, and he began dreaming of a dynasty
at M-G-M, with David carrying on the studio after the Mayer command was relinquished. Nick Schenck saw the value in bringing
Selznick into the company, and negotiations began. Selznick still clung
to his independence and was reluctant to go to work for his father-in-
law. But the lure was too strong: $4000 a week for a two-year term,
his own independent unit with call on any stars, directors or writers
he wanted. Selznick accepted.

Now Mayer faced something he dreaded: breaking the news to
Irving.

The reaction was even more violent than Mayer had feared. Thalberg was in a rage. He believed himself to have been betrayed by

Schenck, and especially by Mayer. Why had they chosen a time when he was weak and ill to bring Mayer's son-in-law into the studio? To Thalberg the plot was transparent—the two men sought to supplant him with a relative. For the first time in the history of M-G-M, Thalberg was no longer in complete charge of the studio's production. His authority had been eroded by creation of an independent unit, and this had been accomplished behind his back! Mayer fled from the house in the face of Thalberg's fury.

Thalberg began to recover. Doctors told him his condition had not been as dire as they first suspected. As his strength returned, he felt the need to get away and refresh his spirit before resuming his command of the studio. He and Norma proposed a trip to their close friends, Helen Hayes and Charles MacArthur. Accompanied by young Irving and little Mary MacArthur, they would take a boat through the Panama Canal to New York, see the latest shows and then sail off for a European vacation. The MacArthurs were in hearty accord with the plan.

Mayer disapproved of the Thalberg-MacArthur journey. He felt that Thalberg was well enough to return to the studio and resume charge of production. Thalberg ignored his pleas. Passage was booked for the two families on the S.S. *California*, leaving San Pedro for New York. Mayer began to feel regrets about his attitude toward Thalberg, and in a rare display of humility he dispatched a letter on February 1933. It began:

> Dear Irving,
>   I cannot permit you to go away to Europe without expressing to you my regret that our last conference had to end in a loss of temper, particularly on my part. It has always been my desire to make things as comfortable and pleasant for you as I know how, and I stayed away from you while you were ill because I knew if I saw you it was inevitable that we would touch on business, and this I did not want to do until you were strong again. . . .

The letter blamed "so-called friends" for stirring up friction in their ten-year friendship. Mayer added that he had striven in the "show must go on" tradition to carry on in Thalberg's absence; that he felt the young man's absence keenly and had done nothing against

Thalberg's interest; that he regretted any suspicions Thalberg harbored against him; that he prayed for Thalberg's quick recovery and return to their film-making partnership. Said Mayer: "I assure you I will go on loving you to the end."

Thalberg responded in kind. Two days later he addressed his own regrets to Mayer: "For any words that I may have used that aroused bitterness in you, I am truly sorry and I apologize." He also assailed the false friends who caused dissension between the two partners, but he pointed out the deep hurt he had sustained because the principles upon which their enterprise had been founded were not defended by his three closest friends—presumably Mayer, Schenck and Rubin. Thalberg coolly offered his "sympathy, understanding and good wishes in the task you are undertaking; and no one more than myself would enjoy your success, for your own sake even more than for the sake of the company." He ended with the wish to see Mayer before his departure and the hope they could part "as good personal friends, if not better, than ever before."

Polite, written words between two men who had been in daily contact with each other for a decade. The courtesies masked the bitterness that could never be erased. Even before his departure Thalberg suspected that Mayer was trying to sabotage the trip. As the time for sailing grew closer, Helen Hayes was still involved in filming *White Sister* with Clark Gable. Thalberg was convinced that Mayer was prolonging the shooting to interfere with his departure. Production was scheduled to end on the night of the sailing, and the Thalbergs and MacArthur waited anxiously on shipboard. Minutes before the gangplank was to be lifted, a limousine arrived on the dock with an escort of siren-screaming motorcycles. Still clad in her nun's habit, Miss Hayes leaped from the car and hurried on board.

The nightmarish encounters with Mayer and Schenck seemed distant as Thalberg rested in the tropical sun and enjoyed the stimulating company of Charlie MacArthur. The two families traveled in utmost comfort with staffs that included nurses for the children, maids for the actress-wives and a manservant whose principal function was to make mint juleps for MacArthur. There was pleasant badinage between the MacArthurs and the Thalbergs, and Irving chided Helen for having brought five hundred dollars in cash. He professed to be an expert in how the rich travel, and he counseled her: "It is not good style to be handing out currency all the time; you should pay with checks."

It was March of 1933, and as the S.S. *California* steamed through the Panama Canal and into the Caribbean, momentous events were happening in the United States. The new president, Franklin D. Roosevelt, declared a bank holiday. "And how does my cash look to you now?" Miss Hayes said gloatingly as the boat docked in Havana. "You wouldn't be able to buy a postcard without it."

The party continued on to New York, where the two couples became enmeshed in a series of parties to fete their departure to Europe. The return to the United States occasioned a revival of Thalberg's anxiety. A political conservative, he was upset by the bold moves of the new President. The bank holiday had thrown Hollywood into a turmoil, and the unrest was compounded by a ruinous earthquake that struck Los Angeles a week after the inauguration. Thalberg feared that Schenck would prevail upon him to return to the studio and help restore order.

One night in Manhattan the MacArthurs were enjoying a *bon voyage* party being hosted by the Harold Talberts. In the midst of the festivities, Miss Hayes was summoned to the telephone. The voice was unmistakably that of Irving Thalberg.

"Listen, Helen," he said earnestly, "I can get us passage on the *Conte de Savoia* tomorrow morning. Let's go. Let's get out of this town."

"But—" the actress replied. "I must ask Charlie."

"Don't ask Charlie," said Thalberg. "Make up your own mind for a change."

"Oh, Irving, it sounds so tempting," she admitted. "I like unplanned things. But I really must ask Charlie." She located MacArthur in the party crowd and told him the proposition. He was incensed and grabbed the telephone from his wife.

"What the hell kind of hanky-panky is this?" he demanded of Thalberg. "Are you trying to get around me? You know Helen is soft. She'll do anything anybody asks."

Thalberg repeated his proposal, but MacArthur's Scottish stubbornness held fast. "You go on with Norma," he said to Thalberg. "We're not ready to leave yet."

But then Miss Hayes came on the telephone and said, "We'll go."

The Thalbergs embark from San Pedro

She spent the night packing, and a truck arrived in early morning for the trunks. She and MacArthur hurried to the dock to board the *Conte de Savoia* and join the Thalbergs. Since no one knew of their departure, there was no farewell delegation. So the Thalbergs and the MacArthurs chose strangers on the dockside and waved fervent farewells to them.

The departure again freed Thalberg from the plight of M-G-M, but he was soon to be faced with other concerns. After a spree with the MacArthurs in Paris, the Thalbergs departed for Bad Nauheim. But this time he did not find the tranquillity he had learned to expect there. Germany was caught up in the disease of Naziism, and Thalberg was witness to ugly incidents of anti-Semitism. He was shaken by the experience.

The Thalbergs and MacArthurs were reunited at Eden Roc, where Irving puzzled over the violence he had seen at Bad Nauheim. Then one night at an hour past midnight, the MacArthurs heard a pounding at their hotel-room door. It was Norma.

"Charlie, come quick," she said. "Irving's sick."

Both MacArthurs rushed down the hall to the Thalberg suite, and they found Irving in bed, his face waxen and translucent. He held in his hand a cable from Louis Mayer. It told the news that he had been relieved of his duties as head of M-G-M production.

"I did this for you," said Mayer.

V

CONCLUSION 1933–1936

He's too good to last. The lamb doesn't lie down with the lion for long.

—*Charles MacArthur*

I

Irving Thalberg returned from Europe in a new, unaccustomed guise. He remained the most respected film maker in the Hollywood industry, but he was a general without an army. For the first time in his adult life, he did not have the vast resources of a studio awaiting his return. The absence of such power bewildered and angered him, and yet he found the freedom exhilarating. He was at last afforded the luxury he had often dreamed of: the time to reflect and plan, without having to feed the insatiable demand by the M-G-M distribution branch for more and more films to put into the theaters. The wresting away of his power over M-G-M production remained in his mind a perfidious event, especially since it had been accomplished in the Mayer-Schenck tradition—without his knowledge or consent. But perhaps—the teachings of William James were taking hold once more —it was for the best. The pursuit of a full production schedule had brought him, he believed, to the threshold of death. If he could be spared for only a few more years, in defiance of the doctors' prognosis, he might be able to do some of the things he had long yearned to do with films. And those few extra years would allow him the infinite pleasure of watching his son grow into boyhood.

He looked a different man when he arrived with Norma and little Irving in New York on July 18, 1933. Reporters and photographers who clambered aboard the S.S. *Majestic* to greet the famous pair noted that Thalberg for the first time in his transatlantic comings and goings looked his age. The addition of several pounds had taken away his boyish appearance and the lines under his eyes gave him the character of a thirty-four-year-old man of importance.

Thalberg announced that he had no plans for the future, which was true. But Nick Schenck had formulated a plan which he hoped would keep the former production chief fruitful and happy. He invited Irving and Norma to spend a week at his Long Island home, and they accepted. Surprisingly, Thalberg displayed not the slightest rancor over what had been done in his absence. He seemed to accept Schenck's explanation that the management of Loew's owed it to the stockholders to make sure there would be a smooth, consistent flow of movies to the marketplace. Since Thalberg was physically incapable of overseeing the entire output, another system had to be devised. There was never a thought of replacing Thalberg, Schenck insisted; such a genius as Irving was irreplaceable. So the authority over M-G-M production had to be widened and extended.

Schenck's arguments seemed to placate Thalberg, and the unpleasantness in Hollywood the previous year became like a half-forgotten dream. The Loew's president made his proposal: Thalberg would head his own, completely autonomous unit; he would have complete freedom to make use of any talent he wanted, as before; instead of supervising all of the studio product, big and small, he could concentrate on handcrafting a few films each year. The terms were hard to resist, especially when the future entailed a more leisurely work pace with no change in his immense salary and participation in profits. Thalberg agreed to the arrangement.

Thalberg arrived back in Culver City on August 19, having been absent from the studio for almost nine months. He and Norma went through the motions of posing for smiling welcome-home photographs with Louis Mayer. But Thalberg's handshake was cold. Events had turned Hollywood's greatest partnership into a forced union beset with distrust.

As he began to look around the studio that he and Mayer had built, Thalberg realized the enormity of what had happened to him.

Welcome home

He learned that no sooner had he left for Europe than Schenck had descended on the studio with a proposal for the men who had for years worked under the aegis of Irving Thalberg.

Schenck, with the support of Louis Mayer, made the proposition to each of Thalberg's associate producers: "We don't know when or if Irving is coming back. When he does come back, God willing, Louie and I want to conserve his health, to relieve him of the terrible burden of running all of the studio's production. So we are breaking the studio up into autonomous units, and we're asking you men to head the units. You will be full-fledged producers, and you will get screen credit for the films you produce. When Irving comes back, he will have his own unit, too."

The opportunity was too tempting to resist. Egos that had long languished in the shade of the mighty Thalberg now had a chance to shine on their own. The Schenck-Mayer proposal seemed perfectly logical; the company had to maintain production, Thalberg or no Thalberg. All of his associates accepted.

All except Albert Lewin. "I'm flattered," he admitted, "but I couldn't make a decision without talking to Irving. Let me take a leave of absence; I'll do it without pay. I'll go to Europe for a long vacation, and when Irving and I both come back, then I'll let you know."

Lewin was the only Thalberg man waiting when the onetime chief returned to the studio. The former college professor told him of the management's offer. "Why didn't you take it?" Thalberg asked.

"Because I didn't want to make a decision before I talked to you," said Lewin. "Either way it's all right—take my own unit or stay with you."

"Well, Al," Thalberg said thoughtfully, "I think it's better for you to have your own unit. But if you were to ask me what I'd prefer, I'd like you to remain."

The diminutive Lewin grinned broadly. "I was hoping you'd ask me," he admitted.

They began discussing the new setup, and Thalberg said he would give Lewin credit on the screen as a producer. "Thanks, anyway," said Lewin, "but I couldn't take it. Everybody will know they're your pictures. I'd feel awfully foolish taking credit for them."

"Well, I'm not going to put *my* name on them," said Thalberg. "So we'll call you associate producer. Okay?"

"Okay," said Lewin. And so Irving Thalberg, who had once commanded the entire personnel of Metro-Goldwyn-Mayer studio, started his new enterprise with a staff of one.

In a gesture of largess, Mayer had ordered new quarters for Thalberg's return. Cedric Gibbons had been commissioned to redecorate the bungalow that Cecil B. De Mille had occupied during his stay at M-G-M. Thalberg's new office was done in grandiose style with high, beamed ceiling, massive fireplace, oversized, pigskin-covered chairs and a huge desk covered with a two-inch-thick glass.

Lewin detected Thalberg's dismay at the sight of the office. "Irving, you haven't deceived me; you don't like this," said his associate.

Thalberg smiled faintly. "To tell the truth, I'm superstitious," he said. "Every time you put on the dog, it's the beginning of the end. We had a lot of success in that lousy little office over there on Washington Boulevard."

Two small-sized men in the enormous office: the poignancy of Thalberg's isolation seemed to be underscored. After the initial effusions that greeted his return, the men who had learned film making under his tutelage stayed away; they had their own ambitions to further. His stars and directors were enmeshed in their own careers and private lives. Even the writers didn't call; their relationships to Thalberg had always been professional, never personal, and there was no reason to come around and wish him well.

It was the time of Thalberg's Valley Forge, Lewin recalled later. The hurt struck deep, but he mentioned it to no one. Not even Al Lewin. The two men sat alone together, facing each other across the lunch table and discussing their plans amid the awesome quiet of the huge room.

As he viewed what had happened to the studio in his absence, Thalberg became more and more disheartened. Louis Mayer had extended his control to every department of the studio, and Thalberg felt that the *esprit* that he had taken such pains to establish over a period of years had been shattered. The respect for high standards of film making, the constant striving to inject new quality into the product—all this had been swept away, Thalberg believed.

Thalberg made no representations to Mayer. He voiced his feelings in a way that was, for Thalberg, most unusual. After shunning publicity throughout his career, he allowed his by-line to appear over an article in *The Saturday Evening Post* of November 4, 1933. Co-authored with Hugh Weir, the story was titled "Why Motion Pictures Cost So Much."

Thalberg began his treatise by pointing out that motion picture companies had not been very profitable during the recent, Depression years. Indeed, the shuttered theaters in many cities offered evidence that money was saved by closing the houses rather than trying to operate them. So the high cost of movies could not be attributed to profit-taking "because in many cases there aren't any profits."

The same was true of other industries, he continued, but the difference was that they have found ways to cut down expenditures in stresssful time. The film industry had not. The producers could not lower prices to theater men, and the theater men could not cut admission costs. So the economy was made in production costs, and this, Thalberg declared, was "committing economic suicide."

Said he: "A bad picture, or even a fairly good picture which is not so good as it should be, may do the company which puts it out many times as much harm as the cost of the picture itself. So, knowing all this, usually from bitter experience, the intelligent producer will go on experimenting—which in pictures means going on spending—until he believes in his own mind that he has made the best possible product."

Thalberg cited the example of *The Sin of Madelon Claudet*. Judicious retakes helped change bathos to pathos and saved the career of "one of the screen's most remarkable personalities," Helen Hayes.

He added: "It is hard to explain a situation like that to a banker. It is hard, as a matter of fact, to explain the whole motion picture situation to a banker—or anyone else. For nobody has been able to say definitely whether picture making is really a business or an art. Personally I think it is both.

"It is a business in the sense that it must bring in money at the box office, but it is an art in that it involves, on its devotees, the inexorable demands of creative expression. In short, it is a creative business, dependent, as almost no other business is, on the emotional reaction of its customers.

"It should be conducted with budgets and cost sheets, but it cannot be conducted with blueprints and graphs.

"That is a hard problem for a banker."

Thalberg described the expeditions of financial experts who periodically came to Hollywood in an effort to straighten out the tangled economics of the film business. Inevitably they decried the extravagance they found. Thalberg admitted there was waste in production and in excessive salaries for stars without a proportionate draw. But he produced figures to prove that during the boom years Hollywood's films cost only 7½ percent ($150,000,000) of their annual intake ($2,000,000,000). Even during Depression times, the cost was no more than 10 percent, far lower than most products. Thalberg hinted broadly that the bulk of the profits was taken by the theater owners.

Returning to production costs, Thalberg cited the instance of *Ben-Hur*. M-G-M inherited the film, which had been started with great hopes by the Goldwyn Company.

"But when we began to get the rushes of the picture in Hollywood, and ran them off in the cold, analytical, almost surgical atmosphere of the studio projections room, we decided that they were not getting anywhere at all. It was then that we made the decision, which was considered at the time a crossing of the Rubicon from sanity to insanity. We sent a new director and a new star to Rome. We junked a half-million dollars in completed film and started all over again. It was the only thing to do. . . .

"Well, with a property like that on our hands, we had a duty not only to our stockholders but to theater owners and to the public as well, to make good. A poor picturization of *Ben-Hur* would have cost us in prestige far more than the half million dollars' worth of junked film. The good picturization, which we did finally make, not only earned back the huge sum of money it cost but it built up a goodwill the value of which it is almost impossible to estimate."

The first place to look for the high cost of motion pictures is in the distribution system, Thalberg declared. He observed that the major companies spent about the same money to sell pictures to a relatively small market of theater owners as was spent on the product itself. This was obviously Thalberg's slap at the superstructure of Loew's, which could blame heavy distribution charges for the fact that his share of the profits wasn't larger.

Thalberg argued that Hollywood made too many pictures, and the failures could easily wipe out the profits of the successes. "The curse of the business is this mad effort to force more and more product on the public so as to hide the extravagant cost of the huge distribution machine and to avoid breaking up huge unwieldy theater chains."*

He concluded:

"To continue the present destructive policy of rushing out pictures poorly made, of destroying stars by robbing them of their glamor and their ability to give distinguished performances, of bewildering the best creative efforts of the best writers through forcing them to work on silly material and rushing them on good material, of loading down good pictures with production costs and selling expenses of pictures which nobody wants to see—to continue any such suicidal policy is to continue giving the one inescapable answer to the question of why pictures cost so much, and to invite a condition of public apathy in which there won't be any pictures at all."

Thalberg had delivered his lecture, one which distressed the power circles of the film companies. Now it was time for him to prove himself as a film maker in a totally new role. His first film was a flop.

2

For his first film as an independent producer, Thalberg was anxious to find a vehicle for Norma. He was grateful for her sacrifice in abandoning her career to be with him during his illness and recovery; it was considered dangerous for a star of her magnitude to remain off the screen for a year, as she had. Thalberg wanted to bring her back in glory.

Unfortunately, he developed a fixation that it would be a wise plan to remake *The Green Hat*, which had been a popular novel by Michael Arlen in the 1920s. Thalberg had filmed it as *A Woman of Affairs* with Greta Garbo and John Gilbert in 1929, and it had been one of her most successful silents. But the Depression had intervened, and Americans were more concerned with their own survival rather than the problems of aristocratic Britishers. Thalberg failed to perceive this, and he went ahead with the film, which was to be retitled *Riptide*.

Al Lewin was against it. So was Charlie MacArthur, who was

---

* The theater chains were wrested from the production companies by government anti-trust decree in 1948; distribution charges remain a source of complaint by film makers.

assigned to write a script. MacArthur despaired of being able to breathe life into the hackneyed plot, and he was personally upset by what had happened to Thalberg at M-G-M. MacArthur walked out on the assignment, and the script was completed by Edmund Goulding, who was also to direct. Thalberg chose Robert Montgomery as Norma's co-star and filled the cast with such distinguished Britishers as Herbert Marshall, Mrs. Patrick Campbell, Ralph Forbes and C. Aubrey Smith. *Riptide* was given the production values befitting a Thalberg picture.

The keynote of the public's reception was sounded at the Pasadena preview. During the early part of the film, the august C. Aubrey Smith was required to speak the grandiloquent line: "Ah, this air of old England; presently I shall hear a nightingale."

A member of the audience commented with an overripe Bronx cheer. The theater erupted in laughter. Razzberries punctuated the unreeling of the film, and Thalberg was desolate. His hopes for a stunning comeback by Norma were shattered. And his own reputation was at issue with *Riptide*. He knew that Hollywood dearly loved a failure, and a flop by Thalberg in his first venture with an independent unit would be welcomed by many of those who outwardly wished him well.

Thalberg did what he could to put *Riptide* into more acceptable form, but the basic elements did not permit much tampering. He released the film and steeled himself for the judgment of critics and audiences. The reaction was not highly unfavorable, but *Riptide* attracted little excitement. As anticipated, the Mayer followers were delighted. The Mayer son-in-law, David Selznick, had been performing with spectacular success with his own unit. He borrowed the *Grand Hotel* formula to combine the Barrymore brothers, Marie Dressler, Wallace Beery, Jean Harlow, Lee Tracy and Billie Burke in *Dinner at Eight*, a popular and critical success. Just as ambitious though not as big a hit was *Night Flight* with the Barrymores, Helen Hayes, Clark Gable, Robert Montgomery, Myrna Loy and William Gargan. Then came a Gable-Crawford musical, *Dancing Lady*, which had the distinction of introducing Fred Astaire and Nelson Eddy to the screen; *Viva Villa!* with Wallace Beery as the Mexican revolutionary; *Manhattan Melodrama* with Gable and a team that showed promise—William Powell and Myrna Loy.

Selznick had achieved results in a manner that transcended nepo-

tism, and Mayer was lavish with his praise. Oddly, Thalberg did not resent Selznick's presence at M-G-M; in fact, the two men had become cordial friends. But the Selznick achievement provided even more reason for Thalberg's determination to succeed on his second independent film.

"To hell with art this time," he said. "I'm going to produce a picture that will make money."

He chose a book by Crosbie Garstin, *China Seas*. It was an undistinguished yarn about adventure in pirate waters, but the locale offered excitement. Also, the shipboard drama afforded an intermingling of characters in the *Grand Hotel* vein. Thalberg was able to call on the services of three stars whose careers he had established as production chief: Clark Gable, Jean Harlow and Wallace Beery. For the role of the English girl he chose a newcomer to M-G-M, Rosalind Russell. Tay Garnett was assigned to direct.

During the filming of *China Seas*, Thalberg displayed an anxiety he had never shown before. His visits to sets had always been perfunctory, and he had never interfered with shooting unless the director or actors sought his consultation. But he visited the set of *China Seas* every day, and he often engaged in lengthy conversations with members of the cast.

One day Garnett noticed a business-like conference between Thalberg and one of the actors. When the director ran through a rehearsal of the scene, the actor protested, "That's not the way Irving wants it done."

"Irving is not the director," Garnett snapped, and he continued to direct in his own manner.

Before filming started, Garnett had reached an agreement with Thalberg that he, as director, would have the privilege of assembling the first cut of *China Seas*. But when he ran some of the early sequences one evening, Garnett noticed something awry. "That's not the way I shot it," said the director.

"Mr. Thalberg ordered it that way," explained the cutter.

On the following day, Garnett noticed another serious discussion between Thalberg and an actor. After Thalberg left the stage, the director asked the performer if he had been coached in how to play the scene. "Yes," the actor admitted.

The next day was Sunday, and Garnett telephoned Thalberg at his Santa Monica home. "I've got to see you," said the director.

Robert Montgomery, Norma Shearer, Herbert Marshall, Riptide

"But Tay—I've got a very busy schedule," Thalberg protested.
"There's nothing more important than this," said Garnett.
Thalberg paused. "All right, come on down."

When Garnett arrived at the beach home, he made a bold beginning: "I've heard stories that you were a son of a bitch where directors were concerned."

Thalberg was astonished. "Jesus, Tay—what did I do?" he asked.

Garnett spilled out his complaints about Thalberg's coaching of the actors. He concluded with, "You hired me as director and gave me the best stars in the business and spent a million dollars for production, and then you wouldn't let me direct the picture. I didn't come to M-G-M to be put in there as a stooge."

Thalberg listened to the tirade and then said quietly, "Is that all?"

"No, that isn't all," Garnett continued hotly. "You countermanded my instructions about the cutting. That was in violation of our agreement."

"Yes, you're right," Thalberg admitted. "What do you want to do?"

"I'll help you find another director."

"No, wait a minute, Tay," Thalberg said. "You're absolutely right. I *have* behaved like a son of a bitch. But I'll make a deal with you. Henceforth I will come on the set only for social purposes— I think I should visit the company now and then for morale. But I promise I won't interfere in the playing of scenes. As to the cutting, I'll not only let you assemble scenes, but you can prepare the rough cut as well. And I'll make no changes in the film without consulting you."

Garnett's anger was assuaged, and the two men parted with an agreement on future conduct of the filming. Thalberg remained true to his word.

China Seas proved immensely popular, as Thalberg had anticipated. It demonstrated to Hollywood that he was still capable of turning out films with a box-office potential.

3

With *The Barretts of Wimpole Street*, Thalberg demonstrated he had not lost his capacity for making films of quality. He had admired the play which had proved a splendid vehicle for Katharine Cornell,

Gable, Harlow and Beery talk with Tay Garnett (under camera) on set of China Seas

and he saw the role of Elizabeth Barrett Browning as ideal for Norma. She had been through her period of playing racy parts, and her husband felt she should return to enacting characters with dignity.

In his eagerness for Norma to portray Mrs. Browning, Thalberg came into conflict with a formidable foe: William Randolph Hearst. The publisher believed that *The Barretts of Wimpole Street* was a perfect screen subject for Marion Davies, and he asked M-G-M to allow her to make it for their Cosmopolitan Pictures. Louis Mayer was caught in the middle between his onetime partner and the vastly powerful Hearst. Mayer realized that Miss Shearer was a more likely candidate for *Barretts*. Hearst, who was unaccustomed to having his will defied, did not take kindly to the decision. After one more film, Cosmopolitan Pictures and Marion's immense bungalow were removed to Warner Brothers. Although he regretted the loss of publicity for himself and M-G-M in the Hearst press, Mayer was relieved. The Davies features had become harder and harder to sell.

Thalberg assembled a distinguished cast for *Barretts*. Fredric March, who had appeared with Norma in *Smilin' Through*, returned to M-G-M to play Robert Browning. The role of Father Barrett went to Charles Laughton, whom Thalberg had placed under personal contract. Thalberg at first deemed the Barrett role too small for Laughton, who had won an Academy award as star of *The Private Life of Henry VIII*. But Laughton wanted the role and was willing to lose fifty pounds and grow side-whiskers for it. Thalberg acquiesced. He enlarged the role of Father Barrett in the film script and eliminated some of the play's more blatant evidence of incest; this was a concession to the newly vigilant censors. "But they can't censor the gleam in my eye," Laughton said slyly.

Production went smoothly under the direction of Sidney Franklin. After the first preview, Thalberg decided the film needed extensive retakes. This presented a problem because Fredric March had been contracted to begin *We Live Again* with Samuel Goldwyn. Goldwyn was willing to release the actor, except for the fact that Rouben Mamoulian was scheduled to begin his contract to direct the film at $5000 a week. Thalberg placed a call to Mamoulian.

"I desperately need Freddy March for three weeks," said Thalberg.

"What's that got to do with me?" asked the director. He found out: Goldwyn didn't want to pay him for the three weeks March would be absent at M-G-M.

"I need March badly, but I'm not going to urge you," said Thalberg.

"All right," said Mamoulian. "You can have him. I'll delay the start of my contract with Goldwyn."

The retakes for *The Barretts of Wimpole Street* were filmed, and Thalberg was satisfied that the picture was ready for release. He didn't forget the gesture of Mamoulian, to whom he sent a telegram expressing his gratitude for Mamoulian's help in enabling him to use Fredric March. Thalberg went on to say that he thought it was a most sportsmanlike attitude and expressed the hope that he soon would have an opportunity to repay Mamoulian's kindness.

Mamoulian, who had lost $15,000 by his gesture, was surprised by the message—and more surprised later when Thalberg made good his word by hiring him for a picture.

The Barretts of Wimpole Street managed to produce the results

Hamming it up on the Barretts of Wimpole Street *set: Frederic March, Norma Shearer, Charles Laughton*

that Thalberg sought: it was acclaimed by critics and audiences alike. The picture and its star, Norma Shearer, were nominated for Academy awards. The Thalberg quality was once again evident on the world's movie screens.

4

The notion of producing a *Merry Widow* with sound—and without Erich Von Stroheim—held immense appeal for Thalberg. He envisioned a new version that would exploit the Lehar music without the Freudian undertones that had marked the 1925 film with Mae Murray and John Gilbert. For his Prince Danilo Thalberg wanted the French charmer, Maurice Chevalier. The time was propitious.

After five years at Paramount, Chevalier had tired of playing the eternally Smiling Lieutenant and was contemplating a return to Paris.

Thalberg and Chevalier had met before. When Irving and Norma were on their honeymoon trip to Europe, they saw the entertainer at the Casino in Paris. Thalberg went backstage and told him: "If you'll make a screen test for me and it turns out well, I'm willing to offer you a Hollywood contract, Mr. Chevalier. Interested?"

Chevalier was unable to take seriously the offer of an American stranger who scarcely looked old enough to vote, much less make offers of film contracts. The Frenchman dismissed him with the statement: "Either people are interested in hiring me or they're not. I don't audition any more."

After his visitors had made a polite departure, Chevalier was informed who they were. He sent word that he had changed his mind, and next day he filmed a test for Thalberg. It proved to be promising, but Chevalier and Thalberg could not agree on terms. Thalberg made a gift of the test reel, which Chevalier used to advantage. It secured him a contract with Paramount.

In 1933, Thalberg telephoned Chevalier and asked him to come to M-G-M for lunch. Thalberg knew that the actor's contract with Paramount was concluding in a few months and he suggested: "You come over with me, and there'll be wonderful parts. You'll make the kind of pictures you've wanted to—I will personally see to it."

After a return to France to contemplate the offer, Chevalier signed a contract with Thalberg. Louis Mayer posed with the pair for press photographers, and an orchestra played the "Merry Widow Waltz" to signalize the first starring vehicle for Chevalier at M-G-M. Ernst Lubitsch, whose *Student Prince* had been a silent hit for M-G-M and who had directed Chevalier in his best Paramount films, was hired as director.

Chevalier and Thalberg clashed at the outset over the choice of an actress to play the Widow. The Frenchman wanted the Metropolitan opera and Broadway star, Grace Moore. Thalberg was not keen on the choice. She had made two early talkie musicals for M-G-M, *A Lady's Morals* and *The New Moon*. During the latter, she began ballooning in size, and Thalberg reminded her that her contract imposed a 135-pound weight limit. She claimed it was the lighting that made her look fat. "Come up and stand on my scales," he urged, but she refused, realizing that she had eaten her way over the prescribed limit. Her contract was dropped at the end of the picture.

The memory of Miss Moore's eating habits influenced Thalberg against her, but the final word was said by Lubitsch: he didn't want her in the role. Even Miss Moore's offer to play the role for nothing was of no avail.

Thalberg and Lubitsch agreed on Jeanette MacDonald for the role of the Merry Widow, much to the disappointment of Chevalier. He had already appeared with her in *Love Parade, One Hour with You* and *Love Me Tonight,* and he felt the need for a new co-star. Besides, there was no real fondness between him and the iron-willed Miss MacDonald.

Lubitsch managed to create new excitement between the co-stars and in the warhorse operetta, and *The Merry Widow* was another achievement for the new Thalberg enterprise. Meanwhile, Grace Moore had met Harry Cohn at a party and had been signed to his

Columbia Pictures, where she scored an immense hit with *One Night of Love*.

Chevalier was surprised when Thalberg proposed their next venture: "How would you like to make a film with Grace Moore, Maurice?" The Frenchman expressed delight, and Thalberg began enthusing about the property he had in mind for the pair. Then he added, "There's one detail to straighten out, Maurice. Cohn insists on top billing for Grace."

Chevalier stiffened. He reminded Thalberg that his contract called for top billing.

"The important thing is to make a good movie, Maurice, and earn money," Thalberg argued. "Isn't that right?"

Chevalier's pride as an entertainer would not allow a compromise. Since they could reach no agreement, Chevalier offered to give up the remaining three years of the contract. Regretfully, Thalberg agreed. Chevalier accepted a cash settlement and departed for France, to remain there until after the war.

5

Irving Thalberg's attitudes stiffened as he reached his thirty-fifth year. It was a subtle change that only those closest to him noticed. To outward appearances he remained the same remarkable Thalberg, a trifle battle-scarred perhaps, but still a mature projection of the boy wonder who had dazzled the film world with his virtuosity.

Those who saw him close-up realized he had changed. Small wonder. Even though he was the most perceptive of men in appraising other persons' motives, he had been subjected to a decade of sycophancy such as few Persian princes had endured. He had grown accustomed to immediate and complete acceptance of his will. Then, during the period when he had been deposed from absolute power over M-G-M, he had known abandonment by those whose careers he had built. The baldness of the plot against him, the uphill struggle to return to eminence, the constant abrasion with Mayer—all these factors combined to make him a different man.

The charm and presence remained. He could be the most persuasive of men, his quiet assurance winning over the most strenuous of arguments. His physical appearance became more impressive with maturity. Always he held himself erect, so that he seemed taller

Jeanette MacDonald, Maurice Chevalier, The Merry Widow

than he really was. He entered a room with the self-contained air of royalty, and all eyes were inevitably directed toward him.

The ravages of his diseased heart added to Thalberg's anxieties. He seemed driven to achieve all he could before his time ran out. Movies became his life, his world, his god. Everything that threatened that life, world, god was to be destroyed. Everything that supported them was to be favored.

Some of his closest friends were alarmed at the changes that had come over Thalberg. Principal among these was Charlie MacArthur, whom Thalberg cherished not only as a gifted utility man with scripts but as a friend who provided frank counsel. MacArthur became heartsick over the pressures and attrition that Thalberg was subjected to. He hated to see Thalberg forced to compete with men who had once been his underlings. The writer became increasingly restless after his wife, Helen Hayes, left her film career and returned to the stage.

Miss Hayes was on tour in Maxwell Anderson's *Mary of Scotland*, and she had left instructions at her Pittsburgh hotel that she was not to be disturbed for the night. But in the early morning, a telephone call awakened her. The operator said she was sorry, but the call seemed urgent.

Irving Thalberg was on the phone: "Helen, are you having another baby?" His inquiry seemed urgent.

"No," she answered sleepily. "What are you talking about?"

"Charlie left here a couple of days ago. He phoned me and said he was going to join you. I can't find him anywhere. I never thought he would do this to me."

Miss Hayes was greatly concerned until she located her husband —at their home in Nyack, New York. He had decided that he could no longer stand the pain of watching the disintegration of Irving Thalberg.

The process was less visible to other associates. His drive seemed no different from that eagerness to excel that Henrietta Thalberg had instilled in him, the quality that had marked his career from the earliest days with Carl Laemmle. And if his political attitudes became more conservative, that also seemed merely a natural progression for the onetime socialist youth who was now earning close to a million dollars a year.

Thalberg's proprietary feeling toward his employees resulted in a misadventure into union politics that forever tarnished his image among writers.

During the early 1930s, screen writers were becoming increasingly dissatisfied with their working conditions. Some of the most important scenarists were earning spectacular salaries, but many more worked for amounts they considered insignificant in relation to their contribution to the finished product. Film writers generally were unhappy with the lack of security in their jobs, the inequities of awarding screen credit, their insignificant status compared to stars and directors.

A number of important scenarists formed the Screen Writers Guild with the aim of improving conditions at the studios. They sought and received support from the Authors League, and a plan was devised to cut off sale of material to the studios at a certain time unless the companies came to terms with the Guild.

Thalberg was appalled. The idea that writers might form into a union was repugnant to him. "Those writers are living like kings," he declared. "Why on earth would they want to join a union, like coal miners or plumbers?"

He was determined to save the writers from such a folly, and he found an ally in Darryl F. Zanuck, who had taken over Fox by merger with his Twentieth Century. Important writers at M-G-M and Twentieth Century-Fox were summoned to executive conferences and offered long-term contracts at handsome figures. They were expected to become members of Screen Playwrights,* a benevolent organization which appeared to some observers to be nothing more or less than a company union.

The leaders of the Screen Writers Guild did not abandon their campaign for recognition. A strike vote was called for. The Guild leaders were aware of Thalberg's feelings about their campaign, but they didn't realize his vehemence until one day when he called a meeting of the M-G-M writers in a large projection room. Writers

* In his notes for *The Last Tycoon*, F. Scott Fitzgerald, who was an observer of the Writers Guild vs. Screen Playwrights struggle, indicated that he was planning a close parallel to Thalberg's activities: "Note also in the epilogue that I want to show that Stahr left certain harm behind him just as he left good behind him. That some of his reactionary creations such as the Screen Playwrights existed long after his death just as so much of his valuable creative work survived him."

whose service dated back to the merger could not recall such a meeting.

Thalberg's manner and voice were cold as ice. He spoke briefly and wasted not a single word. He did not agree with any of the demands presented by the Guild and he would not grant recognition. He reminded his listeners of how he himself had built up the staff of contract writers, had seen that they were handsomely paid, had retained their services year after year, had even kept non-contract writers on salary between assignments.

He touched upon the consequences of a strike. Not only would the "artists"—meaning the actors, directors, designers, etc.—be thrown out of work; the strike would also idle hundreds of carpenters, painters, electricians, janitors, secretaries and others. In carefully measured tones he added: "If you wish to put all these people out of work, it is your responsibility. For if you proceed with this strike, *I shall close down the entire plant*, without a single exception."

His words were received with stunned silence. Not a person in the room doubted that he would carry out his threat. Thalberg was a man of his word, and, although he was no longer in charge of all production, his influence and prestige within the company and the industry continued to be immense. And there could be no mistaking that he was acting with the consent and the support of Louis Mayer.

Thalberg started to leave the room. Then he turned and added his final words: "Make no mistake. I mean precisely what I say. I shall close this studio, lock the gates, and there will be an end to Metro-Goldwyn-Mayer productions. And it will be you—all you writers—who will have done it."

The writers were shaken by the intensity of his threat, and the strike was defeated. The power of the Screen Writers Guild was broken—for a time. But the Guild later prevailed, and its leaders did not soon forget the subverting efforts of Irving Thalberg.

In 1934, Thalberg, along with other conservatives in California, became alarmed at the possibility that Upton Sinclair might become governor of California. The radical novelist had won the Democratic nomination with his campaign to End Poverty in California (EPIC), which appealed to the Depression-weary voters. In the wake of the Roosevelt landslide, Sinclair showed every sign of being able to defeat the Republican nominee, a political nonentity.

The power structure of California was shaken by the prospect of Governor Sinclair soaking the rich with a state income tax, increased property taxes and other measures. Secret meetings were held, and campaigns were formulated to combat the threat of the Socialist-turned-Democrat Sinclair. The radical sayings of his books and pamphlets were emblazoned on the front page of the Los Angeles *Times* and other newspapers. One of the most damaging devices against the Sinclair cause was the use of movie shorts in California theaters. The reels, filmed in newsreel style, purported to be at-random interviews with voters. Those who spoke in favor of the Republican candidate were inevitably well-dressed, articulate persons who gave every appearance of being solid citizens in the community. The Sinclair advocates were unshaven, poorly dressed and obviously uneducated. In one of the films, trainloads of hobos and criminals were depicted on their way to California to seek the easy life that Sinclair promised.

The propaganda did its job well, and Upton Sinclair was defeated. Many citizens, including some who opposed him, were outraged by the tactics used in the campaign. Shortly after the election, a number of Hollywood figures were deploring the anti-Sinclair films at a party given by Fredric March and his wife, Florence Eldridge, both of them liberals. After the denunciations ended, Irving Thalberg said quietly, "I made those shorts."

The guests looked at him unbelievingly. "But it was a dirty trick!" protested March. "It was the damnedest unfair thing I've ever heard of."

"Nothing is unfair in politics," Thalberg replied in his gentle manner. "We could sit down here and figure dirty things all night, and every one of them would be all right in a political campaign."

"It wouldn't be all right with *me*," March insisted.

"That's because you don't know politics," Thalberg continued. "I used to be a boy orator for the Socialist party on the East Side in New York. Do you think Tammany ever gave me a chance to be heard? They broke up our meetings. If there had been any chance that we might beat them in our ward, they would simply have thrown the ballot boxes into the East River, as they did against Hearst."

"But that doesn't mean it's right," said March. "There must be some place where they have honest elections."

"You mean England, I suppose," said Thalberg. "Well, don't kid yourself. Their heckling is just as bad as Tammany breaking up a meeting. But they have something even better up in the high places: the big lie. Do you remember the 'Hang the Kaiser' campaign after the war? And the fake Zinoviev letter that won another election? When an election comes up, all the nice English sportsmanship flies out the window. They take off their gloves and put on the brass knuckles, just as we do. Fairness in an election is a contradiction in terms. It just doesn't exist."

The discussion turned to the rise of Hitler in Germany, and March remarked that Hitlerism should be opposed before it was too late. Thalberg replied negatively, and this angered writer Kyle Crichton, another guest at the party.

"You're a Jew yourself," he said, "and you know what Hitler is doing to the Jews in Germany. It's plain he intends to wipe them out. Doesn't that mean anything to you?"

"A lot of Jews will lose their lives," Thalberg admitted.

"A *lot* of them!" cried Crichton. "Millions of them—maybe *all* of them!"

"No they won't," Thalberg said. "Hitler and Hitlerism will pass; the Jews will still be there."

No amount of argument could sway him from his judgment, and he replied to the heated protests with never a change in his quiet voice.

That detached manner never seemed to leave him; he appeared to take an exterior view of everything, including matters that fired other men's passions. He was capable of intense anger, as he displayed in his contract dealings with Schenck. But in nearly all other affairs, he would not display his temper before other persons; it was at variance with the Thalberg code.

Once Thalberg became upset because of a derogatory article in a trade paper. Instead of ranting about it, as Mayer would have done, Thalberg became so inwardly disturbed that he was forced to quit work for the afternoon.

"Do you mean that you let yourself get sick over a lousy little article in a trade paper?" George Cukor asked him.

"Yes," Thalberg sheepishly admitted to the director. "It was silly of me."

Associates recalled seeing Thalberg in a temper only once. That was during the turmoil over a writers' union, when an underling hoped to gain favor with the boss. The man was a story department official and he proudly reported his findings of perfidy by one of M-G-M's writers, a leader of the Guild campaign.

"I had this man trailed, and he was seen entering another studio," said the official. "I even have copies of the script he submitted to our competitors."

He placed the reports on Thalberg's desk. Thalberg grabbed the papers and tore them angrily. "I won't have it!" he shouted. "Any man who does this again will be fired. And I mean *you!*"

The evidence against the writer was grounds for dismissal, but there were some tactics Irving Thalberg would not employ, despite his claim that all was fair in politics.

On another occasion, George Cukor interceded with Thalberg on behalf of a friend, a competent writer who was unable to find work in the studios. His agent feared that the writer had been placed on a blacklist because of some offense to the bosses.

"There is no such th'ng as a blacklist!" Thalberg replied adamantly. Then he added with a faint smile: "But I'll see that he gets off it."

6

After Irving Thalberg had been relieved of his duties as production head of M-G-M, Louis Mayer sought Darryl F. Zanuck to replace him. The ambitious young man from Wahoo, Nebraska, had established a splendid record as production chief at Warner Brothers and was known to be discontented with his situation there. Mayer staged one of his most intensive campaigns in an effort to persuade Zanuck to make the move from Burbank to Culver City, even lavishing expensive jewelry on Mrs. Zanuck. But Zanuck finally declined; he had other plans.

Mayer decided that he himself would run M-G-M. He knew his limitations as a maker of films and was realistic enough to know that he couldn't replace Irving. Perhaps in time another Thalberg would come along. In the meantime, he, Mayer, would serve as head man of production. He outlined his strategy to Walter Wanger, who had produced such films as *Queen Christina* with Greta Garbo and John Gilbert and *Going Hollywood* with Marion Davies and Bing Crosby.

"Every son of a bitch in Hollywood is waiting for me to fall on my ass now that Irving has gone," Mayer declared to Wanger. "Well, I'm going to fool them. I'm going to build up the biggest collection of talent so that this studio can't fail. I want you to help me. If you come across any actor, director or writer who looks promising, let me know and I'll sign 'em up."

Mayer gave similar instructions to his other producers, and the M-G-M contract list began growing, not without the protests from Schenck over the ascending costs. But Schenck was assuaged by the outpouring of product that resulted from the accumulation of talent. The finished films were being shipped to New York with greater regularity than in the years when Thalberg had insisted on numerous previews and retakes before he pronounced a film completed.

Thalberg himself was alarmed by what he considered was the studio's drift. He wrote a strongly worded letter to Schenck describing the M-G-M personnel as "completely demoralized and uninspired." Standards had slipped tremendously, he wrote, adding: "The pictures that I see, while far from bad and some quite good, are juvenile, immature, and uninspired and lacking that finish that characterized our product for so many years."

A few weeks later, he wrote Schenck again: "I am frankly dismayed at the satisfaction that you have expressed and Louis has expressed with the pictures and the setups for the present and the future." Such letters helped widen the schism between Thalberg and Mayer. The older man became convinced that his one time protégé was trying to denigrate his efforts as studio head and lower his standing with Schenck. It was pure jealousy, Mayer was convinced, because Thalberg was sure no one else could command M-G-M production but himself. Mayer was determined to prove him wrong.

Thalberg felt he had specific grounds for protest. He believed that Mayer was thwarting him at every turn. Time after time, he complained in letters to Schenck, he had been unable to acquire the services of writers and directors he wanted, because they had been assigned elsewhere by Mayer. Thalberg also claimed he had been defeated in efforts to sign certain actors to exclusive contracts.

Mayer's alleged tactics intensified Thalberg's determination to succeed with his independent unit. He pressed forward with his most ambitious project, *Mutiny on the Bounty*.

Thalberg had acquired the Charles Nordhoff-James Norman Hall trilogy by a windfall. Frank Lloyd, a distinguished director who had won an Academy award for *Cavalcade* in 1932, had purchased the screen rights and offered to give them to Thalberg in return for the assignment to direct the film. Thalberg accepted readily.

Louis Mayer was not sanguine about the prospects of *Mutiny on the Bounty*. Throughout M-G-M history, both he and Thalberg had taken special pains to engage the female audience, on the reasoning that the woman of the family selected the film entertainment. At any rate, M-G-M rarely made outdoor adventures or big Westerns, and Mayer was especially concerned about a sea drama with no important female roles.

Thalberg was unworried. "It doesn't matter that there are no women

Laughton as Bligh, with Franchot Tone

Frank Lloyd (in cap) directs Movita, Tone and Gable at Catalina Island

in the cast," he reasoned. "People are fascinated with cruelty, and that's why *Mutiny* will have appeal."

Carey Wilson and John Farrow first worked on a screenplay when the vehicle was intended for Wallace Beery, Clark Gable and Robert Montgomery. Thalberg was dissatisfied with the result and he assigned the script to Talbot Jennings, an Idahoan who had recently come to M-G-M after the London success of his play *This Side Idolatry*. Thalberg met Jennings and told him to work with the associate producer, Albert Lewin. The writer didn't see Thalberg for three months.

Jennings submitted his script in July of 1934, but he received no word whether Thalberg liked it. The only indication that his work was acceptable came when Thalberg loaned him briefly to Samuel Goldwyn to doctor a troublesome sequence in *Resurrection;* Jennings was considered by Thalberg to be reliable.

More script sessions continued, with Lewin and Jennings joining Frank Lloyd and another writer, Jules Furthman. By Christmas, the men had fashioned a script that met Lloyd's satisfaction. Then they began two months of intensive work with Thalberg. They started work in late afternoon and continued until eight or nine o'clock in the evening, with frequent interruptions as Thalberg conducted other items of business. He also was accustomed to having a shave in the evening, and he went to the barber shop for the ritual, often taking Jennings along. After each interruption, Thalberg immediately took up the thread of the *Mutiny* story line.

The script was divided into five major sequences, and Thalberg pored over each of them, striving for every possible improvement. He paced relentlessly up and down the office, slapping the side of his trousers with a small baton he carried, probing the minds of the four men in the room. Over and over again he analyzed what the sequence should be about, what should happen in it, and how it should affect the following sequence. He kept driving forward until the others were word-weary and exhausted. Finally agreement was reached, and the session was over for the evening.

Once he commented on a sequence that failed to please him: "It's like a string of sausages, each one good, but not satisfying. I'm left hungry. I want a big steak!"

Thalberg realized the need for comedy bits to relieve the intense drama. He had recently seen *Lives of a Bengal Lancer*, and he instructed Jennings: "Write me a comedy bit like the cobra scene." Jennings tried, but did not succeed. Thalberg then sent him to collaborate with Robert (Hoppie) Hopkins, a curious fixture at M-G-M —he was a writer who never wrote a script, but wandered from set to set, suggesting gags and comedy bits. Hopkins also failed to produce the needed humor. It was finally provided by Allen Rivkin, who devised the running gag with Herbert Mundin trying to dispose of garbage against the wind.

Thalberg wanted the cast of *Mutiny on the Bounty* to be as perfect as the script. Obviously Beery was wrong for the role of Captain Bligh; he possessed the sadistic qualities, but was too American to be believable. Thalberg wanted Charles Laughton, who had performed brilliantly in *The Barretts of Wimpole Street*, but the casting presented problems because Laughton had contractual commitments in

England. The difficulty was solved by scheduling all of Laughton's scenes at the beginning of the production.

Clark Gable was Thalberg's first and only choice as Fletcher Christian. The actor was attracted to the basic elements of the role, but he rebelled at some of the trappings.

"Look, Irving," said Gable, "I'm a realistic kind of actor; I've never played in a costume picture in my life. Now you want me to wear a pigtail and velvet knee pants and shoes with silver buckles! The audience will laugh me off the screen. And I'll be damned if I'll shave off my mustache just because the British Navy didn't allow them. This mustache has been damned lucky for me."

Thalberg continued his persuasion, but the convincer was supplied by Gable's pal, Eddie Mannix, who pointed out that Fletcher Christian was the only character in the picture who had a romance. Content that his romantic appeal would be preserved, Gable agreed to play Christian.

Robert Montgomery had been scheduled to play the role of the young midshipman, Roger Byam, but he had just negotiated a new contract that granted him a three-month summer vacation. It was to start at the same time *Mutiny on the Bounty* began production, and Montgomery refused to postpone the vacation. He advised Franchot Tone, with whom he was appearing in *No More Ladies*, to apply for the role. That day Thalberg appeared on the set and asked Tone to visit him at lunchtime. The actor did so and was told: "I've decided I don't want Bob Montgomery for the *Mutiny* role. You're going to get your big chance."

Thalberg planned to shoot the major scenes at Catalina Island, but he also sent a camera crew to Tahiti for crowd shots and scenic backgrounds. When the crew returned to Culver City, Thalberg looked at the footage with production manager Joe Cohn. The scenes were well-staged, but film was underexposed.

"What happened, Joe?" Thalberg asked.

"I told them to be sure to dehydrate the film in that tropical climate, and they forgot to do it," Cohn explained "What should we do?"

"There's only one thing we can do: send them back to Tahiti." This time the camera crew followed instructions.

The major part of the production began at Catalina in the summer of 1935. Laughton was troubled with the role of the brutal Captain

Bligh. He telephoned Thalberg at the studio after the first day of shooting and complained, "I can't do this character; I don't understand him at all." Thalberg spent a half hour explaining the nature of the role and how it figured in the story.

For ten evenings, the telephone calls from Catalina continued, with Laughton wailing that he could not come to grips with Bligh. Then the calls stopped. The actor was able to proceed on his own.

Even with production under way, Thalberg did not consider the script completed; he continued honing it to a fine edge. He urged Jennings to rewrite scenes he had already worked over and over. "Put that scene through the typewriter again—just once more," instructed Thalberg. "You might come up with something better." On Sundays Lewin and Jennings reported to the Thalberg house on the beach, and the three men spent the whole day viewing film and working on scenes that Thalberg thought might be improved.

One day a problem developed with one of the cast members, and Thalberg was required to fly to Catalina. He invited Jennings to accompany him. The flight by seaplane took less than half an hour, but Thalberg was ill at ease in attempting to maintain a conversation; he was totally incapable of small talk. On movie matters he could be voluble, or he could discourse on world affairs. But he had established no personal relationship with Jennings, and conversation was difficult. He began by asking Jennings about his background and was surprised to learn that the writer was not English. They had worked in intimate association for months, and yet Thalberg did not even know that Jennings was native-born.

Jennings asked why Thalberg had bought the stage version of *Pride and Prejudice* when the novel was available for nothing in public domain. Thalberg replied that the publicity concerning the play's success made it a good investment. He was beginning to unbend, and he asked if the writer would like to come to his house some day and play bridge.

"Well, I've heard about your bridge games," said Jennings. "What do you play for?"

"Twenty-five cents a point," Thalberg replied in a matter-of-fact tone.

"I'm afraid that's twenty-four cents too much for me," the writer said.

The pair stayed overnight on the island and drove to the *Mutiny* set the next day. Thalberg was silent for a long time as the car bounced over the mountain roads. Then he said quietly: "Sometimes I think I'll quit all this—get out of it."

Jennings was startled. "But what would you do if you did get out of it?" he asked.

Thalberg said nothing for a few moments. "I don't know," he replied.

"What you *do* know is, you never will."

Thalberg didn't answer, his gaze remaining out toward the sea.

Mutiny on the Bounty was plagued with troubles during its filming. A camera barge overturned, sinking the equipment and drowning an assistant. The replica of the *Bounty* was sent out to sea for a storm sequence, but the footage lacked the pitch and toss of an angry ocean. Someone suggested building a smaller model of the *Bounty* so that the contrast with large waves would produce more drama photographically. The studio prop department constructed an eighteen-foot *Bounty* that was big enough to accommodate two men in its hold for steering purposes. It was towed out to sea by a mother ship, and all the crewmen were adjured to secrecy lest the deception reach the public.

Heavy seas were located, and the eighteen-foot replica was launched. But as the filming progressed, rough water separated the two boats, and the midget *Bounty* could not be found.

Thalberg was frantic. "I never should have done it," he fretted. "Two more men may be drowned just to get a movie scene!" He realized that if he called the Coast Guard, to search for the missing boat, the news would reach the public and destroy the illusion of the film. Instead, he hired a flotilla of boats to hunt for the model. After two sleepless nights he received the glad news: the *Bounty* had been found, and the two crewmen were safe.

In long hours of work with his favorite cutter, Margaret Booth, Thalberg trimmed *Mutiny on the Bounty* to a compact two hours and thirteen minutes. He took it out on preview a couple of times and made minor alterations. Then he scheduled another preview at Grauman's Chinese theater. He invited his friend and neighbor, Mervyn LeRoy, to accompany him.

The film drew a strong reaction from the Hollywood audience, and the M-G-M production executives smiled broadly as they gathered

Thalberg accepts the Oscar for Mutiny on the Bounty. *With Gable and Frank Capra*

over the famous footprints in the forecourt of the theater. Each man had a suggestion to make—a little cutting here, a bit of building up there. The smiling Thalberg listened to their proposals without comment.

LeRoy had said nothing about the film, and Thalberg asked him no questions about it on the drive to Santa Monica. LeRoy was puzzled and irate. When Thalberg dropped LeRoy off at his beach house, he said, "Why don't you come over for breakfast in the morning?"

LeRoy agreed. He was still upset when he arrived at Thalberg's house the following morning. As they sat down to breakfast, Thalberg said, "Were you surprised that I didn't ask your opinion about the picture last night?"

"Hell, yes," the director replied. "I was so sore I couldn't sleep."

"Well, what would you do if you had *Mutiny on the Bounty?*"

"I'd ship it, just as it is."

Thalberg smiled. "That's what I thought you'd say, and that's why I didn't ask you. I'm shipping it today."

Mutiny on the Bounty provided M-G-M's biggest gross since *Ben-Hur*—$4,460,000. Because of its lesser cost—$1,905,000—it proved to be a better investment. The Academy award for 1935 went to Irving Thalberg for producing the best picture of the year. Once more he was indisputably the premiere picture maker of Hollywood.

7

Comedy had always been Irving Thalberg's weak suit. His friend, Hal Roach, accused him of having no comedy sense, and the M-G-M films seemed to prove him right. Except for the Buster Keaton pictures, over which Thalberg exercised little control, few of the films had been totally hilarious. Thalberg aimed to improve his reputation as a producer of comedy by his association with the Marx Brothers.

The mad Marxes appeared to have come to the end of their film careers. They had performed in two early talkies, *Cocoanuts* and *Animal Crackers*, to resounding acclaim; they had a faculty of appealing to the mass audience and intellectuals alike with their irreverent humor. They did three more films for Paramount—*Monkey Business*, *Horse Feathers* and *Duck Soup*—with diminishing results. Their comic possibilities seemed to have been exhausted, and Paramount did not renew their contracts.

The Marxes waited for other film offers. None came. Weary of idleness, Groucho accepted an engagement to play *Twentieth Century* in a summer theater at Skowhegan, Maine, his first appearance apart from the family act. "I put everything in your hands," he told Chico before his departure.

Several weeks later, Groucho received a telephone call from Hollywood. "What's new?" Chico asked cheerily.

Groucho, who had been spending his time in the Maine woods, was so struck by the absurdity of the inquiry that he replied, "—— you!" and hung up the phone.

The telephone rang again and it was Chico. "Now wait a minute —don't hang up," he said. "I want to tell you something. I've been playing bridge with Irving Thalberg, and he says he'd like to do some pictures with us. He had to fight with Mayer, who thinks we're all washed up in pictures, but Irving is firm; he wants us to work with him."

"Okay, Chico," said Groucho. "I'll be back in a few weeks and we'll talk to him."

Groucho, Chico and Harpo joined Thalberg for lunch at M-G-M; by this time Zeppo had wearied of the abuse he received as the non-comic, romantic interest in the team, and he had gone into business as an agent.

"I'd like to do some pictures with you boys," Thalberg said. "I think you're enormously talented, but your recent pictures haven't been good."

Groucho bristled. "You don't think *Duck Soup* was funny?" he snapped. "The audiences howled at it."

"Yes, they laughed," said Thalberg. "But after they left the theater, they didn't remember what they had seen. I'd rather get half the laughs, and give the audience some story and romance to remember."

"Romance?" asked Harpo suspiciously.

"Yes, romance," Thalberg replied. "Men like your comedy, but women don't. They don't have as much sense of humor. So we'll give the women a romance to become interested in."

The Marxes were not completely convinced of the wisdom of their choice, but they went along with Thalberg because of the aura of genius that surrounded him. Then the Marx-Thalberg relationship was almost ruined by a familiar hazard: the million-dollar bench.

The brothers' first conference with Thalberg was set for ten o'clock in his office. Having been trained on the split-second schedules of vaudeville theaters, the Marxes arrived on time. They were still waiting at two in the afternoon, when they decided to leave.

On the following day, their appointment was for two o'clock, and they were admitted to Thalberg's office an hour later. The Marxes were seething, and Groucho delivered the ultimatum: "Now look, Mr. Thalberg, we've been stars in three Broadway shows, in vaudeville and in motion pictures. When we have an appointment, we are accustomed to having it kept. Yesterday we waited four hours and finally left. Today we were kept waiting an hour. In the future, don't ever call us unless we can see you at the appointed hour."

Thalberg was apologetic and promised to mend his ways. He was true to his word. When the Marxes came for their next appointment, they were ushered into his office immediately. But after twenty minutes of conversation, Thalberg was called away for an urgent matter; he said he would be back directly.

"Okay, let's show him," muttered Harpo. The brothers pushed filing cabinets against the door. Then they climbed out the window and left the studio.

They met again, and Thalberg was on time; he made no mention of the previous incident. The meeting continued at a lively pace until Thalberg was again called away for urgent business. This time Harpo walked to the commissary kitchen and brought back some raw potatoes. Chico and Groucho built a big fire in the office fireplace, and all three brothers removed their clothes. When Thalberg returned, he found the Marxes squatting stark naked before their roasting potatoes.

Never again did Thalberg leave an appointment with the Marx Brothers.

The problem of a vehicle for the Marxes faced Thalberg, and he summoned his top writers for a meeting. "We've got to come up with a sure-fire idea for the Marx Brothers," said Thalberg. "Paramount milked them dry, but I know there must be other ways to approach their comedy."

A few notions were put forth by the writers, but none sparked any interest from Thalberg. Then James K. McGuinness mused, "You know, the secret of the Marx Brothers is the way they can louse up something dignified."

"Yes?" said Thalberg.

"Well, the most dignified institution in the United States is the Metropolitan Opera House," added the writer.

Thalberg rose and smiled broadly. "You fellows can go to the races today," he announced to the others. "Jim, you stay and work."

McGuinness fashioned the general outline of how the Brothers Marx would bring havoc to an opera company. To write the script, Thalberg chose two of the nation's best comedy minds, George S. Kaufman and Morrie Ryskind, who had written *Cocoanuts* and *Animal Crackers* for the Marxes.

Ryskind found that writing comedy for Thalberg could be unnerving. Once he was summoned to Thalberg's office to deliver a sample of the script. Ryskind read several script pages in breezy style, imitating the voices of Groucho and Chico. He was disconcerted to see Thalberg remain stolid-faced. None of the laugh lines seemed to evoke any hilarity.

The recitation was finished, and Ryskind gazed at Thalberg in despair. "That's the funniest thing I've ever heard," Thalberg commented. It had never occurred to him to laugh.

As the script was nearing completion, the Marxes became nervous about their return to the screen. "The reason our first two pictures were so good was because we played the gags hundreds of times in the theater," Groucho reasoned. "The other three pictures turned out not as good because we never knew whether the gags were going to work or not. And we don't know whether they will in this picture, either."

"Then why can't we play the script before an audience?" Thalberg suggested.

"You're joking, aren't you?" said Groucho. "How can you try out a picture on the road?"

The major award winners of 1935: Thalberg, Bette Davis, Victor McLaglen, standing with Academy president, Frank Capra

"Easy. Take the five big comedy scenes in the script. Play them in vaudeville houses with a connecting narrative on the screen. You'll find out in a hurry whether the stuff is funny."

The Marxes agreed to give it a try. They rehearsed at the studio for a month, then embarked on a six-week tour of theaters in the Pacific Northwest. The first engagement in Seattle was a complete disaster. But Ryskind and gag writer Al Boasberg penned new jokes and pieces of action for every performance and by the end of the run, the material was surefire. The comedy hit of the stage show, as it was in the film, came when Groucho's stateroom filled up with wall-to-wall people.

To direct *A Night at the Opera* Thalberg assigned Sam Wood, who had been associated with dramas as well as light comedies. "Sam hasn't been doing very well for seven or eight years," said Thalberg, explaining the choice to Groucho. "He'll bring a fresh approach to the

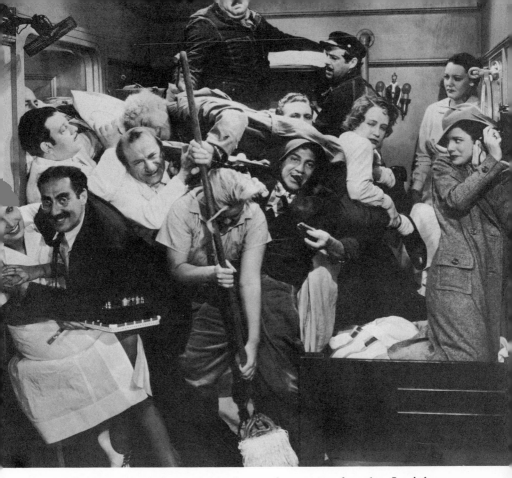

material and he won't be too proud to make any retakes that I might want."

Allan Jones and Kitty Carlisle were chosen to provide romance and songs, and Thalberg himself picked *Alone* by Nacio Herb Brown and Arthur Freed as the feature song.

Sam Wood directed *A Night at the Opera* in brisk style, and Thalberg was pleased with the rough cut. All of the M-G-M executives, including Louis Mayer, accompanied him to the first preview. It was disastrous. The funniest lines were greeted with scattered laughter.

Thalberg was perplexed and dismayed, especially in the presence of Mayer, who had considered hiring the Marxes a folly. Thalberg marched across the street to another theater and announced to the manager: "I'm Irving Thalberg. I just previewed a Marx Brothers picture, and I'd like to run it before an audience once more. Would you play it for me now?"

The amazed manager promptly agreed, but the audience reaction was the same as before. Thalberg spent three days in the cutting room, tightening up scenes to get the most of the comedy. He took the film out again and his judgment was vindicated; *A Night at the Opera* was received with roars of laughter. It proved to be the best and most profitable of the Marx comedies and established them as a bigger attraction than they had ever been before.

8

"I'm getting old," said Irving Thalberg after he had passed his thirty-fifth birthday. His time now was borrowed, since he had lived beyond doctors' predictions. He would not allow a wasted minute.

His personal life remained serene. Norma worked infrequently; she made only three pictures for him during his three years as an independent producer. She was off the screen for two years after *The Barretts of Wimpole Street*, and part of the absence was due to her second pregnancy. On June 13, 1935, a daughter was born to the Thalbergs, and they named her Katherine. Norma had experienced difficulty in the delivery of her first-born, and Irving had been greatly concerned. To save him anxiety a second time, she went to the hospital for the birth of Katherine without notifying her husband. Only after the baby had arrived safely did she place a call to the studio.

Norma continued to make her husband's personal life as simple and restful as possible. They went to an occasional premiere and attended industry banquets and parties given by important members of the film colony. On rare occasions the Thalbergs themselves entertained, usually with dinner parties arranged with Norma's good taste. The occasions were peopled with the bright personalities of the movie world and were inevitably lighthearted and gay.

At one Thalberg party, Elsa Lanchester chanced to notice Jean Harlow placing a small animal in a flower bowl. "What is that?" asked Miss Lanchester. "A grunion," replied Harlow. Miss Lanchester had heard about the silvery, shrimplike fish that came up on the beaches to lay eggs during the full of the moon, but she had never seen one. She rescued the animal from the flower bowl and took it outside to the beach. There she found hundreds of grunion flopping on the wet sand. She dashed back to the party and shouted: "The grunion are running! The grunion are running!"

At the Hollywood premiere of The Great Ziegfeld, *April 1936*

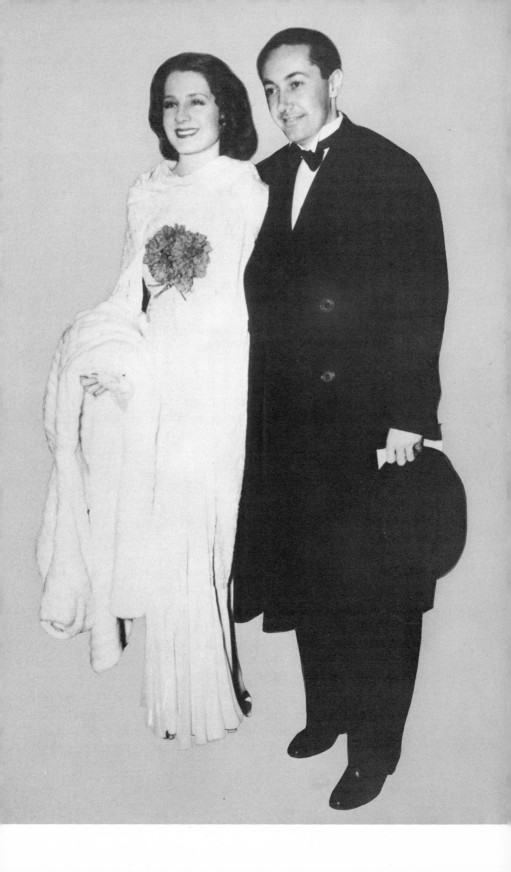

No one seemed the least bit concerned except her husband, Charles Laughton, and Jeanette MacDonald. All three went to the shore to stroll shoeless among the agitated fish while the others at the party continued their usual pastime of talking about movies.

Thalberg remained a leader in the community and served in any cause that might bring honor to the film industry. He was pleased to take part in the ceremonies at Universal City to honor the twenty-fifth anniversary of Carl Laemmle's entrance into the movie world. He accepted, with grave misgivings, the invitation to be master of ceremonies of a testimonial dinner for his old boss. Thalberg could perform in private conversation with complete assurance, but he suffered when called upon to speak in public. He spent hours composing introductions for the various guests and then gave the speeches to his secretary, Goldie Applegate. She copied them on sheets of paper, which he corrected. Then he decided it might be better to type the speeches on individual cards. He practiced the introductions over and over again in his office.

He worried throughout the banquet. After his first speech, he realized to his horror that he had left his cue cards on the lectern. If the speaker were to swoop them up when he finished talking, Thalberg would have found himself speechless. Fortunately that didn't happen, and he got through the banquet with seeming ease.

Thalberg maintained his policy of giving young film makers an opportunity, just as Laemmle had done for him. Like Laemmle, he could be tough.

One of his new assistants was David Lewis, who was introduced to Thalberg by Frances Marion. The meeting was not propitious; Thalberg mistook the young man's self-assurance for arrogance. "We've done a lot of things in pictures," said Thalberg, "and we're not arrogant." But he saw promise in Lewis, who had worked under Selznick at RKO, and he hired him—at half his usual salary. "I'm going to contribute so much to your education that you can pull in your belt a bit," said Thalberg, adding a warning: "If you ask for a raise in the next two years I'll fire you." But at Christmastime he gave Lewis a $10,000 bonus and a gift of Loew's stock.

Thalberg continued searching for new themes and fresh personalities to use on the screen. When Jeanette MacDonald and Nelson Eddy proved a popular combination in Hunt Stromberg's *Naughty*

Will Hays and Mary Pickford present Carl Laemmle with scroll marking his twenty-five years in films. Behind them: Irving Thalberg, Cecil B. De Mille, Louis Mayer, Will Rogers, Junior Laemmle. Others include: Wallace Beery, Buddy Rogers, Sidney Fox, Slim Summerville, Betty Compson, Mary Brian, Gary Cooper, William Haines, Ernst Laemmle, C. E. Sullivan, E. B. Derr, Victor McLaglen, Robert Armstrong, Constance Bennett, Fred Beetson, Al Christie, Sol Wurtzel, Ronald Colman, John Gilbert, Lew Ayres, Jack Cohn, Charlie Murray, George Sidney

Marietta, Thalberg began preparing *Maytime,* which proved to be the most beautiful of the MacDonald-Eddy operettas. Searching for a subject to star Jean Harlow, he chose a Frances Marion original, *Riffraff.* It was a bad selection for Thalberg because it concerned common people, about whom he knew little.

Riffraff was troubled from the start. The script went through many hands until Thalberg was satisfied with it. He asked Tay Garnett to direct, but Garnett declined. "You're making a terrible mistake to put Harlow in this," he said.

Laemmles, Junior and Senior, and Thalberg at testimonial dinner

"Why?" Thalberg asked indignantly.

"Because Harlow is the most famous courtesan in the world; people know her as the lovable tramp. Now you're trying to put her in the role of a madonna."

Thalberg replied, "I'm not destroying a star. I'm giving her career a new dimension."

Garnett remained adamant in his refusal, and Thalberg's impatience rose, although his voice remained calm. "If you play on my team, you've got to play *with* the team," he said meaningfully.

The director countered: "I'll put my shoulder to the wheel if I think there's gold in them hills. But I'm not going to dig holes in the backyard."

"Then I guess that's the end of the line," Thalberg said coolly, and Garnett's contract was terminated.

Riffraff was notable for introducing to M-G-M the figure of

Nelson Eddy and Jeanette MacDonald, Maytime

Spencer Tracy. He had known a faltering career at Fox, and as he was about to be dropped from his contract, Mayer directed Eddie Mannix to seek him out for an M-G-M deal. Winfield Sheehan readily agreed to sell the remainder of Tracy's Fox contract but added: "I'll give you a warning: the guy has no sex appeal." After he was certain he had made the deal, Mannix explained how M-G-M would give Tracy sex appeal: "We're going to put him opposite Jean Harlow, Joan Crawford, Myrna Loy and every other beautiful star we've got. After four or five pictures, the dames will be crazy about him."

Thalberg gave Tracy the role of leader of a cannery strike, and the electricity that sparked between him and Harlow provided the best moments of the picture. But the fate of *Riffraff* was portended by the first preview in Whittier. The cutter, Frank Sullivan, had worked night and day to meet Thalberg's deadline for the preview. On the afternoon before the preview he did not have enough time to complete the usual numbering of the film and the sound track, so the two could be coordinated in case of a break.

The film broke in the middle of the second reel, and the Whittier theater went dark. It was the moment that all studio people dreaded; the impact of many a preview had been destroyed by broken film.

In a few minutes, *Riffraff* resumed. But because the print and sound track numbers could not be synchronized, Harlow's dialogue was coming out of Tracy's mouth. The effect was hilarious to the audience, and the studio people began to sweat. Again the theater went dark while the projectionist tried to make the correction. This time Tracy spoke the words of Mickey Rooney. Dark. Another bad start.

Douglas Shearer dashed up to the projection booth to lend his expertise. Two more tries brought worse results.

"Put on the third reel," ordered Thalberg. While the reels were

being changed, the house lights went up, and some of the audience went into the lobby to smoke. None left the theater.

A courier brought the miserable tidings to Thalberg: the third reel was nowhere to be found; apparently it had been left at the studio.

"Put on the fourth reel," Thalberg said calmly. This was done, and the rest of *Riffraff* played without incident. But with two reels unseen by the audience, the reaction was unsatisfactory.

The cutter, Frank Sullivan, was devastated. After the fourth reel finally started, he could no longer remain in the theater. He stood outside under the marquee, contemplating whether to get into his car and continue driving east. But he remained until the picture's end and prepared himself to face the consequences. Thalberg came over to Sullivan as he emerged from the theater, patted him on the arm and said, "Forget it, Frank. Go home and get some sleep."

Thalberg's relations with Mayer had become almost nonexistent. They met on such formal occasions as the entertaining of visiting dignitaries, but those who arranged such affairs were careful to place the two men at opposite ends of the luncheon table. When he had a problem at the studio, Thalberg often appealed to Schenck rather than face an encounter with Mayer. Schenck's brother, the genial Joseph Schenck, now chairman of the board of Twentieth Century-Fox, often acted as peace-maker between Mayer and Thalberg, and between Mayer and Nick Schenck. Despite his position as head of a competing company, Joe Schenck retained warm personal relationships with all the top M-G-M executives and proved an astute mediator with the warring factions.

The intensity of the Mayer-Thalberg rift was known only to their closest associates. To the great majority of the studio employees and to the Hollywood community, the winning collaboration of the two leaders seemed unchanged. During personal encounters while others were present, Mayer and Thalberg never varied from an attitude of cool politeness; neither raised his voice in anger. But it was nothing like their early years, when they enjoyed the stimulating exchange of ideas.

Thalberg made no effort to mask his disdain for Mayer. One day he was engaged in a story conference with Lenore Coffee when Mayer stormed into the office in a fury. Thalberg displayed no emotion. He turned to the writer and said in a matter-of-fact tone,

Riffraff—in foreground: Vince Barnett, Spencer Tracy, Jean Harlow, Una Merkel, Juanita Quigley, Roger Imhoff, Mickey Rooney

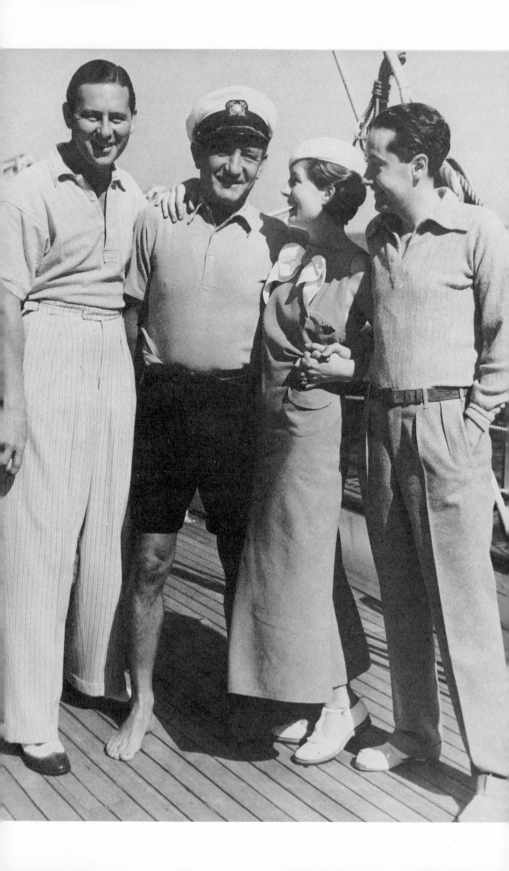

"Would you mind leaving the room, Miss Coffee, while I put Mr. Mayer in his place?"

On another occasion, Mayer was in a conciliatory mood and he begged Thalberg to come to his office for a conference. Thalberg finally agreed, and he took along his new associate, David Lewis. Mayer smiled when he saw Thalberg, then glowered to see Lewis standing behind him. Thalberg walked into the office, and Mayer closed the door in Lewis's face.

Thalberg opened the door and nodded toward Lewis. "Either he stays or I go," Thalberg announced. Mayer grudgingly admitted the young man, who sat uneasily through the brief, unsatisfactory conference.

Mayer was puzzled and perturbed by Thalberg's attitude. He wailed like a rejected father and could not account for Irving's disaffection. "It was for Irving's sake that I took over the studio," he told his associates. "That poor boy was working himself into the grave. I saved him so he can spend more years with Norma and the children. And these are the thanks I get! He rejects me, he fights me at every turn, he undermines me with Schenck. What have I done to deserve it?"

The hopes of Mayer to found a family dynasty at M-G-M were thwarted. Despite his considerable independence within the structure of M-G-M, son-in-law David Selznick was restless. He wanted to produce under his own banner and thus vindicate the memory of his late father, whose independent company had been overwhelmed by the major companies years before. Mayer exerted all his wiles to induce Selznick to stay at M-G-M. In this effort he received unexpected support from Irving Thalberg. Selznick had recently produced *David Copperfield*, *A Tale of Two Cities* and *Anna Karenina*, and Thalberg considered the Selznick output badly needed to bolster the M-G-M reputation of quality. Now one of the important stockholders of Loew's, Thalberg had a proprietary concern about what he considered was a decline in the studio's standards.

The Mayer Group even offered to cut Selznick in on their share of the Loew's profits. But the young producer could not be swayed. Over his father-in-law's predictions of doom, he formed Selznick International Pictures. He told Thalberg of his intention to resign from M-G-M.

"Well," Thalberg sighed, "I think you're doing the right thing."

Ben Lyon, Joe Schenck and the Thalbergs on Schenck's yacht

He joined capitalists John Hay Whitney, Cornelius Vanderbilt Whitney and John Hertz plus Myron Selznick as an investor in the new company, contributing $100,000. David Selznick was thrilled by Thalberg's gesture. He wished he could announce it, so the film world would know the faith that the great Irving Thalberg had in Selznick International. But it seemed more prudent for Thalberg's investment in a competitor to remain secret.

Thalberg's family provided escape from the vexations with Mayer. He remained close to his mother, the imperious Henrietta, who appeared with her husband at all the Thalberg parties. He was deeply devoted to Norma, and their two children brought him great joy. He considered himself to be a very fortunate man, and so did everyone else in Hollywood.

Thalberg's health remained constant during the two years following his breakdown. The reminder of his frailty was with him always in

A luncheon in Marion Davies' bungalow for visiting dignitaries. Standing: William Randolph Hearst, Irving Thalberg, Hal Wallis. Seated: Louis Mayer, Baroness Philippe de Rothschild, Colonel Henry Roosevelt, Assistant Secretary of the Navy, Miss Davies, Baron Henri de Rothschild

the nitroglycerin capsules he carried in case of a heart attack. After a long day's work at the studio, his head vibrated visibly and his pulse could be felt throbbing in his palm. Yet he continued to display recuperative powers that amazed those around him. After a night's rest, he was back at the studio with his customary drive.

Following his long and arduous labors on *Mutiny on the Bounty*, Albert Lewin believed himself to be on the edge of collapse. Always interested in clinical matters, Thalberg asked him what his symptoms were. After hearing Lewin's recital, Thalberg scoffed, "Hell, I get those symptoms all the time!"

One balmy afternoon, Thalberg and Al Lewin were discussing a screen story beside the pool of the Santa Monica house. Norma was in the water with the infant Katherine and young Irving was learning to dive. Lewin contemplated the scene and said to Thalberg, "If I were you, I'd be awfully worried."

Thalberg was surprised. "Why?" he asked.

"Look at you—you've got everything a man could desire: you're still young, you've got millions, you have reached the top of your industry, you have a lovely and talented wife, two beautiful children. The gods hate people like you. They're probably waiting behind that wall over there with a great big bat."

Thalberg laughed. "You're right," he mused. "You're absolutely right."

9

Consciously or unconsciously, Irving Thalberg chose death as a recurrent theme of his next major films.

First came *Romeo and Juliet*. Norma had faced another long absence from the screen because of the birth of their daughter, and Irving wanted to bring her back with a role that would display her beauty and refinement to best advantage. Why not Juliet? Norma was eager. As strong-minded as ever, she relished the challenge of a Shakespearean role, even though, discounting her balcony scene with John Gilbert in *Hollywood Revue*, she had never played one.

Louis Mayer was violently opposed. The masses did not understand Shakespeare, he contended, and the picture would be a failure. Mayer's opposition helped to stiffen Thalberg's determination to go ahead with *Romeo and Juliet*. He was unconcerned by the fact that

Norma was now past thirty and Juliet had been fourteen; he believed that her artistry could overcome the discrepancy. And he harbored the hope that Juliet would win Norma an Academy award in her maturity as an actress, just as *The Divorcee* had done so in her young womanhood.

Thalberg chose Talbot Jennings to arrange the Shakespeare text into a screen play. Jennings completed the screenplay in three weeks, and after several meetings about cuts and additions, the script was set. Thalberg hired George Cukor as director and secured the services of Cornell's Shakespearean scholar, William Strunk, Jr.,* to assure that the spirit of the Bard would not be violated.

"Your job is to protect Shakespeare from us," Thalberg instructed Strunk. The distinguished English actress, Constance Collier was hired to aid in Norma's handling of the iambics.

The casting of Romeo presented problems. Fredric March flatly

---

* Strunk achieved posthumous fame as the author of *The Elements of Style*, edited by his former student, E. B. White.

turned it down. Thalberg sought Leslie Howard, who had twice before appeared with Norma. The British actor was reluctant. He
pointed out that at forty-two he was beyond playing a teen-aged
lover. Furthermore, he argued, "A woman to be interesting does not
have to be anything but in love. . . . But a man who does nothing
but love! If he is as young as Romeo is reputed to be, we do not
take him seriously. And if he is as old as the average actor has to be
to have the necessary experience for this role, he is a bore."

When he learned that Jack Warner would not lend him to Thalberg
for Romeo, Howard changed his mind and decided he wanted the role
after all. A complicated trade was arranged, with Howard and Paul
Muni going to M-G-M for a picture apiece in return for the services
of Clark Gable and Robert Montgomery at Warner Brothers.

Cukor believed that the actors would be more at ease if they were
allowed to play long scenes, rather than the bits and pieces of an
ordinary film. The result was a tedious and expensive production
schedule. But Thalberg did not interfere. He wanted everything about
Romeo and Juliet to be perfect, no matter what the cost.

Having had no previous experience with Shakespeare, Thalberg
was able to bring to *Romeo and Juliet* a fresh and essentially
cinematic viewpoint. The time-worn plot seemed contemporary to
him, and he enthused over Shakespeare as he might have with a
brilliant new screen writer: "What he did with that potion scene!
By his own imagination, poetry and vitality, he had Juliet describe
what the potion was going to do for her. It's brilliant."

Each scene was analyzed for its own merits. Cukor had taken a
solemn approach to the parting scene in which Juliet laments:

> Wilt thou be gone? it is not yet near day,
> It was the nightingale and not the lark
> That pierc'd the fearful hollow of thine ear. . . .

"No, it's overdone," Thalberg commented after viewing the scene.
"It's beautiful, but the parting would have much more poignancy if
it were done with a smile."

Thalberg had been to John Gilbert's funeral that day, and from the
sad occasion he was able to draw support to his argument. He
described how some of Hollywood's leading actresses had engaged
in emotional displays. Marlene Dietrich had even stumbled and fallen

as she walked down the aisle, and she had sobbed loudly through the service. "It's better to underplay a scene than to act as they did at Jack's funeral," said Thalberg.

The balcony scene was filmed in a garden that occupied all of the huge Stage 15. Thirty arc lamps were needed to light the set, and Cukor shot the scene for days, focusing from a variety of angles. During one of Norma's long speeches from the balcony, a set worker noticed a dark figure standing in the shadows offstage. It was Irving Thalberg, and he seemed transfixed as he listened to Norma's lyrical protestation of love. When the scene ended and the stage lights went on, the dark figure had disappeared.

John Barrymore presented problems on *Romeo and Juliet*. Thalberg had cast him as Mercutio in complete confidence that Barrymore would display the same professional behavior as he had in previous M-G-M films. But two years of debauchery had taken their toll. Barrymore was a ruined figure, boisterous and uncontrollable when drunk, vague and ineffective in times of sobriety, as if he were prematurely senile. Barrymore agreed to submit to the discipline of Margaret Carrington, who had coached him for his Richard and Hamlet. "Christ's elder sister," he termed the exacting teacher of elocution. She responded in kind: "If only drink would finally kill the Barrymores, what a better world this would be!"

Barrymore was being pursued by both John Barleycorn and Elaine Barrie, his erstwhile protégée and fourth wife. To escape both, the actor agreed to make his residence during the filming of *Romeo and Juliet* at a sanitarium across the street from the studio, where he had the constant companionship of a male nurse. For a few weeks Barrymore's conduct was exemplary.* Then one Sunday he disappeared, and studio aides hunted frantically for him. Ralph Wheelwright of the publicity department finally located a taxi driver who had driven the actor to his old Tower Road house atop the Beverly Hills. There he was found pacing back and forth, his footsteps echoing in the empty mansion. He was escorted back to the sanitarium.

Thalberg lost patience with Barrymore's peccadillos and determined to replace him, no matter what the cost. He asked William Powell to take over the role of Mercutio.

* Barrymore's experiences in the sanitarium were later incorporated into the script of *A Star Is Born*.

George Cukor and Irving Thalberg confer on the set of Romeo and Juliet

"Mr. Thalberg, that's very flattering," said Powell, "and under any other circumstances I would jump at the chance. But you see, Jack Barrymore gave me my start in pictures. I had been on the stage for ten years and I wanted very much to break into movies. Jack arranged for me to get a part. So you can understand that it would make me very unhappy to replace him in a picture."

"Yes, I understand," Thalberg said resignedly. "Well, maybe we can nurse him through it."

After the shooting finished, the long months of intensive work began to show on Thalberg. An assistant cutter temporarily replaced Margaret Booth during her absence for an appendectomy, and Thalberg snapped at him over a minor error. The first preview in Pomona did not go well, and Thalberg declared that the music had been too loud—he was always impatient with obtrusive scores.

Romeo and Juliet was completed at last, and it was premiered in New York on August 20, 1936, amid much fanfare. The critical

Co-stars appear at a film premiere. Frank Whitbeck, Thalberg, Leslie Howard, Mrs. Howard, Norma, Mayer, William Gargan

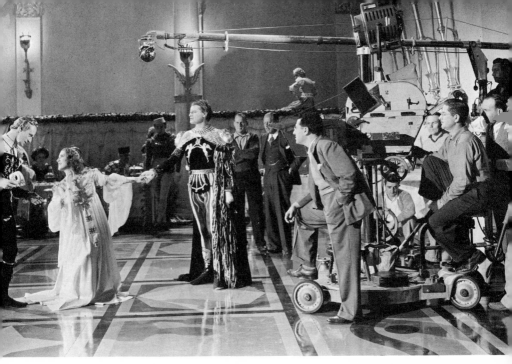

Cukor rehearses the ball scene with Howard, Norma and Ralph Forbes

reception was mostly glowing. Frank Nugent of the *Times* called it "a jeweled setting in which the deep beauty of (Shakespeare's) romance glows and sparkles and gleams with breathless radiance." The public reaction was something else. Louis Mayer was proved right: the movie audience wasn't ready for Shakespeare. In the end *Romeo and Juliet* drew receipts almost equal to its $2,066,000 cost. Because of distribution charges and other expenses, this represented a loss of $922,000. It was the only substantial deficit ever suffered by a Thalberg picture, but he had admitted during its filming that he never expected *Romeo and Juliet* to make money.

10

For three years Thalberg had been striving to fashion a workable script from the Pearl Buck novel, *The Good Earth*, which he had purchased shortly after it had been published in 1931. Louis Mayer did everything he could to discourage him.

"Irving, the public won't buy pictures about American farmers," Mayer argued. "And you want to give them *Chinese* farmers?"

Thalberg was not dissuaded. He told his associates: "*The Good Earth* isn't concerned with farming. It's the story of how a man marries a woman he has never seen before and how they live a life of intense loyalty. The public will be interested in such devotion."

One writer after another had toiled on the screenplay, trying to compress the events of thirty years into two hours on the screen. In 1934, Thalberg sent to China a film company headed by George Hill, whom he selected to direct *The Good Earth*. Hill brought back thousands of feet of film of the Chinese countryside and cities, plus costumes, furnitures and props. Thalberg began the casting, and he chose for his leads Paul Muni and Luise Rainer, the talented Viennese who had won an Academy award for *The Great Ziegfeld*.

Plans for the beginning of production were shattered when George Hill committed suicide. Thalberg was shaken by the loss of another close associate—Hill had directed *Min and Bill, Hell Divers* and other M-G-M successes. *The Good Earth* was assigned to Victor Fleming, another versatile Thalberg director.

Talbot Jennings began work with Fleming and Al Lewin in preparing the script for production. When the writer arrived at Lewin's office, he found the two men surrounded by knee-high piles of scripts that had been written for the film. "Throw 'em all out," said the mercurial Fleming. "We'll start all over again and work from the book."

As the three men continued writing the new script, Thalberg had misgivings about Fleming as director of *The Good Earth*. He was noted as a man's director, and Thalberg had decided to place more emphasis on the woman's saga. When Fleming was forced to leave the picture for an operation, Thalberg gave the assignment to Sidney Franklin, who had drawn fine performances from Norma Shearer and other M-G-M actresses.

Franklin read the script and told Thalberg, "I'd like to direct the picture, but I can't do it as the script reads now."

"Why not?" Thalberg asked.

"Because it's too Occidental. I don't get the Oriental flavor at all. I'd have to work on it from beginning to end."

"Can you do it in a few weeks?" asked the time-conscious Thalberg.

"No, it would take at least three months," Franklin protested.

"I can't wait. I'll give you six weeks."

The script was again rewritten and approved by Thalberg, al-

Sidney Franklin directing Luise Rainer and Paul Muni, The Good Earth

though he continued to rework some of the scenes throughout the filming. Much of *The Good Earth* was filmed in the San Fernando Valley, where an astonishingly authentic complex of Chinese farms had been constructed. It was there that the climactic locust plague, one of the most memorable action scenes in film history, was staged.

Production manager Joe Cohn was concerned about the sequence. "It doesn't reach for a climax," he told Thalberg. "The script doesn't show you the progression of events."

"Now, Joe, don't worry about it," said Thalberg. "If it doesn't work, we'll fix it later."

"Maybe you can, but I'll be the one who's blamed. The difference between us is that you can afford to make a quarter-million-dollar mistake. I can't."

Cohn was right; the locust sequence didn't play to full effect as it was filmed. But Thalberg blamed no one. He asked Bernie Hyman to take the remedial measures, and by trick photography and recutting, the threat of the plague was built to a height of excitement.

The Good Earth cost as much as any M-G-M picture since *Ben-Hur*—$2,816,000—and brought in rentals of $3,557,000 for a profit of a half-million dollars. It added greatly to M-G-M's prestige and provided Luise Rainer with her second Academy award.

I I

One task remained: to bring Greta Garbo to the peak of her artistry. That came with *Camille*.

The Dumas tragedy had been a time-worn vehicle on the stage for Eleonora Duse, Sarah Bernhardt and countless other actresses, and had provided a film subject for Bernhardt in 1912, Clara Kimball Young in 1917, Nazimova in 1920, Norma Talmadge in 1927. The possibilities seemed to have been exhausted, but Thalberg was convinced that Garbo could bring new vitality to *La Dame aux Camélias*.

"We have a problem," he told his staff. "The audience must forget within the first five minutes that this is a costume picture. It must be contemporary in its feeling, but one thing mitigates against that effect: the point that a girl's past can ruin her marriage. That problem doesn't exist any more. Whores can make good wives; that has been proven."

He and his associate on the film, David Lewis, came up with the

Cukor instructs Greta Garbo and Robert Taylor, Camille

solution: instead of being distraught over her past as a courtesan, Armand Duval is jealous of Marguerite's association with the Baron de Varville. Zoë Akins finished the script along those lines, augmenting earlier ones written by James Hilton and Frances Marion.

For Armand, Thalberg chose the handsome, fast-rising Robert Taylor. Although some of the staff feared Taylor was too inexperienced to match the quality of Garbo, Thalberg replied that acting prowess was not required. Taylor needed only to be immensely attractive, which he was, and to portray great love for Garbo, which he could.

George Cukor was selected as director. He had impressed Thalberg with his sensitivity on *Romeo and Juliet*, and the two had formed a close relationship. Cukor often attended previews with the Thalbergs, and once when Thalberg visited the director's impressive home, he said with a grin, "This is the kind of house I like my directors to live in. If they live grandly, like this, they aren't apt to turn down the pictures I offer them. It's the directors who live in bungalow courts who worry me."

Thalberg had his own conception of Garbo's capacities, and he expressed them to Cukor: "She is a fascinating artist, but she is limited. She must never create situations. She must be thrust into them; the drama comes in how she rides them out."

He analyzed the relationship of Marguerite and Armand in *Camille:* "These two people say they are going to get married, but we know that it is an impossible dream. Make it sound as if they are plotting a murder or some other desperate crime."

Thalberg was delighted with the early scenes of *Camille.* "She has never been so good," he enthused to Cukor.

"But you've only seen the shots of her sitting in the opera box," the director pointed out.

"Yes, but I can see a difference in her. She has never been so relaxed, so open to suggestion."

He followed the shooting closely, making frequent visits to the *Camille* set. In time Garbo succumbed to her penchant for privacy, even from her longtime boss. She sent word that it made her nervous to have Mr. Thalberg on the set. He accepted the edict with equanimity. "I've been put off better sets than this one," he cracked,

A Camille *conference: David Lewis, Thalberg, Cukor, actor Rex O'Malley*

although no one could remember when Irving Thalberg had ever been requested to leave a movie stage.

Completed at a cost of slightly under a million and a half dollars, *Camille* proved to be Garbo's most successful film, critically and commercially. "A magnificent and unforgettable performance," said Howard Barnes of the New York *Herald Tribune.* "She is as incomparable in the role as legend tells us that Bernhardt was," said Frank Nugent of the New York *Times.*

12

Irving Thalberg continued to drive himself, and to those close to him, he seemed almost to be testing his destiny. In the first half of 1936, he was pushing forward with the immense production of *The Good Earth.* He planned and put into production *Maytime, Camille* and another Marx Brothers picture, *A Day at the Races.* He finished *Romeo and Juliet* and supervised every aspect of its release. He began intensive work on the next vehicle for Norma, *Marie Antoinette,* which would depict the entire scope of the French Revolution. He was planning *Pride and Prejudice* and *Goodbye, Mr. Chips,* he started work on a film to be based on the Franz Werfel best-seller, *The Forty Days of Musa Dagh.* He asked Rouben Mamoulian to direct it.

Mamoulian, an Armenian who understood Turkish cruelty, relished the assignment and began making notes about how the novel could be translated into film. One day Thalberg told him: "We've run into some trouble with *Musa Dagh.* The Turkish government says if we make it, they'll ban all M-G-M pictures from their country."

"That means—?" said Mamoulian apprehensively.

"To hell with the Turks. I'm going to make the picture anyway."

Thalberg and Mamoulian proceeded with the planning. Then one day Thalberg sent for the director. "I'm sorry, but we'll have to shelve *Musa Dagh,*" Thalberg said unhappily.

"What happened?" Mamoulian asked.

"The Turks got their allies, the French, to ban the picture—and all other M-G-M pictures as well. And they may even go so far as to ban *all* movies from Hollywood. I can't fight that."

Thalberg drew great pleasure from planning the Marx pictures. He adored Chico, with whom he often played bridge; both were expert players. He enjoyed Groucho's cheeky irreverence and Harpo's sweet zaniness. Once again Thalberg sent the Marxes on the road to test their material. When the brothers were finishing up the tour at the Golden Gate Theater in San Francisco, they spotted Thalberg in the audience. Groucho complained afterward: "How come you didn't laugh? Weren't we funny? The audience seemed to think so."

"Of course you were funny, Groucho," Thalberg answered. "But that was the fourth time today I've seen the show."

Thalberg remained for two more days and saw the Marxes perform the same routines at twelve performances. He seemed never to tire of watching them, and he was exhilarated by the backstage atmosphere. Throughout his career, Thalberg had created entertainment in the almost laboratory-like atmosphere of a movie studio. Now, for the first time, he was involved in a form of show business that drew immediate response from the audience. He found it enormously exciting.

Thalberg was enjoying the autonomy of his own company. Most of his decisions were entirely his own; Mayer and Schenck rarely interfered. He felt more at ease than when he had the entire studio as his responsibility, though he still resented the manner in which he was displaced. His recent hits had reaffirmed his pre-eminent position in the film world. The producers who had shunned him when he first returned from Europe were now hovering around, anxious for his advice. Thalberg gave them his opinions without reserve; he bore no grudges.

He drew about him a close-knit staff, and he demanded and received loyalty. He enjoyed the Machiavellian ploy of playing one against the other. One evening he was being driven home by David Lewis. Thalberg asked casually, "Do you like Al Lewin?"

"Yes," Lewis lied.

"He doesn't like you," Thalberg replied. He waited for the remark to sink in. Then he patted Lewis's arm and said with a smile, "It's only an old wife's jealousy of a new young mistress."

The Thalbergs continued to be active in Hollywood's social life, but more and more Norma tried to conserve her husband's strength. She seemed to sense his decline in vitality, as did others who had known him for a long time. To Adela Rogers St. Johns, he "seemed to be a little figure made of white ashes; he had that certain kind of frailness that you see in young people before death, especially those with tuberculosis."

The indefinite future always remained in Thalberg's thinking. Once he was discussing future plans with his young assistant, David Lewis. "Of course you're going to live a thousand years," Thalberg said lightly. "I may not live ten years." He looked directly at Lewis and added with a faint smile, "I may not live ten days."

In reflective moments, he still talked of getting away from the production grind. He wrote to Laurence Stallings in New York that he had just finished *Romeo and Juliet* and for the first time in years, he was undecided about what to do next. Thalberg thought wistfully of the time when he and his mother and Stallings had journeyed out on the train to California, planning *The Big Parade* on the way.

"I'm coming East soon," said Thalberg. "Why don't we rent a place in a rooming house up in New England? You and I could sit on the front porch and talk about ideas for pictures." It was a fanciful idea, and both men seemed to realize it never could happen.

Thalberg felt the urgent need to plan ahead for his company, and he wanted it to be completely independent. In 1935 he began formulating plans for the I. G. Thalberg Corporation, which would release its films through Loew's but would be free of any subservience to M-G-M. Thalberg sought exclusive control over Norma Shearer, the Marx Brothers and any other talent, including non-performers, he might employ during the next four years.

Mayer opposed him fiercely. Such terms would constitute an encroachment on Mayer's autonomy, and he declared he would not permit that to happen. Mayer reminded Thalberg that his present contract would not expire until the end of 1938. As usual, Thalberg was unconcerned about his contractual obligations. He knew what he wanted and he aimed to get it. Mayer was just as determined not to yield.

Samuel Goldwyn became alarmed at the ferocity of the arguments and the effect they were having on his close friend, Thalberg. Not since he had sold out his interest in the Goldwyn Company had Sam returned to the Culver City studio. But now he decided to see Louis Mayer and attempt a solution to the bitter wrangle.

It was a dramatic confrontation between the strong individualists whose names formed two-thirds of the world's biggest film studio.

At a 1936 social gathering: David Niven, Merle Oberon, the Thalbergs

*At an Actors Fund benefit, September 2, 1936. In foreground: the Thal-
bergs, Douglas Fairbanks, Sr., and Lady Sylvia Ashley, Gilbert Roland and
Constance Bennett. Figures behind the Thalbergs: Ray Milland, Margaret
Sullavan, Walter Huston*

They had rarely done business together, and with good reason: they
detested each other. Their antipathy reached a high peak one day
when they were arguing in the showers at the Hillcrest Country
Club. Mayer became incensed about a Goldwyn remark and swung a
fist at Goldwyn's face, knocking him into the towel bin. Goldwyn
threatened a million-dollar lawsuit over the incident until other studio
heads convinced him the publicity would be bad for the industry.

Goldwyn, who had modest quarters during his tenure as head of the
studio, was amused by Mayer's office.

"It's like Mussolini's!" he said. "You need an automobile to reach
the desk." Mayer was not amused.

Without further ceremony, Goldwyn stated his mission: "Louie,

I came to see you about Irving. I don't think you'll ever develop another talent like Irving. I think you'll have to ease up on him. Be a little more careful, a little more considerate. He is a very sensitive boy, and he isn't at all strong."

Mayer was moved by Goldwyn's intercession, and he professed his own concern for Irving. He vowed to make things easier for him. As Goldwyn started to leave, Mayer remarked, "Sam, you are a very brilliant fellow. What you did was kind and thoughtful. Why is it that people don't like you?"

Goldwyn flashed his famous grin. "Louie," he replied, "if you only knew what the people here thought of you, you wouldn't come to work tomorrow."

Mayer acquiesced, and Thalberg signed a new contract that would give him control of talent he had developed until 1939, when he would have his own company. Then Loew's would finance and release his films, but he would operate with complete independence. He would no longer participate in the Loew's profits but would receive profits from his own films, plus a $2000-a-week salary.

The terms were entirely satisfactory to Thalberg, and he began talking of plans for the independent company. But his energies were running out.

One day in late summer of 1936, Al Lewin came to Thalberg with a fifty-page synopsis of a new book that was to be published under the title of *Gone with the Wind*.

"You've got to read this," enthused Lewin, who functioned as Thalberg's literary scout. "It's long, but it's great. The role is made to order for Clark Gable, and the whole story is surefire."

"All right, Al, I'll read it," said Thalberg. But he became engrossed in other matters and put the synopsis aside. Lewin continued reminding him to read it.

One day Lewin asked, "Have you read it?"

"Yes," Thalberg replied.

"And? What do you think?"

"You're absolutely right. It's sensational. The role is great for Gable and it will make a terrific picture. Now get out of here with it."

Lewin looked at him with puzzlement.

"Look," Thalberg explained, "I have just made *Mutiny on the*

Bounty and *The Good Earth*. And now you're asking me to burn Atlanta? No! Absolutely not! No more epics for me now. Just give me a little drawing-room drama. I'm tired. I'm just too tired."

13

The chill in the afternoon air was scarcely noticeable. Norma sensed it, but Irving did not. She knew that he had been exercising, and she was concerned when she saw him sitting on the veranda playing bridge.

"Put on this sweater, dear," she said to him.

"I don't need it," he answered. "Look—are the others wearing sweaters?"

It was Labor Day weekend, 1936, and the Thalbergs were enjoying the quiet elegance of the Del Monte Club on the Monterey peninsula. They had come north with good friends—Harpo Marx, the Mervyn LeRoys, the Sam Woods, Jack Conway and his wife—to spend the holiday at the place that held pleasant memories. It was there that Norma and Irving spent their honeymoon nine years before.

Irving, who had turned thirty-seven three months before, caught a head cold from playing bridge in the cool air. Returning to Hollywood on the day after Labor Day, he ignored the sniffles and continued his usual heavy schedule. After a full day at the studio, he went to the Hollywood Bowl to attend a rehearsal of a production of *Everyman;* he was a sponsor of the pageant, which was to provide funds for Jewish charities. He sat out in the damp evening air to lend his showmanly advice to the show's producers.

Two nights later, Conrad Nagel thanked the Bowl audience of twenty thousand people for their patronage, and he introduced some of the persons responsible for putting on the pageant. Among them were Norma Shearer and Irving Thalberg, who stood and accepted the applause of the throng.

On the next day, Thalberg's cold took a serious turn. He was confined to his bed at the Santa Monica beach house, and his physician, Dr. Philip Newmark, observed that his condition was growing worse. Norma asked Dr. Newmark to send for Dr. Franz Groedel, Irving's old friend and physician from Bad Nauheim, now a refugee from the Nazis and practicing in New York. Dr. Groedel flew to Los Angeles that day.

On the weekend David Lewis received a telephone call from Norma. "Would you fly East with Irving?" she asked.

Lewis recognized the gravity of the request. By mutual agreement, none of the principal members of the Thalberg organization traveled by airplane. Lewis, who had been a pilot himself, replied to Norma: "Certainly, I'll fly East with Irving."

"I'll call you back about the plans," she said. She telephoned back to say that the projected flight was off. Lewis found out later that the doctors were considering flying Thalberg to the Mayo Clinic, where he might be treated with the new sulfa drugs, then not generally available. But Thalberg's condition worsened, and it appeared inadvisable to move him.

On Sunday he developed pneumonia. Bernie Hyman visited him in the bedroom and tried to lift his spirits by commenting how good he looked. When Hyman expressed the certainty that Thalberg would recover, the patient was unconvinced. He smiled weakly and replied, "Nearer My God to Thee."

That Sunday was the day of the annual M-G-M picnic. Irving had been to almost all of them since he and Louis Mayer had opened the studio. This time he would not be joining in the tug-o'-war or the baseball game, and his absence cast gloom over the picnickers. They listened with concern as his message was read over the loudspeaker: "Only illness keeps me from being with you."

His condition worsened through the day, and doctors ordered an oxygen tent. His breathing became more labored, his body more frail. Henrietta Thalberg sat with Norma beside the bed, and the mother's face was masked with grief. Before he lapsed into unconsciousness, Irving spoke softly to Norma. "Don't let the children forget me," he said.

He remained grave throughout the night. On Monday morning, September 14, Thalberg's respiration seemed faintly improved, and there was hope that he was rallying. The doctors were pleased that his heart had suffered no further damage despite the ravages of the pneumonia.

Louis Mayer waited in his office at M-G-M, as he had waited a dozen years before, when his young partner was near death. For Mayer it was a time of unbearable torment. All those years together. Hadn't he, Mayer, been the first to uncover Irving's brilliance in those days on Mission Road? Hadn't he nurtured the boy and loved him like the son Mayer had hoped to have? If Irving were to die now, the tragedy would be compounded, for Mayer had not yet been able to bridge the gulf that had opened between them.

A telephone ring shattered the silence in Mayer's office. Mayer lifted the receiver and listened for a few moments. He put down the receiver and said to the assembled executives: "Irving is dead." Then he hurried from the room.

Mayer was the first to arrive at the Thalberg house at 707 Ocean Front. Other M-G-M executives followed. Rabbi Edgar F. Magnin, who had married Irving and Norma, called to confer about the funeral. A big green roadster drove up before the house and Darryl F. Zanuck emerged. With tears in his eyes, he said to one of Irving's close friends at the door: "Tell Norma I will not ask to see her now. But tell her how deeply we—all of us—sympathize with her. Tell her Irving can never be replaced. We loved him."

Douglas Fairbanks, Sr., and his new wife, the former Lady Ashley, arrived and he gave the message: "Just take our cards to Miss Shearer, and ask her to know that our thoughts are with her."

The doctors told reporters that death had come at 10:16 A.M., the cause being lobar pneumonia. Privately, Dr. Newmark marveled at the performance of Thalberg's damaged heart. "It was magnificent," he remarked. "Even when his temperature rose to 103 and 104, his heart stood up."

The studio was paralyzed with shock. Men and women alike wept openly. Sam Wood arrived on the set of *A Day at the Races* with tears streaming down his face. "The little brown fellow just died," he announced. The film company dispersed, unable to continue with the comedy. Later Groucho Marx muttered, "Why is it the great men always go early? The schlemiels live to be a hundred."

In New York, Nick Schenck issued a statement: "Thalberg was the most important man in the production end of the motion picture industry. He was important personally even more than officially. We all loved him. It is difficult to bear such a blow." Schenck, along with J. Robert Rubin and Howard Dietz, boarded a chartered TWA plane to fly to the funeral.

Sam Goldwyn, who was recovering from a gall bladder and appendix operation, wept uncontrollably for two days. He could not regain his composure to attend the funeral, and Norma called on him to express her understanding.

Helen Hayes was at her home in Nyack, New York, when the telephone call came from Hollywood about Irving's death. She hung up the receiver slowly and contemplated how she could tell the devastating news to Charlie. He was out on the tennis court, playing a few sets with a friend.

For long minutes Miss Hayes struggled with herself, trying to plot what she could do. Finally her courage stiffened. She decided to tell her husband—now.

She walked out to the tennis court and stood outside the fence as he was beginning to serve.

"Charlie," she said.

He didn't turn to look at her. "I know," he answered.

"Irving—"

"I *know!*" he snapped, and he delivered a smashing serve.

Throughout the afternoon Miss Hayes sat in the house, listening to the sound of tennis balls bouncing and being hit. Charlie played furiously for hours, until he was exhausted and spent. Then he came into the house and began to cry.

14

The tributes came pouring in. Louis B. Mayer: "I have lost my associate of the past fourteen years and the finest friend a man could ever have. . . ." Samuel Goldwyn: "I cannot express the terrible grief I feel at the passing of my dearest friend. . . ." Mary Pickford: "No recent news has been as shocking. . . ." Harry Cohn: ". . . the motion picture industry has suffered a loss from which it will not soon recover. . . ." Frank Capra: "I have lost a great friend. . . ." David Selznick: "Irving Thalberg was beyond any question the greatest individual force for fine pictures. . . ." Darryl Zanuck: "More than any other man he raised the industry to its present world prestige. . . ." Adolph Zukor: "Irving Thalberg was the most brilliant young man in the motion picture business. . . ." Cecil B. De Mille: ". . . the greatest conceivable loss to the motion picture industry. . . ." Harold Lloyd: "His pictures will stand as monuments to his artistry. . . ." Jesse Lasky: "It will be utterly impossible to replace him. . . ." Will Hays: ". . . an irreparable loss. . . ."

F. Scott Fitzgerald was in Asheville, North Carolina, where Zelda was a patient in Highland Sanitarium, when he learned of Thalberg's death. He wrote to a friend: "Thalberg's final collapse is the death of an enemy for me, though I liked the guy enormously. . . . I think . . . that he killed the idea of either Hopkins or Frederick (sic) March doing *Tender Is the Night*."*

The New York *Times* editorialized: "He helped, perhaps more than any other man in Hollywood, to make the motion picture a medium of adult entertainment, and by many thousands of theater-goers his talent and vitality will be missed."

It remained for a foreigner to take the full measure of the Thalberg accomplishment. C. A. Lejeune, film critic of the London *Observer* commented: "A temperate man in all his ways of living, in this one respect he was an inveterate gambler. If he believed in a man, or a project, or a story, he would stake everything on his conviction. . . . Everyone who worked for Thalberg loved him. He had the quality, rare among showmen, and precious among men, of standing back after an achievement and letting the other fellow take the credit. There was nothing thrustful about Thalberg; he never wanted to be known as the big promoter. He just saw a little farther than most of the others, and trusted his vision, and worked like a laborer until it came true. . . . In the whole of the film-making world there are perhaps a half-dozen producers whose caligraphy we can identify. Of them all, Thalberg was the most significant, and not alone because he had the resources of the world's most important film company behind him. Genius is an infinite capacity for taking chances, and that genius Thalberg had in full measure. What he also had was a great kindliness, a love for his work, workers, friends and audiences."

All that remained was the funeral.

It was conducted at the Synagogue B'nai B'rith by Rabbi Magnin. All the producers Thalberg had nurtured at M-G-M, all his directors and the stars came to the high-domed temple. The ushers who escorted them to their seats were Clark Gable, Fredric March,

---

* Fitzgerald's suspicions are open to question, since neither Miriam Hopkins nor Fredric March was under contract to M-G-M.

Douglas Fairbanks, Sr., Sidney Franklin, Woody Van Dyke, Moss Hart, Joe Cohn, Sam Wood, Cedric Gibbons, Lucien Hubbard, Carey Wilson, Harry Carey.*

The Barrymore brothers came, and all the Marxes. Charlie Chaplin, Walt Disney, Howard Hughes, Mary Pickford, Will Hays, Fred Astaire, Al Jolson, Harold Lloyd, Carole Lombard, Gary Cooper— all were there. The M-G-M leading men, past and present: Spencer Tracy, Ramon Novarro, Wallace Beery, Robert Young, Robert Taylor, Nelson Eddy, Herbert Marshall, Paul Muni, Conrad Nagel, William Powell, Johnny Weissmuller, Franchot Tone. And the leading ladies: Greta Garbo, Jeanette MacDonald, Joan Crawford, Constance Bennett, Madge Evans, Jean Harlow, Maureen O'Sullivan, Jean Parker, Myrna Loy. Freddie Bartholomew appeared in a black Little Lord Fauntleroy suit. Even Erich Von Stroheim came to the temple to pay respect to his onetime adversary. Gray with grief, Louis Mayer hurried past the respectful crowd and into the synagogue.

The widow sat near the altar in a section partially concealed from the other mourners. With her was Henrietta Thalberg, who seemed almost unable to contain her grief.

The soprano of Grace Moore rang through the temple with a Psalm of David. When she stepped down from her position above the mourners, she broke into tears. Rabbi Magnin intoned the ancient Hebrew ritual for the dead. Then he cited the messages of condolence that had come from throughout the world, including one from Washington: "The world of art is poorer with the passing of Irving Thalberg. His high ideals, insight and imagination went into the production of his masterpieces. I offer assurances of sincere sympathy —Franklin D. Roosevelt."

Rabbi Magnin told of the happiness of the couple he had married

---

* F. Scott Fitzgerald was intrigued with the legend that Harry Carey had been invited to usher by mistake, his invitation having been meant for Carey Wilson. Fitzgerald's notes indicated he intended to use the incident in *The Last Tycoon*. A faded cowboy star, Johnny Swanson, was to have been named a pallbearer for Monroe Stahr, along with Hollywood's most powerful figures. "Johnny goes through with the ceremony, rather dazed; and then finds out, to his astonishment, that his fortunes have been gloriously restored. From this time on, he is deluged with offers of jobs." The Carey incident, alas, was merely legend.

nine years before: "The love of Norma Shearer and Irving Thalberg was a love greater than that in the greatest motion picture I have ever seen—*Romeo and Juliet*."

While the services were beginning at ten in the morning, production and business in every Hollywood studio ceased for five minutes of silent tribute. M-G-M itself was shut down for the entire day.

Twelve limousines filled with family and close friends accompanied the gardenia-blanketed copper casket to Forest Lawn Memorial Park in Glendale for the interment. With them came three truckloads of floral offerings, including a chair of white gardenias, topped with a dove; it was sent by Louis Mayer. Wally Beery, piloting his own plane, flew overhead and dropped three bunches of red roses. One of them fell to earth a hundred feet from the widow as she emerged from her car. Twenty-five M-G-M policemen shielded Miss Shearer from curious eyes as she advanced to the mausoleum on the arm of her brother Douglas. After brief ceremonies, the party emerged. At last the sorrow was too great for Henrietta Thalberg, and she collapsed on the steps of the mausoleum. Her husband helped her to the limousine.

The crowd dispersed, and the mourners returned to their homes. Louis Mayer made plans to complete the films left unfinished at Irving's death. Sam Wood was given the responsibility to complete *A Day at the Races*, and *Maytime* was assigned to Hunt Stromberg; both films were in mid-production. Filming had been completed on *The Good Earth* and *Camille*, and the task of assembling them was handed to Bernard Hyman, Albert Lewin having left M-G-M out of grief over Thalberg's passing. On Mayer's direction, Eddie Mannix instructed Hyman: "These are Irving's last pictures. If anything can be done to make them better, do it, no matter what the expense." *The Good Earth* was virtually complete, but *Camille* went back into production for a new beginning that cost $100,000. The result proved confusing, and David Lewis restored the picture to the version that Thalberg had intended.

Mayer ordered a tribute to Irving to be placed on *The Good Earth* titles, and John Lee Mahin was directed to produce the wording. He submitted four simple lines. For weeks M-G-M executives mulled various versions of the tribute, including some that were long

The casket of Irving Thalberg is carried from the temple

and flowery. Finally the original Mahin wording was adopted. The words with which Thalberg's name appeared on the screen for the only time:

TO THE MEMORY OF
IRVING GRANT THALBERG
WE DEDICATE THIS PICTURE
HIS LAST GREAT ACHIEVEMENT

The tributes continued. The Academy of Motion Picture Arts and Sciences, which had thrice in its first eight years named Thalberg pictures the best of the year, instituted the Irving G. Thalberg Memorial Award for consistently high production achievement. When M-G-M's new administration headquarters was completed, it was designated the Thalberg Building.

Thalberg bequeathed to his family the fortune of $4,469,013.08, of which a half went to taxes and probate costs. Over the years Thalberg's share of the profits from M-G-M films brought another million and a half dollars to his estate, and the payments are still being made.

His legacy to the medium of film was incalculable. Together with Louis Mayer, he invented the big-studio system that kept American movies supreme throughout the world for a generation. But his reputation would not have prevailed if he had only devised the film factory. The touchstone of his genius was quality, the unceasing pursuit of quality. He ventured into uncharted land in his search for improved film entertainment, and his attainments became the goals of his competitors. He was ever seeking refinement in visual images, in sound and music, in acting style and directorial technique. Most of all, in writing.

His own efforts to write, as judged by his co-workers and evidenced by his University of Southern California speech, were lamentable. But the Brooklyn boy who had lain abed in his eighteenth year and devoured the books his mother brought for him—that boy learned what writing was. He recognized when words sang, when characters lost their cardboard and acquired dimension, when events could be so devised to stir the emotions and raise the spirit. Thalberg's films performed those feats to an amazing degree, and no film maker has since achieved his measure.

Most film histories devote only a few sentences to Thalberg; in some, he receives no mention. In 1968, Darryl F. Zanuck wrote to the author:

"No one can possibly write the history of motion pictures without devoting the largest individual share of it to Irving G. Thalberg, who incidentally was my intimate friend until the day he died. In my opinion, he was the most creative producer in the history of films during the period when he was Production Head of M-G-M, and the guiding light of that operation."

A SELECTION OF
THALBERG FILMS

THE MERRY WIDOW
1925

DIRECTION	Erich Von Stroheim
SCREEN ADAPTATION AND SCENARIO	Erich Von Stroheim, Benjamin Glazer
FROM THE MUSICAL COMEDY BY	Victor Leon, Leo Stein
AND THE OPERETTA BY	Franz Lehar
PHOTOGRAPHY	Oliver Marsh

CAST: Mae Murray, John Gilbert, Roy D'Arcy, Tully Marshall, Josephine Crowell, George Fawcett, Edward Connelly

Using the Franz Lehar operetta as basic material, Von Stroheim somehow manages to create a social commentary, complete with Freudian undertones. He begins his film in a small village of a mythical European kingdom, where troops are on the move. Von Stroheim delights in contrasts, as when the royal visitors arrive. The gay-hearted Prince Danilo, John Gilbert, is charmed by the bucolic scene: "Nice little pigs—nice little women." His cousin, the Crown Prince, played with flashing teeth by Roy d'Arcy, is repelled by the squealing swine and the buxom peasants.

Enter Sally O'Hara, premiere danseuse of the Manhattan Follies, portrayed with charm and abandon by Mae Murray. She is unable to find a room at the inn, and the royal cousins both offer their quarters. She declines, but accepts a dinner engagement. Gilbert and D'Arcy are at her side, and Von Stroheim focuses on the trio's feet beneath the table as they engage in an amusing ballet.

Miss Murray displays her talents in the opera house of the capital city. As she dances, three important spectators train their binoculars on her. The Baron Sadoja, enacted with spidery zeal by Tully Marshall, studies her feet. D'Arcy concentrates on her torso. Gilbert has eyes only for Miss Murray's angelic face.

After the performance, Marshall hurries backstage to invite the ballerina to dinner. She fends him off, suggesting three other girls in the company. He inspects their feet and finds them wanting; only Miss Murray's feet will do. She eludes him, only to be accosted by D'Arcy. He tries to engage her attention, but is dismissed with,

MERRY WIDOW, *John Gilbert invites Mae Murray to dance "The Merry Widow Waltz"*

MERRY WIDOW, *A regal quarrel: Roy D'Arcy, John Gilbert, George Fawcett, Josephine Crowell*

"Get out of my way, you big bum." She encounters Gilbert in her dressing room, and he charms her into accepting a dinner engagement at a cafe which supplies private rooms for special patrons.

The Von Stroheim imagination is allowed free rein in the cafe scenes. In one private room he shows Gilbert exerting his immense charm on Miss Murray while two blindfolded musicians, one a faun-like violinist, the other a willowy female, play mood music on the large bed.

"You'd be surprised how many dinners I've run away from because my host got fresh," warns Miss Murray.

In another room D'Arcy and his dissolute companions are engaged in a bacchanale of late-Roman proportions. D'Arcy amuses himself by shooting cigarettes out of the mouths of other revelers. The party plunges into chaos as feather pillows are torn open and their contents thrown into the air.

The two contrasting scenes merge as D'Arcy leads his followers into the apartment where Gilbert is attempting his conquest of Miss Murray. Gilbert scorns the innuendo of his cousin with: "I always knew you were a swine."

Gilbert is dissuaded from his plan to marry Miss Murray after an affecting scene with the king and queen. "What's marriage got to do with love?" the king demands. "Yes," says the queen meaningfully, "what's marriage got to do with love?"

Miss Murray waits in her wedding gown for Gilbert to appear. Instead, D'Arcy arrives to inform her, "You can take that thing off; there will be no wedding." She sits on her bed alone, unbelieving. Then she tears up her veil and agrees to marry the aged, perverse Marshall. She does so, and he succumbs on the wedding bed.

The scene shifts to Paris, and the depravity of the period is depicted in the merriment of Maxim's. Von Stroheim's meticulous attention to detail is shown in restaurant scenes, particularly in the costuming of the military, always resplendent and precise. Gilbert is drunken and disheartened; D'Arcy remains coolly evil. Enter Miss Murray, now the fabled Merry Widow. D'Arcy kisses her hand and his vision of her is blotted out by the brilliance of her diamonds. Gilbert cares only for the widow herself, and they dance the famous waltz.

The next morning, Miss Murray and D'Arcy are riding with his courtiers through the Bois de Bologne when they come across Gilbert, sleeping off a hangover. An argument ensues, and Gilbert challenges D'Arcy to a duel.

The duel scene is staged like a ballet against a backdrop by Seurat. The plot is unraveled in quick order: Gilbert is wounded in the duel; the king dies; D'Arcy returns for the coronation and is assassinated; Gilbert becomes the king and takes Miss Murray as his wife.

THE BIG PARADE
1925

DIRECTOR	King Vidor
STORY	Laurence Stallings
SCREENPLAY	Harry Behn
PHOTOGRAPHY	John Arnold

CAST: John Gilbert, Renée Adorée, Hobart Bosworth, Claire McDowell, Karl Dane, Tom O'Brien, George K. Arthur.

The film opens with establishing scenes of the three male principals: Karl Dane, a primitive working as a steeplejack high atop a new building; Tom O'Brien, a hard-bitten bartender; John Gilbert, a rich wastrel ("Me work? I should say not!"). The tranquillity of peace-time America is pierced by the shrillness of steam whistles signifying war. Gilbert's fancy car is stalled by a parade of recruits passing through the city. His foot taps to the martial music and he hears the cry, "Come on, the whole gang's going over!" He leaps from his car to join them.

In a quick montage, the ragtag group of recruits is converted into precision marchers, and the unit is sent to France, billeting among the cow barns and manure piles of a small village. Gilbert seeks a barrel so he can erect a streamside shower. Hidden inside the barrel as he walks, he encounters a pretty French girl. It is the first of a series of charming romantic scenes.

THE BIG PARADE, *Off to the front: Renée Adorée embraces John Gilbert. To his right: Karl Dane, Tom O'Brien*

THE BIG PARADE, *Renée Adorée, John Gilbert*

Later she arrives on the scene as Dane and O'Brien are showering, and she recognizes Gilbert as the man in the barrel by his fallen legging. He tries to kiss her and receives a slap in the face.

That evening she sneaks away from a family gathering to join him in the courtyard. He introduces her to the American custom of chewing gum, and the lesson goes well until she swallows her gum. The sequence establishes the romance with immense skill.

After the weeks of rural pleasures, the word comes: "*We're moving up!*" Vidor hastens the pace with vivid shots of soldiers racing to their stations, horse-drawn caissons speeding past, etc. The lovers desperately seek each other for a last farewell. Finally they meet, just as Gilbert must leave with the other troops in a truck.

"I'm coming back! Remember I'm coming back!" he tells her, showering her with kisses. The sergeant pulls them apart, and Gilbert climbs aboard the truck. Renée clings to his leg, then to the chain at the truck's rear, then falls into the dirt. Impulsively he tosses her his watch, his dog tags, his extra boot. She clutches the boot lovingly to her breast as the big parade continues toward the front.

The battle scenes are staged with remarkable realism. Especially gripping is the relentless march through the woods with the dough-boys maintaining their pace under brutal fire. Two sequences stand out as classics:

1. Gilbert sees a flower beyond the trench. He reaches for the flower, then withdraws his hand when he attracts enemy fire. Finally he plucks it, thumbs his nose at the Germans, and places the blossom on the chest of the sleeping Dane. Awakening, Dane glances at it and asks, "Am I dead yet?"

2. Gilbert is maddened when Dane ventures into no-man's land and is killed. "They got him! They got him, God damn their souls!" he cries, stalking forth to battle. He wounds an advancing German and crawls into a shell hole with him, holding a bayonet to the enemy's neck. But Gilbert is overcome with compassion and cannot kill him. He lights a cigarette for the German, who then dies. Gilbert then smokes the cigarette himself.*

"Another Big Parade"—the procession of ambulance trucks return-ing from the front. Gilbert is a passenger; he has lost a leg. He returns to the village and finds that it had been caught in the middle

---

* So effective were the two scenes that they were borrowed in part for the much-acclaimed early talkie, *All Quiet on the Western Front*.

of battle. To his distress he learns that everyone has been evacuated, his sweetheart included.

Gilbert returns home (the domestic scenes are the least effective in the film). His family is shocked to discover that he has lost his leg, and he learns that his fiancée has been romanced by his brother.

"Mother—there is a girl in France," says Gilbert. "Then you must find her," says his mother.

He does find Renée as she is plowing a field. She shakes her head in disbelief, then rushes to meet him as he hobbles toward her.

BEN-HUR
1926

DIRECTION	Fred Niblo
FROM THE NOVEL BY	Gen. Lew Wallace
ADAPTATION	June Mathis, Carey Wilson
CONTINUITY	Carey Wilson, Bess Meredyth
PHOTOGRAPHY	Rene Guissart, Percy Hilburn, Karl Struss, Clyde DeVinna

CAST: Ramon Novarro, Francis X. Bushman, May McAvoy, Carmel Myers, Kathleen Key, Frank Currier, Nigel de Brulier, Mitchell Lewis, Claire McDowell, Betty Bronson.

The film opens with a prologue of the Nativity, played in elemental style with Betty Bronson as a Gioconda-smiling Mary and a Bethlehem star that illuminates the startled populace like a noon sun. After the pageant, the intricacies of the plot are quickly introduced: Ben-Hur, one of a long line of Jewish princes, lives in a Palestine palace with his widowed mother and sister. Simonedes is their trusted slave. He has a daughter with whom Ben-Hur becomes infatuated when he meets her by chance. He also encounters his childhood friend, Messala, now a Roman soldier. Says Messala:

"To be a Roman is to rule the world. To be a Jew
is to crawl in the dirt. Forget you are a Jew."

The proud Ben-Hur refuses. Later he watches the procession of

BEN-HUR, *Ramon Novarro*

BEN-HUR, *Francis X. Bushman*

the new Roman governor, who is struck by a rooftop tile Ben-Hur accidentally dislodges. Messala orders him seized and sent to the galleys—and the mother and sister are put in prison.

The film springs to life with the galley sequence. The misery of the oarsmen slaves is captured in grim detail. As the brutish hortator beats the relentless pace with his mallets, a nude male figure hangs lifeless from the wall at his back. A slave is driven to madness and he is whipped to death by guards, then dragged off as another takes his place in the bank of oars.

The sequence is climaxed by a spectacular sea battle with pirates; it is also depicted with sadistic detail: a captured Roman chained to the battering prow of a pirate ship; snakes placed in bottles and thrown onto the Roman ships; severed heads held aloft on swords; bodies impaled on spears.

Ben-Hur saves the life of the Roman admiral and is adopted as a son by him. In Rome Ben-Hur becomes a great athlete, but his honors mean nothing to him. He goes off to Antioch in search of news of his mother and sister. The canny horse dealer, Sheik Ilderim, seeks Ben-Hur to drive his horses in the coming chariot race. Ben-Hur agrees when he learns that his opponent is to be Messala.

The chariot race is a kinetic masterpiece. The buildup to the race is begun with scenes of vast crowds arriving at the stadium. The camera moves through narrow columns and then emerges onto the track, pans upward and shows the enormous stadium packed with people.

The excitement continues to rise with shots of the expectant crowd and the horses rearing and pawing, eager for the race to begin. The white flags are hurled down and the horses charge forward. The camera moves everywhere to capture the excitement from above, from the floor of the track, with closeups of the charging hooves and the flying manes, with longshots of the chariots careening around the turns. Messala topples a Greek in Ben-Hur's path; Ben-Hur's horses leap the wreck. Messala whips Ben-Hur, but Ben-Hur locks his wheel inside Messala's and sends him to his death.

The remaining third of the film is anti-climactic but affecting. Scenes of the last week of Jesus' life—He is never seen full-figure— are interspersed with the major plot. Ben-Hur raises an army to save Jesus from Roman justice; his mother and sister, now lepers, are released from prison. In the procession to the cross, the offstage Jesus advises Ben-Hur to lay down his sword. The lepers are cleansed and reunited with Ben-Hur.

"He is not dead; He will live forever in the hearts of men," says Ben-Hur in the final scene as the camera irises out on the three distant crosses.

Novarro is the perfect Ben-Hur, virile yet aesthetic. The chesty Bushman brings vitality to all his scenes. The acting styles of the women—May McAvoy as Esther, Claire McDowell as the mother, Carmel Myers as an Egyptian siren—are suitable to the histrionics of silent films.

Ben-Hur is most convincing in scenes of crowds and action, less so when the characters are seen close-up.

THE CROWD
1928

DIRECTION AND STORY	King Vidor
SCREEN PLAY	King Vidor, John V. A. Weaver, Harry Behn
TITLES	Joe Farnham
PHOTOGRAPHY	Henry Sharp

CAST: James Murray, Eleanor Boardman, Bert Roach, Estelle Clark.

From the very beginning, Vidor never loses sight of his theme. The opening shot is a realistic scene of a newborn baby being spanked into bawling life. The proud father remarks, "There's a little man the world is going to hear from. Right, doctor?"

At the age of twelve, John is sitting on a fence with a group of companions. "My dad says I'm going to be someone big," he declares as the boys discuss their ambitions. They hear the clang of a horse-drawn ambulance, and John discovers to his horror that it is stopping at his house. Vidor portrays the boy's fear and loneliness as he ascends unbelievingly up the tunnel-like stairway to where his father has died, while the curious crowd mills below.

Title: When John was twenty-one, he became one of the
seven million people who believed New York de-
pended on them.

He gazes at the immense city from a ferry, and a stranger comments, "You gotta be good in that town if you want to beat the
crowd."

The frightening beauty of Manhattan's cityscapes is portrayed
in stark photography, then John—engagingly portrayed by James
Murray—is shown at his new job. He is seated amid vast rows of
desks in a cavernous room, adding up figures. At the stroke of five,
the workers stream out of the building, John en route to a blind
date arranged by a fellow worker, Bert Roach.

The date turns out to be the winsome Eleanor Boardman and the
four revelers—Bert's date is Estelle Clark—board a double-deck bus
en route down Fifth Avenue.

John scorns the sidewalk mobs: "Look at that crowd—the poor
boobs—all doing the same stuff." He points with amusement at a
clown juggling balls to advertise an eating place.

On the subway ride home from Coney Island, John proposes
marriage. The honeymoon trip to Niagara Falls is a masterpiece: John
and his bride, both too bashful to retire, sit in their chairs while all
the other Pullmans in the car have been made up.

The following Christmas presages the troubles to come. John and
Mary are living in a flat with a view of the thundering elevated
train. Her battle-ax of a mother and two disdainful brothers come
to dinner, and John leaves to borrow some gin from Bert Roach.
John comes home drunk hours later.

Months pass, and he arises one morning in a foul mood. The toilet
sticks, doors won't open, and Mary squirts grapefruit in his eye. After
a bitter argument, he storms off to work with the comment: "Take
it from me—marriage isn't a word; it's a sentence!" Distraught, she
calls to him from the window, urging him to return. When he does,
she tells him the news that she is pregnant. He is joyful once more.

Another Vidor touch: when their baby is born, John searches
through the vast hospital, finally finds Mary in a maternity ward the
size of a ballroom. Says John: "This is all I've needed to make me
work harder. I'll be somebody now—honest."

But in the next five years he has achieved only a daughter and a

$8 raise. The girl is seriously hurt by a speeding truck, and the distraught father tries to silence the clamor of the city as the girl lies unconscious. A cop tells him: "The world can't stop because your baby's sick."

The child dies, and John is grief-stricken—

> The crowd laughs with you always, but it will cry
> with you only for a day.

He loses his job and falls deeper into poverty. The family moves to a slum, and Mary takes in sewing. Incensed by his listlessness, she cries, "I'd almost rather see you dead!" He tries to throw himself into the path of an oncoming train, but his son dissuades him by saying, "When I grow up, I want to be just like you."

Encouraged, John seeks a job, but can only find one as a clown juggling balls for a sidewalk advertisement. He takes it and returns home hopefully, only to find Mary being moved out by her two brothers. After a tearful parting, she leaves. But she has a change of heart and returns. John takes his wife and son to the vaudeville show with his earnings. In the final scene they are laughing at the antics on the stage, and the camera pulls back to see the entire vast audience convulsed in laughter.

THE CROWD, *James Murray against the crowd*

THE BROADWAY MELODY

1929

DIRECTOR	Harry Beaumont
STORY	Edmund Goulding
CONTINUITY	Sarah Y. Mason
DIALOGUE	Norman Houston, James Gleason
PHOTOGRAPHY	John Arnold
SONGS	Nacio Herb Brown, Arthur Freed

CAST: Anita Page, Bessie Love, Charles King, Jed Prouty, Kenneth Thomson, Edward Dillon, Eddie Kane, Mary Doran, J. Emmett Beck, Marshall Ruth, Drew Demarest.

After aerial views of Manhattan, the action—and the sound—begins in the offices of the Gleason Music Company. James Gleason strolls down the corridor listening contentedly to the cacophony emitting from the audition rooms. The possibilities of sound are blatantly exploited as the ragtime tunes combine into a large, disharmonious jumble. The noise ceases as the show folk gather around to hear the latest composition of Charles King, a breezy song-and-dance in the Cohan manner. He explains breathlessly that the song has been chosen as the title tune of a new Francis Zanfield revue in which he will star with the Mahoney sisters, a new team from out west. He sings:

> . . . A million lights they flicker there—
> A million hearts beat quicker there—
> It's the Broadway Melody. . . .

A title switches the scene to "A theatrical hotel on 46th Street"—despite the use of sound, an occasional scene-setting title was deemed necessary. The Mahoney Sisters have arrived in New York—"the place we dreamed and talked about; ain't it swell?" The characters are established immediately: Anita Page is the tall beauty, kindhearted but not too brainy; Bessie Love is the spark plug of the act, small and feisty.

King arrives to welcome them to the big city. Bessie is his sweetheart, but he is immediately impressed with her little sister—"I can't

BROADWAY MELODY, *Bessie Love, Charles King, Anita Page*

get over how you've changed!" He proves his newfound prosperity by exhibiting his gold garters, then enthuses about the new Zanfield revue and their part in it. With his customary verve he demonstrates the title song, delivers it with full orchestra in the small hotel room.

Producer Zanfield is unimpressed by the sister act, but offers to hire Anita. The two girls refuse to break up the act, and Zanfield reluctantly agrees to hire Bessie as well. The backstage preparations for a Broadway show are depicted in bright style: the feuding between singer and conductor, the bitchery between chorus girls, the fluttering of the dress designer, the yes-men following the producer, the backers with eyes for the chorus beauties.

One of the backers, played with cool lechery by Kenneth Thomson, picks Anita as his target, and he showers her with roses, jewels and attention. This disturbs both Bessie, who fears for her sister's honor, and King, who has fallen in love with Anita. Bessie discovers this and taunts him: "You're yella, or you'd go out and fight for her!" He leaves, determined to do so, and she finds herself alone in the dressing room. In the film's single affecting scene, Bessie breaks down as she removes her make-up before the mirror. She goes to the telephone and tells her uncle, a booking agent played with a comic stutter by Jed Prouty, to find a new partner for a thirty-week tour of vaudeville.

King arrives just in time to save Anita from Thomson's advances. King offers to battle and is defeated ignominiously. But he wins Anita. After the honeymoon, they urge Bessie to come and live in their Long Island home. But she is determined to make a name on Broadway, and she teams up with a dumb chorus girl with whom she had battled in the Zanfield revue. As they ride to the railroad station with Uncle Jed, Bessie repeats her vow to return as a Broadway star.

The musical numbers are in keeping with the Ziegfeld tradition of the 1920s—lavish in mounting, full of action and empty of meaning. "The Wedding of the Painted Doll" is the most ambitious of the productions, and it is performed in frenetic style by toe dancers and adagio performers, though not without an innocent charm. The most engaging numbers are "Broadway Melody" and "You Were Meant for Me" as sung by King.

THE BIG HOUSE
1930

DIRECTION	George Hill
STORY AND DIALOGUE	Frances Marion
ADDITIONAL DIALOGUE	Joe Farnham, Martin Flavin
PHOTOGRAPHY	Harold Wenstrom

CAST: Wallace Beery, Chester Morris, Robert Montgomery, Lewis Stone, Leila Hyams, Roscoe Ates, Karl Dane, George F. Marion, J. C. Nugent, DeWitt Jennings, Tom Kennedy, Robert Emmett O'Connor.

The mood is established as the credits are being unreeled on the screen. They are played against an endless procession of feet marching in lock-step.

The film begins with a long shot of a huge penitentiary as a van arrives. A new prisoner is unloaded, and he is Robert Montgomery, a patrician young man stricken with apprehensive terror. He has been sentenced to ten years for manslaughter while driving on a drunken New Year's Eve, and he claims his innocence. The guards have heard that before.

Montgomery quickly loses his identity as he is mugged, finger-printed, stripped, measured, numbered and outfitted in prison drab. Then he hears a lecture from the stern warden, Lewis Stone: "Prison does not give a man a yellow streak. But if he has one, it'll bring it out."

After Montgomery leaves, a guard expresses amazement that the new man would be assigned to bunk with Machine Gun Butch, the most incorrigible prisoner of all. Stone replies with a social com-

THE BIG HOUSE, *Chester Morris, Robert Montgomery, Wallace Beery, Roscoe Ates*

mentary: he has no choice but to crowd the prisoners together indiscrimately. The prison was built for eighteen hundred and holds three thousand. Society, he adds ruefully, is ready to lock the wrongdoers up but will not provide adequate facilities.

Montgomery meets his two cellmates: the murdering Butch—Wallace Beery—who boasts of his killings, and a handsome thief, played by Chester Morris. Beery immediately steals the new man's cigarettes, only to have them stolen by Morris.

The mass anonymity of prison is depicted in powerful scenes. On three tiers of the cell block, the doors open simultaneously. The prisoners step out, line up and begin their shuffling march.

The mess hall is seen empty. By a quick dissolve, it is filled with convicts. The camera pans along a row of sullen faces as the men wait for the signal to turn over their tin cups. The food is slopped onto their plates and the faces become hostile. Beery starts the chorus of pounding cups, and the demonstration is broken up by gunfire. Stone declares, "I'm warning you for the last time—I'm running this show," and he sends Beery to solitary confinement.

A knife befalls Montgomery, and during a routine frisking he plants it in the bunk of Morris, who is due for a parole the next day. Morris is sent to solitary.

A notable scene: the camera remains on the corridor of the solitary block. No person is seen; the voices tell the story. Beery calls out to ask who the new arrival is. Morris identifies himself and tells what happened. Beery vows vengeance on Montgomery. The comments are overshadowed by the moaning of a prisoner and the singing of "Goin' Home" by another. "I wish you *would* go home," Beery grumbles.

Morris feigns illness after his release and escapes in a hearse by posing as a cadaver. He visits Montgomery's sister, Leila Hyams, thinking of revenge. But he falls in love instead. Morris is tracked down by the Javert of American films, Robert Emmett O'Connor, and is sent back to prison in time to learn of a break being planned by Beery. He has decided that Montgomery is all right after all, and lets him in on the plan. The cowardly Montgomery, hoping to shorten his sentence, tips the plan to the guards.

Thanksgiving Day has been chosen for the break, and the chapel scene is a portrait of irony. Beery and the others devoutly sing

"Open the Gates and Let the King of Glory in" with repeated choruses of "Open the Gates." During the Lord's Prayer, guns are passed along the pew.

The guards are ready when the dash for the gates comes. The prisoners, heavily armed, are driven back to the cell block, where director Hill provides a brilliant sequence of violent action. Morris prevents Beery from massacring the guards, and the pair shoot it out. Both are wounded, and they reconcile their differences as they crawl toward each other. Beery dies, and tanks arrive to quell the uprising.

Morris is rewarded with freedom, and he walks out the gate to find Miss Hyams waiting. Even as "The End" appears on the screen, the tramping of prisoners' feet can be heard.

ANNA CHRISTIE
1930

DIRECTION	Clarence Brown
ADAPTATION	Frances Marion
FROM THE PLAY BY	Eugene O'Neill
PHOTOGRAPHY	William Daniels

CAST: Greta Garbo, Charles Bickford, George F. Marion, Marie Dressler, James T. Mack, Lee Phelps.

After moody shots of the foggy waterfront, the camera moves into a shabby bar. The early-talkie fascination with things audible is demonstrated in the sounds of a scratchy phonograph, the lowing of fog horns, the blast of steamboat whistles.

Marie Dressler, gloriously dumpy as the long-passé harbor mistress, is being deposed as steady companion of George F. Marion, captain of a fishing barge. Chris is expecting the arrival of his daughter Anna, whom he long ago abandoned to life on a Minnesota farm with brutal relatives. Dressler accepts her exile with equanimity.

Marion is worried about seeing his daughter again, and he is concerned about his fate in general, inveighing against "dat ole debbil

ANNA CHRISTIE, *Charles Bickford, Greta Garbo, George F. Marion*

sea." He departs, leaving Dressler alone in dining section of the bar.

Garbo comes in through the ladies' entrance. She is shopworn and world-weary, and Dressler recognizes immediately what she is. Garbo takes a seat at a table on the opposite side of the room, and she speaks her first words to the bartender:

"Gimme a whisky—ginger ale on the side—and don't be stingy, baby."

The two women begin sparring with each other. Dressler, striving vainly to act dignified, orders a lager. When it arrives, she tries not to betray her eagerness for it. She reaches for it with one hand, then the other, then with both hands. Still she hesitates, struggling against the painful thirst. Finally she grabs the schooner and swallows eagerly.

Garbo gazes sorrowfully at the old wreck and mutters, "You're me, forty years from now." Finally Dressler says, "Aw, let's cut out the scrappin'," and the women seem on the brink of friendship. But

ANNA CHRISTIE, *Greta Garbo, Charles Bickford*

Dressler allows no indication of her identity when her grizzled boyfriend arrives for the poignant reconciliation with his daughter.

Father and daughter go to sea on his barge, and the ocean life seems good for her, despite her complaints of boredom. The scenes of New York harbor are amazingly well done, even though the principal players never left Culver City. Background scenes were filmed and superimposed behind the action in a double-printing device that predated process photography—the filming of scenes against a transparency.

During a storm at sea, Marion rescues a shipwrecked sailor, Matt Burke, played in lusty style by Charles Bickford. Marion perceives the attraction between the seaman and his daughter, and he is opposed to a romance, fearful that "dat ole debbil sea" will work its woes on her.

But Bickford comes a-wooing, and he takes Garbo on a gay excursion to Coney Island. They are interrupted by Dressler, who lurches woozily to their table and recognizes her friend from the waterfront bar. Bickford is angered by the intrusion, and Dressler moves on, being careful not to betray Garbo's secret. Meanwhile she has milked the scene with every trick she learned with Mack Sennett.

Bickford wants to marry Garbo, and he states his intentions to Marion, who becomes furious. Angered by their arguments, she declares, "Nobody owns me, except myself." Then she blurts, "I was in a 'house.'"

The two men are incredulous, then shattered. Later Bickford returns to demand of Garbo the oath that she loves no other man. She so swears, and he again seeks to marry her. Reconciled to her past, the father agrees to the match after he and Bickford return from their voyage—by coincidence they have shipped aboard the same freighter. The film ends abruptly on that note of hope, but a final shot of ominous waters gives hint that "dat ole debbil sea" will take its final toll.

"Anna Christie" evidences none of the technical restrictions of the early talkies, except for the fact that the scenes are filmed in legitimate-stage fashion from only one side of the set. With the clutching of her bosom and running her hands through her hair, Garbo displays some of the silent film technique; but her diction is clear, and her voice only slightly accented. The Marion portrayal is overdrawn, accenting the miracle of Marie Dressler's performance.

TRADER HORN

1931

DIRECTOR	W. S. Van Dyke
BASED ON THE BOOK BY	Ethelreda Lewis
ADAPTATION	Dale Van Every, John Thomas Neville
SCREENPLAY	Richard Shayer
DIALOGUE	Cyril Hume
PHOTOGRAPHY	Clyde DeVinna

CAST: Harry Carey, Edwina Booth, Duncan Renaldo, Mutia Omoolu, Olive Golden (Carey).

The film begins unpromisingly with a longshot of natives paddling a large boat up a jungle river. The river is real; the jungle is painted. But as the journey continues, the boat scenes are interspersed with shots that are astonishingly authentic: flotillas of hippopotamus rising and sounding; crocodiles skittering into the water; fifty elephants on the run at the river's edge.

The boat carries warm-hearted, jungle-wise Trader Horn, Harry Carey at his rugged best, and the greenhorn son of his old partner, enacted by Duncan Renaldo. Carey tries to educate the lad in the perils of Africa, but Renaldo is overwhelmed by the beauty of the setting. They arrive for some trading at a village, and the camera dwells on the everyday activities of the natives. These are shown in fascinating, documentary style.

Renaldo is charmed by the villagers and considers them harmless children. "That's just a little childish prank," comments Carey, pointing to a spread-eagled cadaver hanging from a post.

Carey's trading with the natives is interrupted by the arrival of the fierce Masai and the drumming that indicates a blood bath is under way. The two white men retreat to their boat, where they find two guards speared. The party manages an escape.

While camping beside the river, the party encounters a safari headed by a woman missionary, Olive Carey. Despite Carey's warnings of danger, she insists on heading toward the falls. There she hopes to find the daughter she had lost twenty years before, when natives

had massacred her husband. Later Carey and Renaldo reach the falls, an awesome sight. They find the missionary's body, and Carey vows to carry on her quest.

After more adventures, Carey and Renaldo are captured by a fierce tribe, and they watch the truly terrifying dances preparatory to the executions. "The Good Lord gives you only one death to die, and a fellow mustn't bungle it," advises Carey.

Enter the White Goddess. It is an impossible role, as Edwina Booth demonstrates with her eye-popping outbursts. She orders the two white men and their guide, Mutia Omoolu, tied to crosses and up-ended, ready for burning. But before the wood is fired, she orders the captives freed. Over the wild protests of the witch doctors, she departs with the trio in a boat headed across the lake.

The rest is chase, and it builds and maintains a high degree of excitement. They are threatened by a python, leopards and hunger. They come upon a pride of lions brawling over a kill. They scare off the lions and claim the meat.

Desperate for water, the foursome arrive at a waterhole they share with elephants. Carey objects when Renaldo embraces the girl, and the two men start to fight over her. They are interrupted by the sounds of approaching natives.

Carey instructs the others to flee while he diverts the attack. He does so and is joined by the faithful Omoolu. They escape by swinging on vines across a crocodile-filled river to an island. As the natives are practicing with their spears, the two men float past the camp on a camouflaged log. When Carey reaches safety, he finds that Omoolu has been hit by an errant spear. Carey's mourning of his black companion is touchingly real.

Renaldo and Miss Booth have one more adventure: they are surrounded by pygmies. But the natives turn out to be friendly, and the pair reach the trading post for a reunion with Carey. He realizes that the girl belongs to Renaldo, and he sees them off on a paddle-wheeler headed for civilization. It is a tender farewell, and Carey says, "I'll still be beholdin' the wonders of the jungle that'll never grow old before your eyes, the way a woman does."

A FREE SOUL
1931

DIRECTION	Clarence Brown
FROM A STORY BY	Adela Rogers St. Johns
ADAPTATION	Becky Gardner
PHOTOGRAPHY	William Daniels

CAST: Norma Shearer, Leslie Howard, Lionel Barrymore, Clark Gable, James Gleason, Lucy Beaumont, Edward Brophy, Roscoe Ates.

A masterpiece of story-telling, *A Free Soul* features one strong scene after another, each one furthering the plot and delineating character. Each scene plays concisely, has a beginning, middle and end, its conclusion signaled by a brief fade-out.

The story is based on the real-life relationship of Adela Rogers St. Johns and her father, the famed criminal lawyer, Earl Rogers. He was a flamboyant man, noted for his courtroom tricks and his drinking, and Lionel Barrymore captures the humanity of the character without neglecting the circusy aspects.

The action begins as Barrymore is defending a gangster on a murder charge. He takes his daughter, Norma Shearer, to court and she meets the defendant, Clark Gable. He strides in from the jail with manly confidence, and Miss Shearer, as well as the audience, is impressed by his entrance. Barrymore takes a swig from the flask of his retainer, James Gleason, and goes to court.

The state's case against Gable is largely based on a hat bearing his initials which was left at the scene of the crime. Barrymore dwells on this fact, then asks Gable to stand before the jury. Barrymore places the hat on Gable's head and it proves a couple of sizes too small. The courtroom erupts in laughter. Fadeout.

At a birthday party for Barrymore's mother, Miss Shearer announces her engagement to the refined Leslie Howard, a polo champion. Members of the socialite family approve. Then they are shocked by the entrance of the family's black sheep, Barrymore, roaring drunk and accompanied by his newly freed client, Gable. Miss Shearer is shocked by the family's rudeness to Gable, and she goes off with

A FREE SOUL, *Norma meets Gable. Lionel Barrymore, seated*

A FREE SOUL, *Lionel Barrymore, Norma Shearer*

him in his speedy roadster. They are nearly machine-gunned by a passing sedan, and he takes her to his hideaway headquarters, where he is a planning a gambling house.

Weeks later, Barrymore is drinking heavily in Gable's establishment. The genial host announces he wants to marry Miss Shearer. Barrymore is astounded. "The only time I hate democracy," he snarls, "is when one of you mongrels forgets his place."

Police raid the place, and the drunken Barrymore is thrown into Gable's apartment. There he finds his daughter, dressed in a slinky Adrian gown. The anguish in their faces tells everything. Wordlessly, he gives her the wrap and takes her home.

In a scene of high emotion, they try to justify their actions. She offers a bargain: if he will quit drinking, she will never see Gable again. He agrees, only after she predicts he will die insane from drink, as his father had.

For three months they camp out in Yosemite, and he appears to have conquered his alcoholism. But when they return to the railroad station, he wanders off to buy liquor at a drugstore. She watches in horror from the other side of the tracks as he staggers out of the station. A train stops between them, and when it has gone, he has left on it.

She returns home to find she is rejected by the respectable members of her family. She turns to Gable. He announces his intention to marry her. She is repulsed by the idea, but he persists brutally. "Don't worry about your old man," he says; "drunks like that never come back." She reflects, "Suddenly the moonbeams turned to worms," and escapes when he is out of the room.

Gable storms into her apartment the next morning and again makes his threats. Howard arrives, and Gable warns him not to interfere. That night Howard goes to Gable's office and calmly shoots him dead.

Howard is on trial for murder and will not defend himself. Miss Shearer frantically searches the San Francisco waterfront and finds Barrymore in a flophouse. At the climax of the trial, Barrymore walks into the courtroom. Over the heated objections of the prosecution and Howard himself, Barrymore is allowed to represent the defendant. He calls one witness, his daughter, and exacts from her the tearful story of how she became Gable's mistress.

In a profoundly moving speech, the kind that Academy awards are built upon, Barrymore faces the jury and puts himself on trial: "There is only one breast that you can pin the responsibility for this murder on. . . ." He collapses and dies. After Howard's acquittal, Miss Shearer leaves for a new start in New York, and he vows to follow her.

THE SIN OF MADELON CLAUDET
1931

DIRECTION　Edgar Selwyn
FROM THE PLAY *The Lullaby* BY　Edward Knoblock
DIALOGUE CONTINUITY　Charles MacArthur
PHOTOGRAPHY　Oliver T. Marsh

CAST: Helen Hayes, Lewis Stone, Neil Hamilton, Robert Young, Cliff Edwards, Jean Hersholt, Marie Prevost, Karen Morley, Charles Winninger, Alan Hale, Halliwell Hobbes.

The sentimental tale is related in flashback by Jean Hersholt in one of his first portrayals of a kindly doctor. He surprises Karen Morley, the wife of a young doctor friend, as she is about to leave her husband. She explains he is too busy with his career to devote any time to her. Hersholt bids her to sit down and listen to a story.

It begins with Helen Hayes as a Normandy farm girl being urged by a romantic American, Neil Hamilton, to run away with him. Even as her father pounds at the bedroom door, she agrees. The pair take up life together in a Paris garret, and he tries to paint. A friend, Lewis Stone, brings a critic to view the work, and the man sniffs to Miss Hayes, "If you love him, which God forbid, steal his brushes."

Hamilton is called home to America by his father's illness, and he vows to return. But his sweetheart's fate is depicted in a dissolve from a laundry tub she is stirring to a closeup of a champagne glass he stirs with his finger. He is at a bachelor party on the night before his wedding to an American girl.

Miss Hayes gives birth to his baby, and she is embittered. "I wish he was dead," she snaps. But then the child is placed beside her, and in a profoundly moving scene she extends a mother's love.

She calls upon Stone to sell him the painting he had admired. He has another idea: why doesn't she come and live with him? She declines, saying that her father has arranged a marriage with a farm neighbor. But the farmer, Alan Hale, won't accept the shame of her baby, and she won't be parted with the boy. So she accepts Stone's offer and sends the son to live with her friends, Cliff Edwards and Marie Prevost.

Now Miss Hayes is transformed from a farm beauty to a bejeweled woman of the world, and she plays the role convincingly. Stone is kind and undemanding, and their life together is serene—until he is arrested as a dealer in stolen jewels. He kills himself, and his mistress is sent to prison for ten years as an accomplice.

SIN OF MADELON CLAUDET, *The unmasking of Lewis Stone*

At the end of her sentence, Miss Hayes seems every bit like a woman who has spent ten years in confinement; her movements are cramped, her attitude timorous. She immediately goes to see her son in a home for boys and there meets the doctor, Hersholt. He says the boy has the talent to be a surgeon and mentions that a bad family background could hold him back in the profession. She has a tearful meeting with her son, but doesn't admit she is his mother. She vows to give him every advantage.

His life in school and hers in the world are depicted in scenes that literally shift, moving horizontally from one to the other with a black strip between. The son, Robert Young, excels in his studies. She picks up men in the street, blackmails men in bars, steals wallets—anything to provide money for her son's education.

In the end she is a ruined jade, and she seeks to commit herself to a hospital from which she can never emerge. But first she must see

SIN OF MADELON CLAUDET, *Madelon and an underworld type*

her son once more. She goes to his house and lovingly fingers the brass plate that reads DR. CLAUDET. Tricking the help, she gains entrance and slips into the doctor's study, there to caress the chair in which he receives patients.

Young enters and suspects she wants to steal the silver frame she is holding, the one that contains the picture of him as a boy with his mother. He agrees to examine her, and when he listens to her heart, she stifles the urge to embrace him. As he goes to mix her some medicine, she slips away.

The flashback returns abruptly to Hersholt and Miss Morley. Touched by the account of a mother's sacrifice, she discards her plan to desert her husband. Hersholt says the mother is being supported by her son in a home outside Paris, though he still is unaware of her relationship. When Young returns from his work, Miss Morley greets him warmly and urges that they bring the old woman to live with them. He agrees, and the film ends as it began, with strains of Brahm's "Lullaby."

The film has obvious deficiencies: pedestrian direction; a transparently artificial ending; clouded moral aspects. But Miss Hayes' performance shines through with brilliant humanity.

THE GUARDSMAN
1931

DIRECTION	Sidney Franklin
FROM THE PLAY BY	Ferenc Molnar
SCREENPLAY	Ernest Vajda
CONTINUITY	Claudine West
PHOTOGRAPHY	Norbert Brodine

CAST: Alfred Lunt, Lynn Fontanne, Roland Young, Maude Eburne, Zasu Pitts, Herman Bing.

Maxwell Anderson's *Elizabeth the Queen* is being played with solemnity on the stage of a Vienna theater. Lynn Fontanne is the aging queen and Alfred Lunt the ardent Essex, and they reach an emotional

THE GUARDSMAN, *Alfred Lunt, Lynn Fontanne, Roland Young*

climax as he marches off to the headsman despite her entreaties of love. They take curtain calls as the audience marvels at what a talented and happy married pair they are. But even as they bow to the applause, they are muttering insults to each other behind their smiles.

The argument continues in their dressing rooms. When she drops a bracelet, he snaps, "It is of no consequence; I only gave it to you on your thirtieth birthday."

"Twenty-ninth," she corrects. They go on bickering after the arrival of their friend, Roland Young, a bemonocled critic who is amused by the frailties of the acting breed. In his own dressing room Lunt complains to Young that his wife has been daydreaming and playing Chopin in a darkened room. It is a sure sign that she is anticipating the arrival of a new lover, probably a military man.

"Some day a soldier will come into her life, and I'll kill her, I'll kill her!" Lunt exclaims. Meanwhile he has been studying his hairline in the mirror and he adds, "Yes, it is getting thin."

Lunt softens when he arrives home, and he advances toward her boudoir with designs of love. But he is infuriated to find her in the dark—playing Chopin.

He devises a bold plan to test her love. He showers her with anonymous gifts, then appears on the street underneath her window in a close-cropped hairpiece, fake beard and the regalia of a Russian guardsman. She tosses him a note. He takes it and hurries off, only to be followed by the ever-observant Young. Lunt loses the chase and confesses his plot: He will feign an engagement as Hamlet in an outlying town, then appear as the guardsman to woo his own wife.

Returning home, Lunt prepares to leave "for the most serious role I've ever played." Fontanne is impatient for him to go. When he leaves, she busies herself with preparations, aided by her mother, irrepressible Maude Eburne, and the maladroit maid, Zasu Pitts. The guardsman, equipped with fur hat and heavy accent, arrives and seeks her favors without delay. She spurns him and out of earshot he exults, "I knew it, I knew it! She's true!" and dances a Luntian jig.

He comes back as the husband, claiming to have missed his train. The pair argue, and she insists on escorting him to the railroad station this time. She meets the guardsman again at the opera and spurns him once more: "I never want to see you again." But Young counsels him: "If you don't follow her now, you'll never know—nor will I."

She again refuses him at her doorstep and he exclaims, "She's true to me! I'm the happiest man in the world!" But then she tosses him her key from the bedroom window. Heavy of heart, Lunt enters the house.

On the following morning, the husband reappears. As he talks with Fontanne from the bathroom, he changes into his guardsman disguise, then appears over her with knife in hand, threatening, "Have you prayed tonight, Desdemona?" For one instant she loses her bemused calm, then she laughs. He refuses to believe her claim that she had recognized him the night before. But then a creditor, Herman Bing, arrives and sees through Lunt's disguise immediately.

That bolsters her argument, and she claims to have recognized his kiss —and his eyes. "And then—"

"Oh, yes, I was afraid of that, too," he adds.

Young enters and witnesses the tender reconciliation. "So you recognized him from the very first moment?" he asks, and she nods in a most enigmatic way.

A Molnar trifle, one which would barely extend the length of a short story. But it is played with feathery skill by two great professionals who maintain the illusion throughout.

GRAND HOTEL
1932

DIRECTOR	Edmund Goulding
ADAPTATION	William A. Drake
FROM THE PLAY BY	Vicki Baum
PHOTOGRAPHY	William Daniels

CAST: Greta Garbo, John Barrymore, Joan Crawford, Wallace Beery, Lionel Barrymore, Lewis Stone, Jean Hersholt, Robert McWade, Purnell B. Pratt, Ferdinand Gottschalk, Rafaela Ottiano, Morgan Wallace, Tully Marshall, Frank Conroy, Murray Kinnell, Edwin Maxwell.

The entire action takes place within the Grand Hotel of Berlin, a fact that contributes dramatic unity to the diverse plot structure. After the opening scene of the hubbub in the lobby of a deluxe hotel, the human situations are artfully delineated by conversations in the public telephone booths:

1. Lionel Barrymore as the pitiable Kringelein tells of leaving his bookkeeper's job to spend his dying weeks amid the luxury of the Grand.

2. John Barrymore, the suave Baron von Gaigern, discloses his plot to cure his financial reverses by stealing the jewels of the famed ballerina, Grusinskaya, played by Garbo.

GRAND HOTEL, *Greta Garbo and John Barrymore*

GRAND HOTEL, *Wallace Beery and Joan Crawford*

3. The dancer's maid reports that her mistress is suffering a malaise and doesn't feel able to perform that evening.

4. Wallace Beery as the hard-headed industrialist Preysing—and curiously the only cast member to employ a German accent—describes his desperation to win a merger with a Manchester firm, his only chance to escape ruin.

5. Jean Hersholt, Senf the porter, telephones the maternity hospital for news of his wife, overdue in delivering their child.

All five tell of their plights, then the tempo quickens by intercutting of brief pieces of conversation by each. Back in the lobby, Lewis Stone, the hotel doctor badly scarred by the war, delivers the irony:

"Grand Hotel . . . People coming, going . . . Nothing ever happens."

The interplay of the characters is a marvel, especially in the relationship of the two Barrymores. Joining the principal figures is Joan Crawford, the ambitious stenographer Flaemmchen, who is engaged to take something more than dictation from Beery and who befriends the mournful bookkeeper. The lives of all intermingle, except for Garbo. She remains fittingly aloof, playing most of her scenes with John Barrymore, who comes to rob her and remains to be her lover. Even he at first is rebuffed with the line, "I want to be alone." Barrymore is at the peak of his powers, cleverly underplaying to Garbo's effusiveness.

At the climax Beery is defeated in the business deal. Desperate for money, John Barrymore attempts to rob Beery and is killed by him. Garbo goes off to the railroad station, expecting to meet Barrymore for a rendezvous in Vienna. Beery's arrest rules out Crawford's plan to become his mistress, and she leaves for a Paris fling with the dying Lionel Barrymore.

The performances are uniformly excellent. Crawford is ideal as the slangy stenographer, and Beery offers the proper note of Prussian brutality without straining credulity. The long-suffering Stone provides solidity as commentator and sometime participant. But it is Lionel Barrymore who contributes unity to what might have been a series of disjointed episodes. His Kringelein remains humanly provocative throughout, and he helps propel the other characters to fulfillment of their destinies.

Goulding's achievement in directing such diverse temperaments is noteworthy. The film provides some neat touches: Parting with Crawford after making a date for cocktails, John Barrymore gives her a playful pat on the behind. . . . Unaware of her lover's death, Garbo telephones his room—but the ring is heard only by his dachshund . . . Barrymore's body is loaded into a hearse as sides of beef are delivered to the hotel.

Life resumes. A pair of chirping honeymooners arrive in their touring car and register at the Grand. The porter finally receives the news that he has become the father of a baby boy. The tempo of the big-city hotel becomes hurried once more.

The scarred doctor surveys the scene dourly and comments:

"Always the same . . . People come, go . . . Nothing ever happens."

RASPUTIN AND THE EMPRESS
1932

DIRECTION   Richard Boleslavsky
SCREENPLAY   Charles MacArthur
PHOTOGRAPHY   William Daniels

CAST: John, Ethel and Lionel Barrymore, Diana Wynyard, Ralph Morgan, Tad Alexander, C. Henry Gordon, Edward Arnold, Mischa Auer, Jean Parker.

The film begins slowly—too slowly—as director Boleslavsky dwells on newsreel shots and studio-staged processionals celebrating the three hundredth anniversary of Romanoff rule in Russia. John Barrymore enters first, as the semi-fictional Prince Chegodieff investigating the bomb-murder of a high-ranking member of royalty. He is suave and sardonic, yet concerned for Russia's plight.

Next comes Ethel, unchallengingly regal as the Czarina. "What have we done to these people of yours that they hate us so?" she asks of her ineffectual husband, played by Ralph Morgan. Her early scenes are over-played with stage techniques of eye-rolling and

RASPUTIN AND THE EMPRESS, *Lionel, Ethel and John Barrymore with their director, Richard Boleslavsky*

hand-wringing; later she seems to have learned the restraint of her film-trained brothers.

John Barrymore halts a mass execution of plotters and pleads with the Czar to begin the reforms his people are demanding. Morgan agrees to institute a duma to help him rule.

The Crown Prince, charmingly acted by Tad Alexander, suffers a fall and becomes deathly ill because of his hemophilia. Diana Wynyard as Princess Natasha, the Empress's lady-in-waiting and sweetheart of John Barrymore, brings to the palace the monk Rasputin, in whose healing powers she believes.

The entrance of Lionel Barrymore finally brings excitement to the tale. He plays Rasputin full-bearded and mad-eyed, a rapaciously ambitious man in search of lust and power. He finds both after hypnotizing the boy back to health, thus winning the confidence of Miss Barrymore.

Lionel is capital in his infamy. He makes a deal with the head of the secret police, Henry Kolker, for favors in return for information on high-ranking officials. He destroys men with his information and seduces women. He arrives late at a dinner party in his honor, belches in remembrance of a fine dish of borscht he had just enjoyed, and insults an admiring dowager, Louise Closser Hale.

His host, John Barrymore, invites him into the den and urges him not to meddle in the formation of the duma. John prophetically whips a duelling foil as he speaks. Lionel is not intimidated. "I know my destiny; I know my power," he rants. "In less than a year *I* will be Russia."

After Sarajevo, John urges the Czar not to defy the Kaiser's ultimatum; Lionel counsels the Czar otherwise. John is convinced the evil monk must be destroyed. Miss Wynyard learns of this and hurries to Lionel's home to warn him. John interrupts Lionel's partying with his harem and calmly fires a pistol at him. But Lionel is wearing armor and is unharmed. John is seized.

The Czar is convinced to begin the war, and he goes off to command the forces, leaving Lionel in complete power at the palace. When he starts making advances to one of the young princesses, Jean Parker, Miss Wynyard warns Miss Barrymore. When confronted by her, Lionel proclaims, "*I* am the Czar of all the Russias!" Miss Barrymore eloquently expresses her dismay over the consequences of her trust in the madman.

This time John aims to complete his mission. He and the court physician, Edward Arnold, inject "enough poison to kill five men" into small chocolate cakes that Lionel favors. He eats three of them at a wild party and doesn't even falter. Then he recognizes John's waiter, Mischa Auer, and exposes the plot. He leads John to the cellar at pistol-point, intending to execute him.

In the most electrifying scene of the film, John and Lionel spar verbally until the poison at last begins its work. John gains control and he beats Lionel furiously over the head with a poker. Still Lionel refuses to die and he staggers toward John like a wraith, blood streaming down his face. John finally takes him into the storm outside and drowns him in the ice-choked river.

John is publicly rebuked but privately thanked by the Czar for his service. John is sent into exile for his own good and urged to "take Natasha with you." He pleads with the Czar to send his wife and children out of the country in view of the growing unrest. But the ruler answers, "We have never injured our people. They will never injure us."

The film ends with the Revolution accomplished and the royal family sent off on a journey from which they would not return.

Aside from its convincing portrait of court intrigue, the main attractions of *Rasputin and the Empress* are the Barrymores, especially the brothers. They play splendidly in concert, lending credulity to what might have been an empty pageant.

THE BARRETTS OF WIMPOLE STREET
1934

DIRECTION	Sidney Franklin
FROM THE PLAY BY	Rudolf Besier
SCREENPLAY	Ernest Vajda, Claudine West, Donald Ogden Stewart
PHOTOGRAPHY	William Daniels

CAST: Norma Shearer, Fredric March, Charles Laughton, Maureen O'Sullivan, Katharine Alexander, Una O'Connor, Marion Clayton, Ferdinand Munier, Ian Wolfe, Ralph Forbes, Leo G. Carroll, Flush.

The sepulchral voice of Charles Laughton is heard from behind the dining room door as the tyrannical father of the Barrett family intones the benediction before the evening meal. Upstairs, his beloved Elizabeth—Norma Shearer—is being examined by a doctor for her prolonged and unexplained ailment (in reality, a burst blood vessel in her lungs). "You've got to help; you've got to *want* to get well," she is told. She urges the doctor, Ferdinand Munier, to intercede with her father and prescribe warm milk instead of her daily portion of porter, which she detests. He agrees.

Her six brothers and two sisters join Miss Shearer after dinner, and all are joyful that their father is going away on a trip. The most rebellious of the children, Maureen O'Sullivan, expresses her feelings by dancing a polka, which is summarily ended by the entrance of Laughton. The cocker spaniel, Flush, scurries for cover.

"I am most displeased," Laughton announces, and he sweeps the others from the room, concentrating his attention on Miss Shearer. He countermands the doctor's prescription and urges her to continue drinking the porter for its healthful attributes. After much protest, she consents. The maid, Una O'Connor, brings in the despised tankard with her characteristic walk, as if she had rollers under her hoop-skirt. Miss Shearer swallows the drink with great distaste, and Laughton reproves her for her attitude: "If you love me, you can't be afraid of me."

THE BARRETTS OF WIMPOLE STREET, *Fredric March, Flush, Norma Shearer*

The first real excitement in her secluded life comes when Robert Browning admires her poems and begins a correspondence. Impulsively he comes to pay a call. She is panicked, but agrees to see him.

Fredric March sweeps into the room and carries off that most difficult of portrayals, that of a famous poet. He is ardent but not effusive, fluent but not flowery. They discuss their works, and she asks him to explain a difficult portion of one of his poems. He studies it, then admits: "When that passage was written, only God and Robert Browning understood it. Now only God understands it."

He professes his devotion to her in a long, beautifully sustained scene unbroken by closeups. "But I'm a dying woman!" she protests. "We all are dying," he replies.

Wimpole Street undergoes a change of season, and Miss Shearer has been freed from the invalid's couch. She even proposes to go downstairs to meet March, much to the horror of her maid, Miss O'Connor. Miss Shearer manages the feat and she happily tells March of her doctors' recommendation: that she winter in Italy. He also has plans to go to Italy.

Laughton enters and registers his disapproval of the visitor. He warns, "You can't do it," when Miss Shearer tries to climb the stairs. When she falters, he pushes March aside and carries her to the bedroom. He is incensed about the Italy plan and accuses her of plotting against him—"I, who used to be your whole world; who loved you; who *loves* you."

She is defeated in her plan, but March persists. When Laughton recognizes the romance, he makes plans to move the entire family to a country home in Surrey. He arrives home unexpectedly as Maureen O'Sullivan is showing off to Miss Shearer the man she hopes to marry, Ralph Forbes. Laughton cruelly dismisses Forbes and any possibility of a marriage.

Finally Miss Shearer turns on him. "You're like a shadow over our lives," she says. In a scene of subtle horror, Laughton reveals his unnatural love for his daughter, then adds, "Forgive me, my dear, I was carried away." Now she is convinced she must flee.

She makes her escape as Laughton is delivering his sanctimonious grace at dinner. The family is plunged into hysteria when her departure is discovered. "Her dog must be destroyed," announces the stunned Laughton. Miss O'Sullivan says triumphantly that the dog has escaped, too.

The final shot depicts a wedding witnessed only by Miss Shearer's two co-conspirators, Una O'Connor and Flush.

Most of the film takes place in the bedroom of Elizabeth Barrett, yet there is no sense of confinement—except for the desired one portraying her cloistered life. The literate dialogue, the interplay of the characters, and brilliantly sustained performances make it engrossing drama.

CHINA SEAS
1935

DIRECTION	Tay Garnett
FROM THE BOOK BY	Crosbie Garstin
SCREENPLAY	Jules Furthman, James K. McGuinness
PHOTOGRAPHY	Ray June

CAST: Clark Gable, Jean Harlow, Wallace Beery, Lewis Stone, Rosalind Russell, Dudley Digges, C. Aubrey Smith, Robert Benchley, William Henry, Live De Maigret, Soo Yong, Carol Ann Beery, Akim Tamiroff, Ivan Lebedeff, Edward Brophy, Hattie McDaniel, Donald Meek.

The film demonstrates what the Thalberg system could accomplish with undistinguished material, technique triumphing over content. The technique was to fill the screen with bright personalities, give them pseudo-sophisticated dialogue to talk at a rapid rate, and play the whole thing so fast and furiously that the audience had no time nor inclination to question the inadequacies.

The point of embarkation is Hong Kong, which is established in brief location shots. Then the gallery of characters begins walking up the gangplank of the rusty China Sea steamship: the hard-driving captain, Clark Gable, nursing a three-day hangover; Jean Harlow, his sometime doxy; Rosalind Russell, the English lady with whom he once had an affair before she was widowed; Wallace Beery, a Scottish merchant with a piratical air; Lewis Stone, a defrocked sea captain

CHINA SEAS, *Clark Gable, Rosalind Russell, C. Aubrey Smith, Jean Harlow*

being given a second chance; C. Aubrey Smith, doughty owner of the shipping fleet; Robert Benchley, a novelist in search of local color but unable to find it because he is permanently soused.

Scarcely have the passengers and crew arrived on board before, the plot is determined: the ship will pass through pirate waters on its way to Singapore, and it is carrying £250,000 of gold, hidden by Gable in a steamroller.

Gable shows his mastery before sailing. He notices that several of the Chinese women in steerage have big feet. Figuring that women dodge a thrown object and men catch it, he tosses a cigar at them. One catches it, and Gable rips off their clothes, revealing men's attire underneath. He hands them over to police.

The early part of the voyage is taken up with romantic maneuverings by Miss Russell, who came from England in search of Gable, and Miss Harlow, who warns him, "You can't quit me any more

CHINA SEAS, *Jean Harlow, Wallace Beery*

than I can quit you, and you can kiss a stack of cookbooks on that!" Much of the dialogue is devoted to such give-and-take. Benchley floats above it all in an alcoholic haze, musing, "Once when I was ten, I played ten simultaneous games of chess blindfolded. Lost every one of them."

A typhoon blows up, and passengers are herded into the saloon. A piano rolls across the floor, almost crushing a young girl, played by Beery's real-life daughter, Carol Ann. Gable saves her in time.

Then the steamroller comes loose on deck, and rolls crazily, crushing coolies underneath. In a thrilling action sequence, Gable is almost pushed overboard by the careening machine, but he finally secures it.

Spurned by Gable, Miss Harlow steals the key to the arsenal for Beery, who is after the gold. His operatives take over the ship while the captain is asleep, and a junk-load of pirates headed by a Malay prince, Ivan Lebedeff, comes alongside. The passengers are panicked.

Gable cooly opens the strong box at gunpoint, but the gold containers reveal only sand. The pirates apply an iron boot to make him reveal the whereabouts of the gold. He faints twice but keeps his secret. Beery, who has not revealed his part in the plot, declares, "There can't be any gold or he would have talked. Nobody can be that tough."

The pirates begin to evacuate. Lewis Stone, gravely injured, redeems his previous cowardice by assaulting them with grenades. He is killed by gunfire, and Gable destroys the junk with a cannon.

Afterward Gable interrogates Miss Harlow and Beery, and she confesses that she betrayed him out of pique. His guilt disclosed, Beery takes poison and dies after telling her, "Lovin' you is the only decent thing I ever did in my life, and even that was a mistake."

As the ship arrives in Singapore, Gable realizes he would be miscast sitting beside a fire in England with Miss Russell. "Yes, I love her," he admits to Harlow, "but not the way I do you." He vows to testify for her at the trial.

The voyage over, Benchley steps off the boat and lands in the bay. "These streets are in deplorable condition," he comments.

MUTINY ON THE BOUNTY
1935

DIRECTION	Frank Lloyd
FROM THE BOOK BY	Charles Nordhoff and James Norman Hall
SCREENPLAY	Talbot Jennings, Jules Furthman, Carey Wilson
PHOTOGRAPHY	Arthur Edeson

CAST: Charles Laughton, Clark Gable, Franchot Tone, Herbert Mundin, Eddie Quillan, Dudley Digges, Donald Crisp, Henry Stephenson, Francis Lister, Spring Byington, Movita, Mamo, Ian Wolfe, Ivan Simpson, De Witt Jennings, Stanley Fields.

The portent is established in the first scenes as Clark Gable, portraying Fletcher Christian, leads a press-gang through Portsmouth saloons in search of a crew for the *Bounty*. One of his captives asks who the captain is, and he is told. "Bligh!" exclaims the unfortunate, and he bolts for the door. As the aristocratic Franchot Tone takes leave of his mother for service as a midshipman, he hears Henry Stephenson describe Bligh as "a sea-going disaster."

There is much carousing on the deck of the *Bounty* prior to sailing, with vendors and harlots plying their wares. At length the captain arrives—a sneering, slouching Charles Laughton. His first words: "Mr. Christian, clear the decks of this rabble!"

The crew gets a foretaste of Laughton's sadism when a Navy boat arrives with a sailor to be flogged for striking his captain. The man is dead, but Laughton orders the flogging to continue.

The excitement of the voyage is depicted in quick cuts showing the men about their duties of unfurling sails, lifting anchor, etc. The

MUTINY ON THE BOUNTY, *Clark Gable and Charles Laughton*

basic difference between the two antagonists is established as Laughton remarks to Gable his pleasure at sailing with a gentleman and underscores the fact that he is himself a self-made man.

Laughton piles cruelty upon cruelty. When Tone engages in a scuffle with another midshipman, he is punished by being sent to the masthead during a gale. Floggings are handed out for minor offenses, and a sailor is keel-hauled to his death. Laughton cuts the cheese ration, accusing the crew of stealing two large cheeses. He becomes enraged when he is reminded that the cheeses were delivered to his house in England.

Whn Gable refuses to sign the register that would approve the captain's command, Laughton snarls, "You mutinous dog!" Gable almost retaliates, but the cry goes up, "Tahiti!"

The island scenes display a sensual beauty, and Gable engages in a romance with Movita that establishes his choice between the idyllic life of Polynesia or the brutality of the *Bounty*.

The *Bounty*'s mission—loading breadfruit trees for shipment to the West Indies—is completed, and the crew takes reluctant leave of Tahiti. Laughton continues hammering at Gable, accusing him of stealing cocoanuts, of misappropriating two large pearls given him by Movita. The break comes when Laughton orders on deck the bibulous, ailing surgeon, Dudley Digges. Digges staggers topside and dies.

"Bligh, you've given your last order on this ship," Gable declares. "We'll be men again if we die for it."

The confusion and violence of mutiny is shown in brief, exciting scenes, then the punishment is meted out: Laughton and his followers are cast off in an open boat, the nearest safe landfall being Timor, thirty-five hundred miles distant. Laughton drifts away with his imprecation: "I'll live to see you—all of you—hanging from the highest yard-arm in the fleet!"

A memorable shot: the dumped breadfruit plants floating in the wake of the *Bounty* as it returns to Tahiti.

The highpoint of the film has been reached; but the consequences of the mutiny must be portrayed. Laughton miraculously conquers the sea and returns to Tahiti for the mutineers. Gable manages to escape with his followers on the *Bounty;* Tone and others stay behind and are clapped in irons despite their claims of innocence. Laughton pursues the *Bounty* with such zeal he wrecks his ship. Tone is sentenced to death by a Portsmouth court-martial, but is reprieved by George III. Laughton has triumphed, but he is snubbed by his superiors. And Gable has sailed on to Pitcairn, burning the *Bounty* and his previous life behind him.

The final events are anticlimactic, but the over-all effect of the film is one of rare adventure. The motivating character of *Mutiny on the Bounty* is Charles Laughton, and his Bligh is excessively mannered, almost in silent-screen style. It is Clark Gable who maintains the film's equilibrium throughout. He makes no attempt to portray an English gentleman. But as a man of goodwill and common sense, he is utterly convincing.

A NIGHT AT THE OPERA
1935

DIRECTION	Sam Wood
SCREEN PLAY	George S. Kaufman, Morrie Ryskind
ORIGINAL STORY	James K. McGuinness
PHOTOGRAPHY	Merritt B. Gerstad

CAST: Groucho, Harpo and Chico Marx, Allan Jones, Kitty Carlisle, Margaret Dumont, Sig Rumann, Walter (Woolf) King, Robert Emmett O'Connor.

Margaret Dumont, that S.S. *Mauretania* of dowagers, waits impatiently in a Roman restaurant for her escort to arrive. She is about to leave when Groucho Marx, seated back-to-back with her at the next table, finishes his meal and is presented with a check. He hands it to the nubile female opposite him and comments, "That's outrageous. If I were you, I wouldn't pay it." Then he joins Miss Dumont at her table.

The basic element of the labyrinthine plot is outlined immediately: Groucho, alias Otis P. Driftwood, proposes to introduce the rich widow to New York society by having her back an opera company headed by Sig Rumann. The star of the company is Walter King, a tenor of prodigious ego. He is on the make for the leading lady, Kitty Carlisle, but her heart belongs to an obscure singer, Allan Jones.

Harpo is introduced as King's maladroit dresser, and Chico is—well, Chico. He elects himself agent for Jones, and he negotiates a contract with Groucho, both tearing off portions of the document as they eliminate clauses.

All ship aboard a New York-bound liner, giving rise to the most famous of Marx Brothers scenes. Groucho, sprawling atop his steamer trunk, is trundled to his tiny stateroom. "It would be simpler," he tells the porter, "if you would just put the stateroom in the trunk."

Alone inside the room, Groucho opens the trunk to discover Chico and Jones. Groucho pulls open a drawer and finds Harpo asleep. "Those aren't my shirts; my shirts don't snore," Groucho complains.

The stowaways refuse to leave until they are given dinner. So Groucho orders an elaborate meal ("Do you have any stewed prunes? Well, give 'em some hot coffee—that'll sober 'em up."). Two chambermaids arrive to make up the beds. An engineer enters to turn on the heat. Next, a manicurist who asks, "Want your nails long or short?" Groucho: "Better make 'em short; it's getting crowded in here." Then comes the engineer's assistant and a young girl looking for her Aunt Biddie.

A mop woman joins the throng, and Groucho advises her to start on the ceiling, where there's room. Four waiters arrive bearing the dinner on trays, atop which Harpo climbs. Finally Miss Dumont appears for a rendezvous with Groucho. She opens the door and all fifteen persons pile out onto her.

The stowaways manage to land in New York posing as bearded air heroes and receive tributes at City Hall. All goes well until Harpo spills too much water on his face and the beard disappears. The classic cop, Robert Emmett O'Connor, trails them to Groucho's hotel room and almost makes an arrest. But he becomes so confused while chasing them in and out of rooms that he is ready to turn in his badge.

The plot is complicated helplessly when Groucho is fired as Miss Dumont's mentor and Miss Carlisle loses her job as prima donna for rebuffing King's advances. Groucho masterminds the solution: by fouling up the opera opening so that Rumann and King are foiled in their plans.

The orchestra begins the stately overture. But Harpo and Chico

A NIGHT AT THE OPERA, *Groucho Marx, Margaret Dumont, Sig Rumann*

A NIGHT AT THE OPERA, *Harpo, Allan Jones, Chico, Groucho*

have tampered with the sheet music, and the musicians launch into a rendition of "Take Me Out to the Ball Game." Harpo and Chico play catch in the orchestra pit, and Groucho strolls down the aisle selling peanuts.

Backdrops fly up and down like windowshades, Harpo swings across the stage Tarzan-style, yet the opera goes on. Finally King is abducted. The show must go on, and Jones and Miss Carlisle are in the wings, ready to perform. They sing to enormous applause, and the Marxian plot succeeds in the end.

A Night at the Opera is the perfect Marx Brothers vehicle, allowing each to display his disciplined madness. Groucho is given wide opportunity for his native irreverence (to waiter: "You got change for ten dollars?" "Yes, sir!" "Then you won't need that dime I was going to give you.") Harpo has a variety of sight gags, and Chico, the most underrated of the trio, complements his brothers in richly inventive style.

ROMEO AND JULIET
1936

DIRECTION	George Cukor
FROM THE PLAY BY	William Shakespeare
ARRANGED FOR THE SCREEN BY	Talbot Jennings
DANCE DIRECTION	Agnes De Mille
PHOTOGRAPHY	William Daniels

CAST: Norma Shearer, Leslie Howard, John Barrymore, Edna May Oliver, Basil Rathbone, C. Aubrey Smith, Andy Devine, Ralph Forbes, Reginald Denny, Maurice Murphy, Conway Tearle, Henry Kolker, Robert Warwick, Virginia Hammond, Violet Kemble-Cooper.

A large, decorative tapestry filled with Elizabethan figures comes to life amid a flourish of trumpets, and a herald describes the two households and the star-cross'd lovers whose tale will comprise "the two hours' traffic on our stage."

ROMEO AND JULIET, *Leslie Howard and Norma Shearer*

The prologue over, Verona occupies the screen in its medieval splendor. To the cathedral come two great families in full retinue, and the courses of their processions seem aimed at collision. They deflect at the church entrance. Servants idling outside the church exchange insults and a sword fight between the two houses ensues. Montagues and Capulets pour out of the cathedral to join the fray, which is staged in exciting cinematic style. The Prince of Verona, magnificently played by Conway Tearle, subdues the brawlers and warns of dire consequences if the feud again erupts in violence.

Juliet is introduced in her chamber with her mother, Violet Kemble-Cooper, and the nurse, the purse-lipped Edna May Oliver, who takes the role and runs with it. Miss Shearer is at first annoyingly girlish, tripping about and posing with hand to cheek. But the mannerisms vanish, and she emerges as the romantic heroine. Her voice is sure and musical; she seems to understand both the meter and the meaning of the lines.

Romeo is first seen in a setting that is pretentiously pastoral, complete with grazing sheep and a Roman ruin. Howard plays the role dreamily, almost distractedly. Yet his very underplaying adds credulity to the role that is too often overwrought.

The lovers meet at the Capulet masque, the most beautifully staged sequence in the film. Cukor keeps the camera moving through the assemblage of guests and into the Agnes De Mille dances, and the sudden love between Miss Shearer and Howard is both credible and poignant.

The earlier portions of the action are blessed with the presence of John Barrymore as Mercutio. He seems not in the best of figure or of voice, yet his authority is unquestionable. He is every bit the de-bauched Mercutio as he leers at the whores on the balcony above the square and belches and prances his way through the Queen Mab speech. His bawdy exchange with Miss Oliver is capital; he flips up her skirts roguishly and exclaims, "'Tis no less, I tell ye, for the bawdy hand of the dial is now upon the prick of noon." His death at the hands of Tybalt, played with splendid style by Basil Rathbone, is touching loss.

The balcony scene is imaginatively staged, and the two players bring freshness to the time-worn phrases. Yet something mitigates the scene's effectiveness. Perhaps it is the enormity of the set, and the length of the journey by which he must pass through the garden and up walls to come within a few feet of her.

With the death of Mercutio, the inexorable events begin. This is the least interesting portion of the film, as it is of the play, because the sense of doom is overwhelming. But the action is portrayed with grace and style. The Capulet servants are seen garlanding the house on the morning of Juliet's wedding to Paris (Ralph Forbes). After her lifeless body has been discovered, the servants now shroud the place with black.

The tomb scene exacts the full impact of its tragedy, and the film ends with the two sorrowing families agreed to amity. The Prince of Verona concludes with

> For never was a story of more woe
> Than this of Juliet and her Romeo.

The story is told with no violence to its author. The text has been judiciously cut, but the archaisms remain and there are no Olivier-like simplifications. *Romeo and Juliet* through most of its length is a felicitous joining of Shakespeare and film.

THE GOOD EARTH
1937

ASSOCIATE PRODUCER	Albert Lewin
DIRECTOR	Sidney Franklin
SCREENPLAY	Talbot Jennings, Tess Slesinger, Claudine West
BASED ON THE NOVEL BY	Pearl Buck
PHOTOGRAPHY	Karl Freund

CAST: Paul Muni, Luise Rainer, Walter Connolly, Charley Grapewin, Tilly Losch, Jessie Ralph, Soo Yong, Keye Luke.

Dawn on a Chinese farm. Paul Muni, convincingly made up to be Chinese, awakens to the joyful realization that this is his wedding day. He performs his morning chores oblivious of the crankiness of

his aged father, Charley Grapewin. Then he goes to the Great House of the village to claim his bride, who has spent her girlhood as a kitchen slave. He finds Luise Rainer huddled frightenedly near the stove. She follows him as he marches proudly back to the farm, and she rescues a peach seed he has discarded. After the wedding feast that night, she plants the seed outside the humble house.

The passage of seasons is depicted in an idyllic montage of tilling the soil and caring for the crops. The peach tree is now a flowering twig and the wife is with child. A storm threatens the wheat and she joins the men in the field to rescue the crop. When she collapses, Muni carries her to the house and starts to fetch a midwife. "No, go back to the wheat," she tells him, and she delivers her own child. To celebrate his fatherhood of a son, Muni goes to the Great House and buys more land.

In time he has five fields and three children, and prosperity seems to be his. But then he sees travelers streaming from the north. His wife knows what is happening: "It was famine that made me a slave."

The earth cakes dry and crops wither. Muni resists entreaties of relatives to sell his land for food: "Before I sell it, I'll feed it to my children." His avaricious uncle, Walter Connolly, adds, "Yes, and you'll bury them in it." When starving neighbors storm his kitchen, they find Miss Rainer cooking—mud.

"O-lan, the earth has forgotten us," Muni cries, but his wife will not allow him to sell it. She gives birth to a fourth child but snuffs out his life rather than add to their burden. The family decides the only chance for survival is to go south to the city.

The film receives a charge of excitement as the pastoral countryside is left behind for the tangle of the city. Survival is scarcely easier, but Miss Rainer teaches the children to beg, and they manage. Now revolution and terror grip the city, and she is carried along by a mob bent on looting the palaces. She is crushed underfoot and regains consciousness to find a bag of jewels nearby. Captured, she is saved from the firing squad when the revolutionary soldiers are summoned elsewhere. The family returns to the land, and the jewels finance their new prosperity.

The peach tree grows to a sturdy height, and the sons are now grown and educated. Expansive with his wealth, Muni moves his

THE GOOD EARTH, *Paul Muni, Luise Rainer*

family into the Great House, and he is swayed by Connolly's sly
remark, "You are rich; you could even take a second wife." She is
Tilly Losch, a teahouse dancer who brings discord to the house. Miss
Rainer accepts the second wife without complaint: "I know that
I'm ugly and not to be loved."

Muni visits his farms and his longtime friend and overseer blurts
out the secret—that the second wife has seduced Muni's son. Muni
is unbelieving and banishes the overseer from the land. Throughout
their exchange can be heard an ominous sound: the chirping of
cicadas.

When he returns home, Muni discovers the son with Miss Losch
and beats him. Then workers come from the farms with the dread
news that the locust plague is coming. If he loses his crops, Muni
will be ruined, and no escape is known from the locusts. But his
first-born, Keye Luke, has learned in school that the plague can be
combatted.

All rush to the farms, and they fight the fearsome masses of insects with fire, spades, gongs and hands. The victory is won.

Muni sells the Great House and moves back to the land with his
wife and family. There is a gala wedding feast for the son, but Miss
Rainer is too ill to take part. In a scene of great tenderness Muni
says he would sell all his land if he could heal her. "No, I would not
allow that," she says, "for I must die sometime, and the land will
always be there."

When she dies, Muni goes into the night and stands beside the
peach tree. "O-lan, you are the earth," he says.

The hymn to the earth is over, and it ends on the proper note.
For, although Muni and the others are totally convincing in their
portrayals, it is the performance of Luise Rainer that gives power
and dimension to the tale.

CAMILLE
1937

DIRECTION George Cukor

SCREENPLAY Zoë Akins, Frances Marion, James Hilton

FROM THE NOVEL BY Alexandre Dumas

PHOTOGRAPHY William Daniels, Karl Freund

CAST: Greta Garbo, Robert Taylor, Lionel Barrymore, Elizabeth Allan, Jessie Ralph, Henry Daniell, Lenore Ulric, Laura Hope Crews, Rex O'Malley, Russell Hardie, E. E. Clive, Douglas Walton, Marion Ballou, Joan Brodel, June Wilkins, Fritz Lieber, Jr., Elsie Esmonds.

A beautiful courtesan with a fondness for gaiety and camellias, Marguerite Gautier—Garbo—drifts through the Parisian demi-monde with scant regard for her own precarious health. The decadence of the mid-nineteenth century is brilliantly portrayed in opening scenes at the theater, where the ambitious belles vie for attention of the rich and affluent men, particularly the Baron de Varville, the coolly sadistic Henry Daniell.

Through a mixup, Garbo encounters the young, inexperienced Armand Duval, portrayed with masculine beauty by Robert Taylor, believing him to be the baron. Garbo discovers the error and comments to him: "I am not always sincere; one can't be in this world. But I am sorry it happened." She drops him for a liaison with Daniell.

Later she meets Taylor again and it is apparent that he is in love with her—he carries the handkerchief she left at the theater. She invites him to a dinner at her apartment, and he attends with a gathering of her so-called friends. They are a study in glittering depravity —Laura Hope Crews as a cigar-smoking couturiere, Lenore Ulric as a competitive bawd—and Taylor resents the telling of spicy stories at the table of his beloved.

She is indulgent of his concern, and she invites him to return after the party is over. But Daniell comes back from a trip, and Taylor is thwarted once more.

CAMILLE, *Robert Taylor and Greta Garbo*

CAMILLE, *Greta Garbo, Rex O'Malley, Laura Hope Crews*

The young lovers meet again, and he urges her to go with him to the country to regain her health. She does so, after exacting 40,000 francs and a slap in the face from Daniell.

The romance reaches full flower in the country, and Garbo gives a wedding for her friend, Elizabeth Allan. But such bliss is not for the tragic Camille. Taylor's father, played by the ubiquitous Lionel Barrymore, comes to plead with Garbo to give up the young man lest his promising future be destroyed.

She returns to Daniell. Later she finds herself overcome with consumption and debts and declares, "Nothing will help me but Armand's return." He comes back from his foreign exile and learns of her desperate illness. He hastens to her apartment.

In a classic scene, she hears of his arrival, and her face, almost masked by death, suddenly becomes animated. She greets him as the Marguerite of old.

But she understands her fate, and she tells him, "Perhaps it's better if I live in your heart, where the world can't see me." The camera focuses on her lifeless face as Taylor cries, "Marguerite, don't leave me!"

Camille brings Garbo to the climax of her career. In none of her films did she find such a happy wedding of characterization and vehicle. Cukor provides the proper blend of taste and restraint in a subject that could easily have leaned to bathos. The mounting is lavish without overwhelming the story, and Adrian designed a succession of gorgeous gowns to enhance the star. The supporting cast is well-nigh perfect, especially Daniell with his casual villainy and Laura Hope Crews in one of the most amusing of her fluttery characterizations.

Appendix A

The Irving G. Thalberg Memorial Award

The plan to memorialize Thalberg with a special award was announced at the annual dinner of the Academy of Motion Picture Arts and Sciences on March 4, 1937, with the first presentation to be made the following year. The purpose of the award:

"To carry on the ideals represented by Irving G. Thalberg is the privilege of the Academy in sponsoring this award. It shall be given each year for the most consistent high level of production achievement by an individual producer, based on pictures he has personally produced during the preceding year. It shall be in the form of a specially designed trophy which will, each year, become the permanent possession of the producer to whom it is awarded."

Recipients of the award have been:

1937–Darryl F. Zanuck	1951–Arthur Freed
1938–Hal B. Wallis	1952–Cecil B. De Mille
1939–David O. Selznick	1953–George Stevens
1941–Walt Disney	1956–Buddy Adler
1942–Sidney Franklin	1958–Jack L. Warner
1943–Hal B. Wallis	1961–Stanley Kramer
1944–Darryl F. Zanuck	1963–Sam Spiegel
1946–Samuel Goldwyn	1965–William Wyler
1948–Jerry Wald	1966–Robert Wise
1950–Darryl F. Zanuck	1967–Alfred Hitchcock

APPENDIX B
Major Academy Award Winners and Nominations for Thalberg Films
(*Winners are denoted by asterisks.*)

1927–28

ARTISTIC QUALITY OF PRODUCTION	*The Crowd*
DIRECTION	King Vidor, *The Crowd*
TITLE WRITING	Joseph Farnum, *Laugh, Clown, Laugh; Telling the World; The Fair Co-ed**
CINEMATOGRAPHY	Charles Rosher, *The Tempest*

1928–29

PICTURE	*Broadway Melody** *Hollywood Revue*
ACTRESS	Bessie Love, *Broadway Melody*
DIRECTION	Lionel Barrymore, *Madame X*
WRITING ACHIEVEMENT	Josephine Lovett, *Our Dancing Daughters* Bess Meredyth, *Wonder of Women*
CINEMATOGRAPHY	George Barnes, *Our Dancing Daughters* Clyde De Vinna, *White Shadows of the South Seas**

1929–30

PICTURE	*The Big House* *The Divorcee*
ACTOR	Wallace Beery, *The Big House* Laurence Tibbett, *The Rogue Song*

ACTRESS Norma Shearer, *The Divorcee**
Norma Shearer, *Their Own Desire*
Greta Garbo, *Anna Christie*
Greta Garbo, *Romance*

DIRECTION Clarence Brown, *Anna Christie, Romance*
Robert Leonard, *The Divorcee*
King Vidor, *Hallelujah*

WRITING ACHIEVEMENT Frances Marion, *The Big House*
John Meehan, *The Divorcee*

CINEMATOGRAPHY William Daniels, *Anna Christie*

1930–31

PICTURE *Trader Horn*

ACTOR Lionel Barrymore, *A Free Soul**

ACTRESS Marie Dressler, *Min and Bill**
Norma Shearer, *A Free Soul*

DIRECTION Clarence Brown, *A Free Soul*

1931–32

PICTURE *Grand Hotel**
The Champ

ACTOR Wallace Beery, *The Champ**
Alfred Lunt, *The Guardsman*

ACTRESS Marie Dressler, *Emma*
Lynn Fontanne, *The Guardsman*
Helen Hayes, *The Sin of Madelon Claudet**

1932–33

PICTURE *Smilin' Through*

WRITING (ORIGINAL STORY) Frances Marion, *Prizefighter and the Lady*
Charles MacArthur, *Rasputin and the Empress*

1934

PICTURE   *The Barretts of Wimpole Street*

ACTRESS   Norma Shearer, *The Barretts of Wimpole Street*

1935

PICTURE   *Mutiny on the Bounty**

ACTOR   Clark Gable, *Mutiny on the Bounty*
Charles Laughton, *Mutiny on the Bounty*
Franchot Tone, *Mutiny on the Bounty*

DIRECTOR   Frank Lloyd, *Mutiny on the Bounty*

WRITING (SCREENPLAY)   Jules Furthman, Talbot Jennings. Carey Wilson, *Mutiny on the Bounty*

1936

PICTURE   *Romeo and Juliet*

ACTRESS   Norma Shearer, *Romeo and Juliet*

1937

PICTURE   *The Good Earth*

ACTRESS   Luise Rainer, *The Good Earth**
Greta Garbo, *Camille*

DIRECTION   Sidney Franklin, *The Good Earth*

CINEMATOGRAPHY   Karl Freund, *The Good Earth*

APPENDIX C
Printed Sources

BOOKS

ALPERT, HOLLIS, *The Barrymores*, Dial Press, New York, 1964.

BAINBRIDGE, JOHN, *Garbo*, Doubleday, Garden City, 1955.

BARRYMORE, LIONEL (as told to Cameron Shipp), *We Barrymores*, Appleton-Century-Crofts, New York, 1951.

BICKFORD, CHARLES, *Bulls, Balls, Bicycles and Actors*, Paul S. Eriksson, New York, 1965.

BILLQUIST, FRITIOF, *Garbo*, a Portrait, Putnam, New York, 1960.

BLESH, RUDI, *Keaton*, Macmillan, New York, 1966.

BROWN, CATHERINE HAYES, *The Story of Helen Hayes*, Random House, New York, 1940.

CHAPLIN, CHARLES, *Autobiography*, Simon and Schuster, New York, 1964.

CHEVALIER, MAURICE, *With Love*, Little, Brown, Boston, 1960.

CONWAY, MICHAEL, DION MCGREGOR and MARK RICCI, *The Films of Greta Garbo*, Bonanza, New York, undated.

CONWAY, MICHAEL and MARK RICCI, *The Films of Jean Harlow*, Bonanza, New York, 1965.

CRAM, MILDRED, in *American Spectator Year Book*, Frederick A. Stokes, New York, 1934.

CRAWFORD, JOAN (with JANE KESNER ARDMORE), *A Portrait of Joan*, Doubleday, Garden City, 1962.

CRICHTON, KYLE, *Total Recoil*, Doubleday, Garden City, 1960.

CROWTHER, BOSLEY, *Hollywood Rajah, The Life and Times of Louis B. Mayer*, Henry Holt, New York, 1960.

————, *The Lion's Share*, E. P. Dutton, New York, 1957.

DE MILLE, CECIL B., *The Autobiography of Cecil B. De Mille*, Prentice Hall, New York, 1959.

DRESSLER, MARIE, *My Own Story*, Little, Brown, Boston, 1934.

DRINKWATER, JOHN, *The Life and Adventures of Carl Laemmle*, Putnam, New York, 1931.

FITZGERALD, F. SCOTT, *Babylon Revisited* and Other Stories (including "Crazy Sunday"), Scribner's, New York, 1960.

————, *The Last Tycoon*, Scribner's, New York, 1941.

FOWLER, GENE, *Good Night, Sweet Prince*, The Viking Press, New York, 1943.

GRAHAM, SHEILAH and GEROLD FRANK, *Beloved Infidel*, Henry Holt, New York, 1951.

GREEN, ABEL and JOE LAURIE, Jr., *Show Biz: From Vaude to Video*, Henry Holt, New York, 1951.

HAYS, WILL H., *The Memoirs of Will Hays*, Doubleday, Garden City, 1955.

HECHT, BEN, *Charlie, the Improbable Life and Times of Charles MacArthur*, Harper, New York, 1957.

HOWARD, LESLIE RUTH, *A Quite Remarkable Father*, Harcourt, Brace, New York, 1959.

JACOBS, LEWIS, *The Rise of the American Film*, Harcourt, Brace, New York, 1939.

KEATON, BUSTER (with Charles Samuels), *My Wonderful World of Slapstick*, Doubleday, Garden City, 1960.

LANCHESTER, ELSA, *Charles Laughton and I*, Harcourt, Brace, New York, 1938.

MACGOWAN, KENNETH, *Behind the Screen*, Delacorte Press, New York, 1965.

MARSHALL, ARTHUR CALDER, *The Innocent Eye; The Life of Robert J. Flaherty*, W. H. Allen, London, 1963.

MIZENER, ARTHUR, *The Far Side of Paradise*, Houghton, Mifflin, New York, 1959.

MOORE, GRACE, *You're Only Human Once*, Doubleday, Doran, Garden City, 1944.

NOBLE, PETER, *Hollywood Scapegoat, The Biography of Erich Von Stroheim*, The Fortune Press, London, 1950.

PERELMAN, S. J., *The Most of S. J. Perelman*, Simon and Schuster, New York, 1958.

PIPER, HENRY DAN, *F. Scott Fitzgerald*, A Critical Portrait, Holt, Rinehart and Winston, New York, 1965.

RAMSAYE, TERRY, *A Million and One Nights*, Simon and Schuster, New York, 1964.

SINGER, KURT, *The Laughton Story*, John C. Winston, Philadelphia, 1954.

TALMEY, ALLENE, *Doug and Mary and Others*, Macy-Masius, New York, 1927.

TAYLOR, DWIGHT, *Joy Ride*, Putnam, New York, 1959.

TURNBULL, ANDREW, *Scott Fitzgerald*, Scribner's, New York, 1962.

TURNBULL, ANDREW, editor, *The Letters of F. Scott Fitzgerald*, Scribner's, New York, 1963.

VIDOR, KING, *A Tree Is a Tree*, Harcourt, Brace, New York, 1952.

ZOLOTOW, MAURICE, *Stagestruck: The Romance of Alfred Lunt and Lynn Fontanne*, Harcourt, Brace, World, New York, 1964.

PERIODICALS

BENÉT, STEPHEN VINCENT, "Fitzgerald's Unfinished Symphony," *The Saturday Review of Literature*, Dec. 6, 1941.

COLLINS, FREDERICK L., "Meet the Boy Wonder of Hollywood," *Collier's*, Aug. 2, 1924.

Fortune, "Metro-Goldwyn-Mayer," December 1932.

THALBERG, IRVING, and HUGH WEIR, "Why Motion Pictures Cost So Much," *Saturday Evening Post*, Nov. 4, 1933.

THURBER, JAMES, "Taps at Assembly," *The New Republic*, Feb. 9, 1942.

TULLY, JIM, "Irving Thalberg," *Vanity Fair*, October 1927.

Also: various editions of New York *Times*, *Variety*, *Film Daily*, Los Angeles *Examiner*, Los Angeles *Times*, Los Angeles *Herald-Express*, *Photoplay*.

INDEX

PHOTOGRAPH CREDITS

Academy of Motion Picture Arts and Sciences, Title page, 173, 282
Culver Pictures, Inc., 233
Research Reports, 38
Universal Pictures, 43, 46, 49, 55, 57
Ken Murray, 201, 220, 221
Lucien Hubbard, 59
Kelly-Springfield Tires, 67
John Springer, 110, 238
King Vidor, 117, 138
Museum of Modern Art, 120, 212, 220
Wide World Photos, 168, 235, 296, 314
United Press International, 243
M-G-M, 73, 74, 76, 77, 78–79, 81, 85, 87, 88, 89, 99, 101, 102, 103, 104, 105, 107, 109, 110, 112, 120, 121, 123, 125, 127, 137, 141, 142, 143, 144, 148, 149, 152, 154, 155, 157, 160, 162, 163, 165, 166, 168, 170, 171, 175, 177, 182, 187, 199, 200, 203, 205, 209, 211, 214, 215, 225, 227, 230, 249, 256, 259, 261, 263, 265, 273, 274, 284, 285, 287, 291, 292, 294, 298, 300, 301, 302, 305, 307, 309, 313, 323, 330, 333, 336, 340, 342, 344, 347, 348, 351, 354, 357, 358, 360, 363, 366, 369, 372, 373, 375, 379, 381, 384, 388
Ray Stuart, 279
Junior Laemmle, 289, 290